"Executive coaching is no longer a luxury. In the fast-paced world of e-business, leadership has become the essential element of success. Coaching has proven itself as the most effective way to develop the cadre of leaders that Internet businesses rely on. *Coaching for Leadership* is packed with knowledge that will maximize the impact of the coaching process."
—Kevin R. Walsh, vice president, Oracle Corporation

"In this fast-changing, highly competitive environment, coaching has become one of the most important leadership skills. *Coaching for Leadership* is a treasure of practical ideas on how to build this critical skill in individuals and in the organization."
—Jim Moore, director executive development,
Sun Microsystems, dean, SunU

"Coaching is a critical skill for leaders in high-performing businesses. *Coaching for Leadership* provides a wealth of techniques and approaches to the many and varied coaching challenges leaders face in today's highly competitive marketplace."
—Ray Vigil, vice president, Enterprise Networks
Global Learning Solutions, Lucent Technologies

"An invaluable work . . . *Coaching for Leadership* is eminently practical, but also lays out the theoretical basis of a profession that blends human psychology with a concern for achieving measurable business goals."
—Sally Helgesen, author, *The Web of Inclusion: A New Architecture for Building Great Organizations* and *The Female Advantage: Women's Ways of Leadership*

"A valuable and wide-ranging reference volume providing thoughtful and practical guidance by leading experts."
—Robert B. McKersie, Society of Sloan Fellows
Professor (emeritus), MIT

COACHING FOR LEADERSHIP

How the World's Greatest Coaches Help Leaders Learn

Edited by
Marshall Goldsmith
Laurence Lyons
Alyssa Freas

JOSSEY-BASS/PFEIFFER
A Wiley Company
San Francisco

Copyright © 2000 by Jossey-Bass/Pfeiffer.
ISBN: 0-7879-5517-5
Jossey-Bass/Pfeiffer is a registered trademark of Jossey-Bass Inc., A Wiley Company.

Library of Congress Cataloging-in-Publication Data

Coaching for leadership : how the world's greatest coaches help leaders learn / edited by
Marshall Goldsmith, Laurence Lyons, Alyssa Freas.—1st ed.

    p. cm.
    Includes bibliographical references and index.
    ISBN 0-7879-5517-5
    1. Executives—Training of. 2. Leadership—Study and teaching. 3. Mentoring in
business. 4. Business consultants. I. Goldsmith, Marshall. II. Lyons, Laurence. III.
Freas, Alyssa.

HD30.4.C63 2000
658.4'07124—dc21   00-035209

Copyright page continues on pp. 393-394

Printed in the United States of America

Published by

JOSSEY-BASS/PFEIFFER
A Wiley Company
350 Sansome St.
San Francisco, CA 94104-1342
415.433.1740; Fax 415.433.0499
800.274.4434; Fax 800.569.0443

www.pfeiffer.com

Acquiring Editor: Matthew Holt
Director of Development: Kathleen Dolan Davies
Senior Production Editor: Dawn Kilgore
Editor: Rebecca Taff
Manufacturing Manager: Becky Carreño
Jacket Designer: Richard Adelson

FIRST EDITION
HB Printing   10 9 8 7 6 5 4 3

CONTENTS

EXHIBITS AND FIGURES

Exhibits

Figures

FOREWORD

Coaching is a rapidly growing vocation these days because so many of us are searching for a qualified person to help us develop and improve. But being a coach wasn't always a legitimate profession.

Just ten years ago, Jerre Stead put the job title Head Coach on his business card at Square D. (He was the chairman of the company at the time.) Many people stared at the word, puzzled about what it meant. Some snickered about this New Age title for the leader of an old-line company. The press turned hostile when he put Head Coach on his business card and changed all the managers' titles to coach after joining NCR. When he carried his Head Coach title to Ingram Micro, some journalists carped that it was the kind of fuzzy thinking that gets a company into trouble.

But all that is behind us, and coaching now occupies a place of honor on the management stage. Being a coach is not only legitimate; it has become highly desirable.

What is a coach anyway? What do great coaches do? Quite simply, coaches help people become more than they realize they can be. How do people learn to be great coaches? That's what this book is all about.

"Coach" is an old French word meaning "a vehicle to transport people from one place to another." Today, a coach helps a person move up a level—by expanding a skill, by boosting performance, or even by changing the way a person thinks. Coaches help people grow. They help people see beyond what they are today to what they can become tomorrow. A great coach helps ordinary folks like you and me do extraordinary things. In short, a great coach provides sturdy shoulders to stand on—so you can see farther than you might see on your own.

Your parents were your first great coaches. Recall your first steps. You likely stood up, unsteadily, took a short step, fell unceremoniously on your rear end, and burst out crying. Your parents didn't swat you and say, "Stupid kid. Give it up. You'll never walk. Just crawl around and stay out of our way." No, they could see you walking, running, and even winning marathons—activities you could not even imagine through your tears. As your coaches, they helped you move toward a tomorrow you couldn't then see.

Coaching is *not* a spectator sport. A productive coaching relationship begins with two people with fires in their bellies: one who wants desperately to move forward and another who yearns to help that person make the journey.

To be coached successfully you must want—desperately—to move, to learn, to grow, and you must be truly dedicated to spend the time and energy to do so. Coaching isn't something that happens *to you;* it happens *through you*. As a person being coached, you must be an active player in the game, not a spectator in the second row.

Being a coach requires a deep dedication to helping another person get to where they want to be. It means enduring many painful silences while you wait for the person being coached to come up with an answer. It also means surviving the withering glances of disappointment when, after someone has poured out his or her latest soap opera to you, you ask, "And what do *you* think would be best?"

But a coach does more than ask questions. A great coach can often see possibilities that the person being coached does not even know exist. A great coach helps an individual clarify which goals he or she wants to reach for, and then—through careful and caring questioning—helps that individual move more quickly along the journey of realization.

Coaching is destined to be *the* leadership approach of the twenty-first century. Yesterday's leader was a decision maker and resource allocator who asked how to best exploit an employee's abilities for the organization's gain. Employees were seen as tools and resources for accomplishing the organization's goals. Today's leader is a people developer and relationship builder who asks, "How can I help this person become more valuable as an individual—as well as to all of us?" Today's leader is a coach.

In today's free agent world, both leaders and followers are able to choose whether to participate fully in the relationship or not. Each must provide a path for the other's success. True influence comes from the mutual commitment to help others achieve their goals. This is the essence of coaching—and of leadership. A follower follows, much like a person seeks a coach's guidance, because doing so helps the follower achieve his or her destiny. A leader leads, much like a coach coaches, to achieve his or her destiny of helping others achieve their destinies.

Coaching is one of the deepest, mutually satisfying experiences a person can have. The coach helps the person being coached to learn and grow and to realize their dreams. At the same time, the person being coached brings out the noblest sentiments and provides the deepest gratification for the coach. Coaching is the quintessential win-win experience.

This book will help you achieve your destiny, whether it is to coach others or to be coached—or both. Now, open your mind and get ready to learn from the great coaches.

James A. Belasco

May 2000   *San Diego, California*

"We have a duty to pass on our learning."

RICHARD BECKHARD

This book is dedicated to Dick Beckhard, a wonderful coach, a professional colleague, and a personal friend and mentor to many of the authors of this book.

PREFACE

Motivation: Toward a Better Way

Every so often—perhaps once in a lifetime—we have a chance to anticipate a radical and pervasive change that is truly fundamental in nature. This book exists because we are at this very moment at the pinnacle of such change in the world of work. With the passage of every business day, yesterday's "management" approach becomes less relevant while we struggle to find a better way.

Peter Drucker's "knowledge worker" is replacing the factory worker at such a rate as to become today's stereotypical worker. The flatter, shamrock organization typified by Charles Handy is evolving as modern networks are becoming as familiar as traditional pyramids. Whereas in the past we were taught how to work with managers, now we must ask: How can we learn to work with peers?

Ideas stemming from Edgar Schein's "process consulting" are escaping from the closed professional consulting world to reach a much wider group of practitioners—that growing number of people doing all sorts of work who now recognize themselves as leaders. Business is going global. Work is more turbulent and stressful. The "job for life" has disappeared, thus challenging each individual to take care of career and personal development—paradoxically at a time when organizational memory, knowledge, and learning are becoming more valuable and sought after. Consumers are pressing for products that deliver more value and continue to demand more service. Even the "office" is redefining itself in new places, allowing us to work at all times of the day as technology offers to make our style of work more flexible. The "better way" must somehow accommodate all these major shifts and offer some answers to the really hard questions.

We were motivated to write this book because we could see that a number of individuals and organizations had found a better way. At a time when managers were being urged to re-engineer the processes of their businesses, we noticed that some organizations were making even greater strides by focusing on *people*. Their approach is *coaching*. It is far too easy to dismiss coaching as yet another technique in the management toolbag. The editors see coaching quite differently. For us, a leadership attitude is essential if individuals and organizations are to flourish in the new business world: good coaching offers both dialogue and etiquette, which together provide the structure and process in which leadership can work well. For us, coaching is the style of choice that rehumanizes the modern worker.

The goal of the editors, then, was simply to bring together the thinking of the world's greatest coaches at a critical time when leaders and managers need to learn about good coaching. This need has been met in this book with tested guidelines that promote responsible and effective coaching. We feel we have a duty as a progressive group to articulate our experiences, ideas, theories, and practices into one book that consolidates and positions the coaching subject into mainstream leadership and management topics.

Our Audience

Naturally, there are many audiences for this book. Those who already recognize themselves as leaders will find valuable reference material to help develop and improve their own leadership style. All those who see themselves as "managers" will find here a route along which to explore and experiment in leadership activities. Our book is for those who sponsor coaching, those who provide or receive coaching, the designers of coaching programs, and anyone who will integrate coaching into his or her own personal style whenever relating to others in the workplace.

Our Authors

We did not expect to write this book alone. At the outset it was clear that we needed to consolidate the thoughts, experiences, and insights of the world's greatest coaches and thinkers on management and leadership. We feel that their generosity in contributing chapters and their enthusiasm toward this ambitious project has validated our own beliefs about the importance of coaching. We take this opportunity to thank our authors warmly, for their willingness to share, for their perseverance in keeping to deadlines, for working with us on making changes to their chapters, and for their unanimous encouragement and support. Their response has built this book into a unique collection of chapters offering an entry point into our subject to readers from all backgrounds.

We have read and edited all the chapters. In areas where we have found different authors writing about the same idea, we have tried to adjust the language so that the same word or expression in one place will refer to the same idea in another place, in a uniform way throughout the book.

We have been editors, never censors. While we have diligently applied a uniformity of language, we have deliberately avoided any insistence on a uniformity of ideas beyond a commitment to coaching. Ours is an emerging subject in which specific situations can be as important as tested techniques in determining outcomes. Practice concepts that today might appear to us as ambiguous, paradoxical, or even contradictory will compete in the real world of experience; they will synthesize, and our collective thinking will make progress into the future.

Our Subject

In order to describe our subject area, we make a few general comments. There is something fundamental about coaching that enables it to fit into organizations of all kinds. Coaching is a behavioral approach of mutual benefit to individuals and the organizations in which they work or network. It is not merely a technique or a one-time event; it is a strategic process that adds value both to the people being coached and also to the bottom line of the organization.

Coaching establishes and develops healthy working relationships by surfacing issues (raw data gathering), addressing issues (through feedback), solving problems (action planning), and following through (results)—and so offers a process in which people develop and through which obstacles to obtaining business results are removed. Coaching can also be looked at as a peer-to-peer language expressed in a dialogue of learning.

Coaching is transformational. Through a behavioral change brought about in individuals, a leader may transform the organization and gain commitment. Coaching can offer a new propellant to organizational change. In coaching, people are offered the chance to align their own behavior with the values and vision of the organization. By helping people understand how they are perceived when they are out of alignment—and then putting these individuals back into alignment, one person at a time—coaching can make real impact and build healthy organizations—top-down, and from the grass roots up.

As to a formal definition of "coaching," how it relates to "leadership," and questions such as the difference between coaching and "mentoring," or whether the "sports metaphor" is appropriate—here we have let our authors speak for themselves. Of course, each of us has a personal view, and we take the opportunity to share this in our own individual chapters, which open the book.

Our Hope

Our hope is that, through the reading of this book, the reader will gain an understanding of the importance of coaching as a preferred and tested route to achieve leadership; the dramatic impact that can be achieved through coaching; why managers need to develop into leaders; and how coaching fits in with other techniques and approaches (consulting, therapy, organizational development, and so forth).

You will gain a thorough grasp of how—and for whom—coaching should be applied in your own organization and in your career, and also how to perform in your role as a coach, a person being coached, a sponsor, or as a buyer or supplier of a coaching service. Lastly, you can return to this reference work when you need to see how the world's top forty-five leading professionals have successfully responded to difficult coaching problems and successfully applied their own ideas in diverse situations.

Ultimately it is you—our reader—who we hope will complete the quest of this book by bringing good coaching practice into the world of work for the benefit of all.

Structure of the Book

How do you approach a subject so vast and eclectic as *Coaching for Leadership?* Our subject is at the vortex of so many disciplines related to management, leadership, personal, and organizational development.

The abundance of so many starting points is reflected in the wide range of authors who have come together to contribute to this book. The reader can approach our subject by starting with any contribution that seems interesting or familiar and progress through the book in any order. This is an ideal book to "dip into" when looking for an approach, a technique, or even for some inspiration on the subject.

For those who prefer a more structured approach, we have divided the book into parts, each representing an important aspect of coaching for leadership. These are:

Foundations of Coaching.   Here we introduce our subject, identifying the "foundation elements" that we see as essential and setting the book in a familiar and supporting context. This part of the book is intended to make our subject accessible to readers from any background.

Role and Identity.   The collection of chapters in this section explores the many and varied roles that we might take in a coaching activity and in our day-to-day behavior as leaders.

Moments and Transitions. Sometimes a new situation gives us the opportunity to take a coaching role. In this part of the book, we look at coaching activities that are inspired by a change of circumstance or by our participation in some process that may, of itself, not seem to be related to coaching on the surface.

Practice and Techniques. In this part of the book we have collected some of the best tried-and-tested, practical approaches to coaching. This valuable reference work will help the reader to develop a style based on the best practices of coaching pioneers, who explain what works—and also what derails effective practice.

Expanding Situations. This part of the book collects the ideas of leaders who have applied the coaching concept to real and important leadership situations. These authors provide a compendium of case studies and other situations in which the ideas of coaching can and do make a difference in achieving results.

ACKNOWLEDGMENTS

We have many people to thank for the creation of this book.

This book was made possible by a virtual, distributed, networked, and wonderful team. Sarah McArthur made sure all our words made sense, Samantha Broitman has been our gateway to the authors, while Amelie Davis and Kristina Corzatt helped in various ways. As a whole, the team did whatever became necessary to get the book produced. We have much to thank them for.

Many people collaborated in peer review of the material. Special thanks go to Rachael Joy Lyons for inspiring this book and to Nathan S. Lyons for his expert help in articulating difficult concepts simply. Thanks also to Mike Fuhr for reviewing copy.

Matthew Holt, Dawn Kilgore, and the team at Jossey-Bass simply became an extension of the editing team and provided us with an excellent practical example of what it means to work well in a networked and distributed team. Their hand has put the final touches to this volume.

Marshall Goldsmith
Rancho Santa Fe, California
May 2000

Laurence Lyons
Reading, England

Alyssa Freas
La Jolla, California

A PERSONAL NOTE

We would like to personally thank Larry Lyons for his incredible effort in the development and completion of *Coaching for Leadership*. Larry is truly the key editor of this book. He originated the idea, reviewed all of the manuscripts (many several times), gave the book a consistent "voice," and parented this project from beginning to end. During the entire project, Larry maintained a wonderful attitude. He never let late chapters, missing information, or tight deadlines dampen his enthusiasm. Without Larry, *Coaching for Leadership* would never have happened!

We would also like to thank the members of the Learning Network, an association of many of the world's leading professionals in the field of leadership development. The group meets annually in Del Mar, California, with the purpose of helping one another, helping our profession, and helping the world to be a better place. We are proud to note that twenty-three of the chapters in this book were written by members of the Learning Network.

May 2000   Marshall Goldsmith and Alyssa Freas

ABOUT THE EDITORS

Marshall Goldsmith is a founding director of Keilty, Goldsmith & Company (KGC). A recent study by Penn State University listed KGC as one of seven key providers of customized leadership development in the United States. Marshall is one of the select few consultants who has been asked to work with over fifty CEOs of major organizations. KGC's leadership development, coaching, and feedback processes have impacted over one million people in seventy leading organizations around the world.

Laurence S. Lyons is a senior vice president of Executive Coaching Network, Inc. He has been described by Henley Management College as a leading authority on organizational transformation. With a twenty-five-year background, including senior line and staff management positions in small, medium, and large organizations, he is an accomplished coach, consultant, public speaker, and author. He is also director of Metacorp Consulting in the U.K. He lectures widely on leadership and also on the application of information technology to new work practices, strategy, and change management. Larry is co-author of the highly successful book *Creating Tomorrow's Organization.*

Alyssa M. Freas is president and CEO of Executive Coaching Network, Inc. (ExCN), a global company whose primary mission is to help organizations achieve results by improving the effectiveness of their executives. ExCN has attracted a highly qualified group of coaches, including authorities on teambuilding, strategic planning, e-business, change management, succession planning, retaining talent, and the customer-employee profit chain. Through ExCN's Strategic Executive Coaching Process[SM], Alyssa has helped executives translate their vision into action, align corporate values, improve employee competence and commitment, manage transitions, improve executives' abilities to coach emerging leaders, and implement lasting improvements in executives' performance and business results.

ABOUT THE CONTRIBUTORS

Nancy J. Adler is a professor of organizational behavior and cross-cultural management at the Faculty of Management, McGill University, Montreal, Quebec, Canada. Nancy conducts research and consults on strategic international human resource management, global leadership, international negotiating, culturally synergistic problem solving, and global organization development. She has authored numerous articles, produced a film, *A Portable Life,* and published several books, including *International Dimensions of Organizational Behavior, Women in Management Worldwide,* and *Competitive Frontiers: Women Managers in a Global Economy.*

John Alexander is president of the Center for Creative Leadership, an international, nonprofit, educational institution with headquarters in Greensboro, North Carolina. John has presented to audiences worldwide on topics related to leadership and leadership development, and has published widely. He has a special interest in leadership in nonprofit and community settings. Before joining CCL in 1990, he worked for more than twenty years as an award-winning newspaper editor and columnist.

David Allen has more than twenty years of experience as a management consultant, productivity coach, and educator. He has conducted performance enhancement workshops for more than 250,000 professionals, with current ongoing programs in government, aerospace, financial services, retail, and information technology. President of the management consulting and training company David Allen & Co., he is also founding partner of Actioneer, Inc., a San Francisco-based software company that computerizes the best practices of personal productivity.

Judith M. Bardwick is president and founder of the influential management consulting firm Bardwick and Associates. Since 1978, she has concentrated on issues relating to improving human and organizational effectiveness. Currently a clinical professor of psychiatry at the University of California at San Diego, she has also worked as a psychological therapist. In addition to her most recent book, *In Praise of Good Business,* she is the author of *Danger in the Comfort Zone, The Plateauing Trap, In Transition,* and *The Psychology of Women.*

Richard Beckhard During his career, Richard Beckhard was an organization consultant, author, and professor of management and organizational behavior at the Sloan School of Management at MIT, where he served on the faculty for twenty-one years. His practice consisted primarily of working with managing complexity and change and organizational and institutional development. Dick is considered one of the "fathers" in the field of organization development. He authored eight books and numerous articles and, along with Edgar Schein, was the creator and editor of the Addison-Wesley OD Series. Dick's most recent book, *Agent of Change: My Life, My Practice,* was published in 1997. He was co-editor of the best-selling Drucker Foundation Future Series, which included *The Leader of the Future* (a *Business Week* "Top 15" bestseller), *The Organization of the Future,* and *The Community of the Future* (ranked by Amazon.com as number one in its field).

James A. Belasco is a professor at San Diego State University; the author of several best-selling books, including *Teaching the Elephant to Dance, Flight of the Buffalo,* and his newest, *Soaring with the Phoenix;* a consultant to major organizations; and a speaker. He is also a successful entrepreneur and coach-leader in specialty chemicals and computer software companies.

Chip R. Bell is senior partner and manager of the Dallas, Texas, office of Performance Research Associates, Inc., a consulting firm that specializes in helping organizations create a culture that sustains customer loyalty. In the late 1970s, he was vice president and director of management and organization development for NCNB (now Bank of America). Chip is the author or co-author of fourteen books. His newest book, *Customer Love: Attracting and Keeping Customers for Life,* is scheduled for publication in late 2000.

Roger Chevalier is an independent performance consultant who specializes in integrating training into more comprehensive performance improvement solutions. With more than twenty-five years' experience in performance improvement, Roger is a former vice president of Century 21 Real Estate Corporation's performance division and a former training director for the U.S. Coast Guard's West Coast Training Center.

Thomas G. Crane is a consultant, facilitator, author, and coach, specializing in assisting leaders to create high-performance teams. Tom's passion (and also the title of his first book) is *The Heart of Coaching*, which focuses on changing a leader's mind-set from that of the "boss" to the mind-set of the "coach." Tom has worked as a consultant and engagement leader for fifteen years in small and large organizations that are going through strategic change and cultural alignment.

Bert Decker is a major figure in the communications field. He has been on NBC's *Today* show as their communications expert, often commenting on the presidential debates. He is the author of the best-selling book, *You've Got To Be Believed To Be Heard,* as well as video and audio programs, such as "High Impact Communication" and "Creating a Powerful Presence." His book, *Speaking with Bold Assurance,* is scheduled for publication in mid-2000. Bert is chairman and founder of Decker Communications, Inc., a PROVANT company specializing in training executives and managers in the spoken word.

Alan Fine, founder of InsideOut Development, has more than twenty years of experience coaching world-class athletes and executives in Fortune 500 companies. His work extends to some of the most demanding companies. Alan's interest in how people learn and perform under pressure led him to develop a coaching method of performance improvement. He is the author of *Mind Over Golf* and a columnist for *Golf World* magazine.

Joe Folkman is a managing director at Novations Group, Inc.—a PROVANT company. He leads the firm's survey feedback practice. His book, *Turning Feedback into Change!*®: *31 Principles for Managing Personal*

Development Through Feedback, suggests how to use feedback in intelligent ways to bring about genuine and positive change in personal behavior. Joe is also the author of two books on employee surveys: *Making Feedback Work: Turning Feedback from Employee Surveys into Change* and *Employee Surveys That Make a Difference*.

Robert M. Fulmer is the W. Brooks George Professor of Management at the College of William and Mary and Distinguished Visiting Professor of Business at Pepperdine University. Recognized as an expert on leadership development, he is author of four editions of *The New Management* and co-author of *Executive Development and Organizational Learning for Global Business* and *Leadership by Design*. Robert is a senior fellow and special advisor to the president of the EastWest Institute, and he served as subject-matter expert for a 1998 global benchmarking study of leadership development.

Don Grayson is directing Keilty, Goldsmith & Company's team development practice. A management psychologist for the past twenty years, his areas of specialty include team building, meeting facilitation, executive coaching, 360° feedback, leadership training, and management of organizational change. Don conducts psychological assessments to aid clients with selection and promotion decisions, and he co-authored the *Professional Development Report*, a computer-generated, workplace-oriented personality profile.

Cathy Greenberg-Walt is the change management managing partner of Andersen Consulting's Global New Business Models Team, a partner in charge of the Executive Leadership Theme Team at the Institute for Strategic Change, a frequent keynote speaker, and an author. With an interdisciplinary doctorate in the behavioral sciences, she focuses on the successful management and integration of business strategy, process, technology, and leadership.

Victoria Guthrie is a senior fellow and director of innovative program initiatives at the Center for Creative Leadership (CCL). She co-designed three of CCL's leadership development programs: LeaderLab; Leading Downsized Organizations; and Leading Creatively. She is the author of

Coaching for Action: A Report on Long-Term Advising in a Program Context, as well as a number of other publications, and two chapters in CCL's *Handbook of Leadership Development.*

Bill Hawkins is an independent consultant specializing in leadership development, performance management, and organizational change. In association with Keilty, Goldsmith & Company and Innovative Resources Consultant Group, Inc., he has worked with and conducted leadership training in over twenty Fortune 500 companies in seventeen countries. Listed in *Who's Who in International Business,* Bill was a contributing author in the Drucker Foundation's book, *The Organization of the Future.*

Tom Heinselman is a principal with Keilty, Goldsmith & Company (KGC), one of America's key providers of customized leadership development. He specializes in providing consultation and training services in the areas of leadership development, team building, and executive coaching. Prior to joining KGC, Tom gained firsthand leadership experience as vice president of human resources for a personnel consulting firm and in various management positions at IBM.

Paul Hersey has helped train over ten million managers and salespeople from more than one thousand businesses and organizations. Recognized as one of the world's outstanding authorities on training and development in leadership, management, and selling, he is also a teacher and a consultant to industrial, government, and military organizations. Paul has authored or co-authored numerous books, papers, and articles, including *Management of Organizational Behavior: Utilizing Human Resources; Organizational Change Through Effective Leadership;* and *Selling: A Behavioral Science Approach.* His most recent books include *The Situational Leader* and *Situational Selling: An Approach to Increasing Sales Effectiveness.*

Maya Hu-Chan has been an international management consultant, coach, and trainer for over twelve years, specializing in executive coaching, 360° leadership feedback, organizational transformation, diversity, and cross-cultural communications. Maya has coached over three thousand leaders in Global 100 companies to improve their leadership competency and worked with leaders in twenty-one countries. Maya is co-author of *A Study in Excellence: Management in the Nonprofit Human Services, Global Business Skills,* and *Manager's Resource Guide.*

Julie M. Johnson is an executive coach who helps companies improve business results by maximizing the performance of key individuals. Julie's work focuses on leadership-needs assessments, high-potential employees, people who have just been promoted, and resolution of interpersonal, business-related conflicts. Julie holds a B.A. in liberal arts from Carnegie Mellon University, an M.A. in social psychology from Southern Methodist University, and an M.B.A. from the Harvard Business School. Julie conducts an international coaching practice, the Reid Group in Fairfield, Connecticut.

Beverly Kaye is president of Career Systems International, Inc. Her cutting-edge management style and career development programs are used by leading corporations. She is a prolific writer, popular lecturer, and a management consultant. In the early 1980s, Bev published her now classic book, *Up Is NOT the Only Way,* which forecast how individual careers would be affected by the move to leaner and flatter organizations. She has recently co-authored *Love 'Em or Lose 'Em: Getting Good People to Stay.*

James M. Kouzes is chairman emeritus of the Tom Peters Company. He is also the dean's professor of leadership in the Leavey School of Business at Santa Clara University and an executive fellow at its Center for Innovation and Entrepreneurship. Jim is co-author of the award-winning and best-selling book *The Leadership Challenge: How to Keep Getting Extraordinary Things Done in Organizations* and the recently released *Encouraging the Heart* and *The Leadership Challenge Planner.*

Kerry Larson has worked as an internal coach for AT&T Wireless, McCaw Cellular Communications, Teledesic, and Avia. Currently, he is a senior partner with Leadership Strategies International and vice president of people development at Teledesic. Previously, Kerry was senior vice president with AT&T Wireless Services. He also worked for Avia International as vice president of organizational development.

Richard J. Leider is a founding partner of The Inventure Group, a firm devoted to helping individuals, leaders, and teams discover the power of purpose. As a pioneer in the field of life/work designing, Richard has become an internationally respected author, speaker, and executive coach, as well as a noted spokesman for "life skills" needed in the twenty-first century. He has written four books, including the international bestseller *Repacking Your Bags,* and is now an online columnist for the nation's fast-growing business magazine, *Fast Company.*

Bruce Lloyd is principal lecturer in strategy at South Bank University, London, England. He is the author of over one hundred papers and articles on strategy-related topics, with a recent focus on the future of office and office work; the relationship between power, responsibility, leadership, and learning; and the role of wisdom in knowledge management. He is the editor of two books, *The Best of Long Range Planning on Creating and Managing New Ventures* and *Creating Value Through Acquisitions, Demergers, Buyouts, and Alliances.*

Carlos E. Marin is a senior consultant with Keilty, Goldsmith & Company. He is the former vice president of the Human Development Training Institute in San Diego and the former academic dean and chancellor of National University. Carlos has extensive national and international experience as an organizational, management, leadership development educator, consultant, and executive coach. He has designed and implemented many programs targeted at aligning business strategies with organizational culture modifications.

Howard Morgan is a director of Keilty, Goldsmith & Company and Leadership Research Institute. Since joining the firm in 1988, Howard has specialized in executive coaching as a strategic change management tool leading leading to improved customer/employee satisfaction and overall corporate performance. His recent achievements include the development of an internal coaching model for a large international organizations and coaching executives on the skill of leading leaders.

David Noer is an author, researcher, and consultant. He has written six books and numerous academic and popular articles on the application of human spirit to leadership. He heads his own consulting firm in Greensboro, North Carolina. His practice involves executive coaching; team development; dealing with the human aspects of mergers, acquisitions, and downsizing; mission, vision, and value development; and strategic planning. The common thread of his work involves helping organizations and people through transitions by harnessing the power of applied human spirit.

Tom Pettey is the chief of the Human Resources Division for the California Public Employees' Retirement System (CalPERS). As key policy advisor on human resource issues, he has primary responsibility for the implementation of human resources strategies to support the CalPERS strategic plan. In addition to directing the core human resources functions, over the past two years he has devoted particular attention to the development of specialized and innovative programs to recruit and retain a top-quality workforce.

Elizabeth Pinchot is an executive coach, consultant, and author. Co-founder and president of Pinchot & Company, she has coached senior executives in large organizations and entrepreneurs in startups and has advised the executive directors and senior staff of nonprofit companies. As president of a consulting company, she has been responsible for the development of dozens of employees. Elizabeth is also co-author, with Gifford Pinchot, of *The Intelligent Organization: Engaging the Talent and Initiative of Everyone in the Workplace.*

Gifford Pinchot is an author, speaker, coach, and consultant on innovation management and related topics. He has coached teams that have launched over five hundred new products and services. His best-selling book,

INTRAPRENEURING: Why You Don't Have to Leave the Corporation to Become an Entrepreneur, defined the ground rules for an emerging field of enterprise—the courageous pursuit of new ideas in established organizations.

Barry Z. Posner is dean of the Leavey School of Business, Santa Clara University, and professor of leadership. Barry is co-author (with Jim Kouzes) of the award-winning and best-selling leadership book: *The Leadership Challenge: How to Keep Getting Extraordinary Things Done in Organizations.* An internationally renowned scholar who has written many research and practitioner-oriented articles, Barry is a frequent conference speaker and workshop facilitator and has worked with many organizations.

Alastair G. Robertson heads Andersen Consulting's worldwide leadership development practice. He is also a partner in the organizational and human performance line of business, providing in-depth expertise in strategic change and organizational strategy. He is a specialist in individual, team, and organization leadership assessment and behavior development, building on personal motivational strengths, and is an advisor and coach to many European and U.S.-based executives.

Edgar H. Schein is Sloan Fellows Professor of Management Emeritus and senior lecturer at the MIT Sloan School of Management. He is co-editor of the highly acclaimed Addison-Wesley series on organization development. Professor Schein has consulted with a range of organizations around the world on culture, organization development, and careers. He is considered one of the founders of the field of organizational psychology.

Deepak (Dick) Sethi is director of executive and leadership development for the information company, The Thomson Corporation. He is a leading authority in the field of executive and leadership development, and the program he helped design and direct at AT&T is widely considered a leading-cdge benchmark program.

Jeremy Solomons is an independent consultant, speaker, and writer, who provides customized coaching, facilitation, and training in career development, conflict resolution, cross-cultural communication, global leadership, international management, multicultural team building, and strategic planning to individuals and groups around the world. Jeremy has just completed a year-long research project, which will be part of the forthcoming book, *The Global Leader of the Future.*

Iain Somerville is a partner in Andersen Consulting's Strategy practice, based in Los Angeles, California. He serves the leaders of global organizations, primarily in technology-based service industries, such as communications, media, and education. Over the past twenty-five years, as a top management consultant and executive coach, he has served many of the world's leading private, public, and social sector enterprises. Iain is the founder of the Andersen Consulting Organization Strategy practice and the Institute for Strategic Change—the firm's global business "think tank."

Liz Thach is director of leadership and organization development for MediaOne Group, a $7.4 billion broadband and international wireless business. With over sixteen years' experience in the field of human resource development, she specializes in international leadership development and the application of communication technology to workplace performance. Her experience includes organization development, executive and leadership development, and team building.

R. Roosevelt Thomas, Jr., is founder and CEO of the management consulting firm R. Thomas Consulting and Training. He is also founder of and senior research fellow at the research-based American Institute for Managing Diversity. Known for his pioneering work in diversity management, he is author of two groundbreaking books, *Beyond Race and Gender: Unleashing the Power of Your Total Workforce by Managing Diversity* and *Redefining Diversity.*

Dave Ulrich is professor of business administration at the School of Business at the University of Michigan. He is co-author of *Results-Based Leadership, Human Resource Champions, The Boundaryless Organization,* and

Organizational Capability. Business Week hailed him as one of the world's top ten educators in management and the number one educator in human resources. Dave also edited *Human Resource Management Journal* 1990–1999.

Robert Witherspoon, a seasoned executive coach, speaker, and author, is president of Performance & Leadership Development Ltd. He helps clients improve their business results by developing the performance and leadership of key people. Formerly a partner at Arthur Andersen, he has over thirty years experience in business and consulting. Robert is the lead author of *Four Essential Ways That Coaching Can Help Executives,* a bestseller from the Center for Creative Leadership. He lives and works out of Washington, D.C.

COACHING FOR LEADERSHIP

PART ONE

FOUNDATIONS OF COACHING

Part One introduces the reader to the foundations of coaching, which we see as a modern and success-driven approach to leadership. We explain how coaching offers an appropriate style of working in the post-management era. The leadership era—in which knowledge workers already operate in a more turbulent, flexible, and dispersed work setting—demands a new work-style approach, and we show how coaching delivers it.

In its very essence, we see coaching as a mainstream and purposeful activity. Coaching helps every executive build an individual path to achieve personal or organizational aspirations. When consolidated, all these paths transform today's managers into tomorrow's leaders. In setting the scene, Laurence Lyons introduces a new and broader way of thinking about strategy to incorporate the ambitions of the individual as well as the work team and organization. We see this idea of mutual strategy as one of the foundations of coaching. To make the coaching activity capable of delivering results in the real business world, there must be some mechanism for actually bringing about real and durable change on the ground. Marshall Goldsmith explains the importance of integrating a practical, behavioral change mechanism as another and vital foundation element that must be at the root of successful coaching. In order to flourish within an enterprise (or, equally a not-for-profit organization), coaching must support the creation of core value in delivering genuine and measurable economic business results. Alyssa Freas clearly shows the practical steps that can create the powerful links between executive coaching, customer satisfaction, and bottom-line business results. These three foundations of coaching—mutual strategy, behavioral change, and core value—introduce the reader to key themes that run through the entire book.

We believe that coaching should be seen as a holistic and integrative approach that has developed over time from a range of leadership approaches and development techniques. Elizabeth and Gifford Pinchot discuss the links between psychotherapy and coaching and introduce the reader to some ethical considerations that surround our subject area. To finish and consolidate this section, Edgar Schein raises and answers fundamental questions about the purpose and nature of coaching and shows how it can be regarded as a branch of process consulting: both embrace common systems ideas, such as problem identification and responsibility for outcome, within the context of a "helping relationship."

CHAPTER ONE

COACHING AT THE HEART OF STRATEGY

Laurence S. Lyons

Observing the Coaching Scene

Imagine them, perched at the corner of a highly polished mahogany table in some elegant boardroom. They take turns at drawing on a whiteboard, one passionately elaborating on a point, the other deep in thought. A fresh pattern of thought sparks insight: highly animated, they evaluate every possible angle, moving toward a considered plan of action.

Now picture them meeting in a hotel lounge. Here they speak in more hushed tones, punctuated with sips of expensive coffee which has, in fact, generously paid for their admission. Their conversation is accompanied with gesticulation. At times they argue aloud. Equally, there are protracted periods of contemplative silence. They appear to be business colleagues, come together to clinch a deal. The observer may suppose them to be friends—or perhaps adversaries—working through some evidently complex problem. And in some ways, they are.

We will see their meetings reconvened regularly, the vital encounters often arranged at point-blank notice. Emergencies demand urgent, intense contact.

If recently successful, their conversation accompanies dinner in a prestigious restaurant. In more pressing moments, they will make whatever arrangements are expedient—a hurried trip to an airport lounge may fit the bill. Sometimes they will have no choice other than to talk on the telephone. For them, the venue is hardly relevant. The value is in the quality of the dialogue and in its consequences, not in its location. This is therefore a meeting of the utmost importance. The outside world cannot interrupt them, even if it were to dare to try.

Strategy

To the casual observer, the practice of executive coaching may appear to involve little more than holding an animated conversation. But behind the immediate "here-and-now" setting in which such an exchange takes place, many worlds are to be found. One describes the executive's career that stretches beyond today, well into the past and future. Any modern career is set within a world of work in which the ground rules are in a state of flux. Central to this, we find the immediate present, the world of today, populated by colleagues in various teams, managers, direct reports, associates, suppliers, and customers. The specific configuration of relationships can include government, trade unions, banks, shareholders, stock markets, and so forth. Permeating this is the competitive or purposeful world of the organization in which the executive works. And then again, there is a world beyond the boundary—one all too often neglected in management books—desperately needing to be acknowledged, though not explored, during the coaching process. This is the non-business, non-work, social, personal, family world. We must accept that within work there is life beyond work.

In order to be fully effective, a coaching dialogue must be able to integrate these worlds. Good coaching has the capacity to help an executive or team develop competencies and business effectiveness within any or all of the domains.

To complicate this picture, membership in the work teams to which the executive belongs (for example, project team, task force, or committee) is often fluid: people come and go. Team, personal, and organizational objectives also change over time. In addition, the organization itself is often in a state of reformulating its own identity, mission, and structure.

Yet, this apparently simple coaching dialogue does take place. Our research shows that it is consistently successful when performed well. Amazingly, a seemingly simple "coaching conversation" accommodates turbulence and uncertainty, yet repeatedly succeeds in producing outstanding results. For the practitioner who has a limited perception of coaching as simply a collegial conversation, coaching will undoubtedly fail to deliver durable success. But coaching will be successful both in a strategic sense and over time when acted out as a structured dialogue of emerging purpose. Practitioners and their clients have a mutual interest in knowing how this can be brought about.

A Structured Dialogue of Emerging Purpose

Good coaching is difficult to do. Perhaps the greatest challenge is to engage the executive in a dialogue of emerging purpose. The disarmingly simple question, "What should we talk about?" can be hard to answer well. Thus, the coach often works with the executive as a kind of scout, together selecting an appropriate path. Coaching is potentially both high-impact and high-risk. Dire consequences can result from setting off in the wrong direction—disappointing to both the executive and the business. In contrast, identifying the right path will reap high reward.

Dialogue is at the heart of coaching. In an interview, we find two people. One is typically a senior executive of a large corporation, responsible for a significant part of the business, the other an executive coach—neither an employee of nor a technical consultant to that corporation. The executive has million-dollar spending authority. The coach has no corporate authority whatever. But through dialogue alone, the external coach exercises considerable influence. With neither formal authority nor direct accountability, the coach's greatest ambition is to profoundly affect the way that the executive thinks and behaves.

Rapport is vital to make sure that the dialogue gets off the ground. The "chemistry" of the pair must quickly establish trust and credibility; the executive must have confidence that the coach is not simply wasting time.

Good listening skills on the part of the coach, together with the ability to deliver honest feedback, are crucial to keeping the dialogue grounded in reality—not on fabricated supposition or unsupported beliefs. Between them, coach and executive need to agree on how to separate transient, situational factors from those that are innate and require attention. This sifting can often require delicate judgment when the setting is a turbulent corporate environment. Every effort made in teasing out fact from raw data is well rewarded: carefully validated data is a key determinant of the quality of the outcome of the coaching venture.

The directional or strategic power of any coaching dialogue lies primarily in its ability to question. Questions may be asked to surface submerged issues or may be asked to help the executive to reconsider some position or proposed course of action. The executive's attitudes or opinions may become either reinforced or challenged: the person's current path will be either confirmed or probed. Even when the dialogue confirms the validity of a person's existing game plan, it adds value—boosting the executive's confidence while keeping business risks in check.

Coaching re-engages with reality when good questioning is followed by inspired analysis, detailed action planning, and follow-through back in the work environment. Working together with the executive, the coach crystallizes their conversation in an action plan. The end point of a coaching interview invariably involves the executive planning to try out some new behavior. Most importantly, the full value of any coaching activity can only be realized when a new behavior is actually performed in the real world. At this stage—after the coaching interview has ended—the coach encourages the executive to follow up and execute the plan. In a sense, the coach now acts as both a memory and a conscience. Thus, coaching is best seen as a complete and ongoing process, not just a single interview event.

A good coach need not be an expert in the executive's job type or industry. A good coach does not even have to possess as wide a range of social skills as the executive. With a sound appreciation of business and interpersonal dynamics, a good coach is simply a process person who can establish rapport; is informed about the executive's immediate environment; is honest and courageous in providing feedback; is a good listener;

asks good questions; is visionary and analytical; and is a good planner who seeks follow-up and closure.

The sheer power unleashed in the coaching process must surely obligate the executive and coach to consider several serious questions, such as: What constitutes success in this dialogue? Who, specifically, is my client? How should confidential issues be treated? Which topics fall outside the purview of coaching, and how do those affecting work performance get recognized? In the face of these ethical conundrums, the coach must strive to align dialogue in a direction punctuated by validated objectives. The coach must be brave enough to urge the executive to move forward—often by confronting some taboo topic, hitherto deliberately ignored. The dialogue will always help the executive pursue selected objectives—yet not be overly directed by the coach. After all, coaching is concerned with facilitation, not giving advice. Although the necessity remains for the executive to persevere along the most successful route that can currently be identified, there is no promise that the path will be simple to find or easy to travel.

This brings us to two crucial insights into good coaching. First, it is necessary to look behind a dialogue to realize that it will not simply "happen" without background. The most robust coaching relies on broadly informed dialogue. Quite a lot of work may have to be undertaken in the collection, validation, and analysis of information before real coaching can begin. The kind of information that is assimilated might include current facts about the markets, technology, or political environment in which the executive is working. Impressions held by colleagues, associates, and direct reports might provide vital indications about the executive's personal interaction. Sometimes the only alternative is to begin with an executive's own anecdotal information, but coaching in a vacuum is a dangerous game.

The second insight to be gained takes us beyond executive coaching. By incorporating the ethos of the organization within the coaching dialogue, it becomes possible to relate an individual's behavior to purposeful organizational change. When the whole organization is engaged, coaching becomes strategic. Moreover, within a modern learning organization, team coaching and the development of strategic thinking may become one and the same thing.

For the coach, strategy need not reside in quarterly profit targets alone. Those committed to strategic coaching will expand the meaning of strategy to at once embrace individual, team, and corporate actors. Strategic executive coaching is an inclusive, practical approach, incorporating the idea of a dashboard or balanced scorecard, and it is well-adapted to a complex world in which even the ground rules are in a state of change.

Transforming People

For the sponsor, a coaching initiative might be viewed as a self-contained project, rather than as part of an integrated corporate strategy. However, whenever coaching succeeds in aligning the needs of the business with the developmental needs of its people, it cannot help but be strategic in nature.

Many organizations face a situation in which an entire block of talent shifts when issues of succession and development emerge. Typically, this occurs during mergers, downsizing, or block retirement. The creation of a career path to retain top talent and a drive to expand into global markets are also examples of situations demanding a strategic coaching response. Whatever the cause, a gap opens up that has to be filled for the organization to remain strategically healthy. So, at one leading automobile manufacturer, fast-track engineers are today being coached to become tomorrow's senior leaders. Elsewhere, a Fortune 500 IT innovator has implemented coaching within a program that has integrated five separate operating countries into a cohesive and highly successful business region.

For the person being coached, the experience is invariably strategic. Coaching offers the executive a golden opportunity to step back and reflect on personal development. By expressly allocating precious work time, the coaching interview momentarily suspends the immediate pressures of the day and encourages the individual to think about "just me." From this viewpoint, the coaching intervention is able to break the pedestrian logic of mere reaction and repetition. For once, the executive has time to look dispassionately and proactively at more broad-brush issues in a far wider context. The individual may well start to consider the interface between work and life. Work is within life; work is a part of life. In order that the executive may learn and develop at work, that individual must first understand where they are in their career and in their life. Often, reflection on one's purpose will validate or challenge one's current position. Such consideration may encourage an individual to move forward or to move on to something new. To the extent that coaching sensitizes people to reflect and act in a more purposeful way, it is again strategic in nature, helping to align the organization with the people who are in it.

In times of major organizational change, coaching often provides the necessary impetus for building and motivating teams. Team coaching helps establish and then build a collection of individuals into a fully functioning business network. The resulting team unites people across functions and divisions, often including members outside the formal organization. Time and again, we have seen a team-coaching process motivate people to coalesce. Provided that the group contains that critical mass of people needed for the business to move forward, a nascent transition team starts to emerge. Many team members will have recently taken part in individual coaching sessions, and so will be ready to think strategically at the moment the team starts to form. When a foundation of trust has been established, the conditions for cohesion are in place and the team spontaneously ignites in a dialogue of business improvement. Such teams are enthusiastic; such teams have solutions that will work; such teams are unstoppable. A well-designed team-coaching process brings together the right people and raises the broadest challenge, in an environment in which failure is not an option.

Coaching also plays a special role at the most senior level in an organization (that is, with the board of directors or senior management team). At this level, issues are often motivational rather than technical. Technically, the coach will play a unique role as interpreter by insisting that jargon gets transformed into business concepts that are commonly understood. Motivationally, members may differ significantly in their beliefs about the purpose of the business and may hold conflicting expectations about what success means and how to measure it. Then again, business owners may hold wildly different views about asset valuation and a preferred exit or merger strategy. Located at an intermediate level in large companies, divisional and regional boards often grapple with a particularly perplexing question: How can we find ways to add value from our unique vantage point in the overall structure? In all these cases, coaching offers yet another framework for dialogue. Coaching provides a climate within which vital, though seemingly intransigent, issues may be brought to the surface, confronted, and then dealt with. Coaching offers the senior team a practical tool to break any logjams that are in the way of progress.

In all of these cases—for individuals, teams, and boards—coaching offers a structured dialogue of emerging purpose, directed toward success. As Figure 1.1 shows, with the right conditions in place coaching is organizational transformation; coaching is team development; coaching is strategy in motion.

FIGURE 1.1. THE STRATEGIC COACHING MODEL

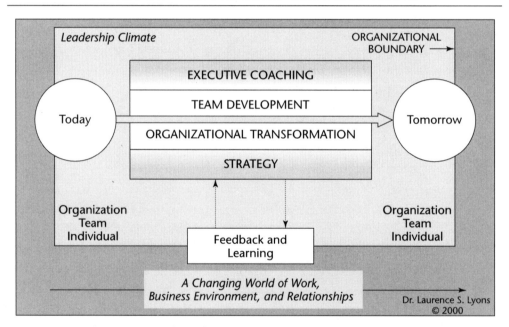

Strategic Coaching gets people, teams, and organizations from where they are today to where they want to be tomorrow. The leader is committed to ensuring the existence and maintenance of the coaching process and its alignment with business results.

Leadership

In an era in which leadership is replacing management and learning is replacing instruction, coaching is surfacing as the accessible face of strategy. Business strategy no longer commands an exclusive domain secreted within the impersonal body of an abstract "organization." Today, as demands on everyone's time intensify, strategy is manifest in the flesh and blood of each executive. Coaching is not simply a passing fad: it offers a pragmatic supporting context in which modern strategy flourishes. In today's turbulent world, strategy has developed into something that emerges, always tracking a moving target. And the preferred vehicle—responsive enough to reduce the risk in successfully traveling toward that ever-changing destination—is to be found in the dialogue of coaching.

Any dialogue that brings an executive closer to goal achievement in the real world truly succeeds at a strategic level. Achievement-oriented dialogue reaches outside the immediate interview to make real things happen. Coaching has the power to let strategy come alive and therefore to work in practice. Executive coaching has become current simply because it has become relevant. Coaching facilitates success and is congruent with the way we want to work and the way we have to work. It is relevant to the modern world of business because it is holistic and adaptive. Coaching is also a method that respects people as individuals, not merely as cogs in the business machine. Rooted in conversation, coaching is evolving as a natural form of leadership.

A Radically Different World of Work

As knowledge work relentlessly replaces manual work, we are witness to the dawn of perhaps the most meritocratic workplace environment in history. Management is no longer perceived in terms of maintaining the business machine, but is seen as the motivator and leader of men and women. Our understanding of the essence of management is reeling from radical change.

The management metaphor has, until now, been extremely useful in helping executives become more systematic and better organized in order to plan, motivate, and control. But, the word "management" has come to represent an attitudinal straightjacket that can stifle, and often excuse the need for, that kind of truly innovative thinking that has become a prerequisite for success. As markets become more efficient and intensively competitive, ideas of coercion and control—together with a reliance on rigid rules—hinder, rather than help, businesses succeed.

Noticeably, the adjectives used to describe management work have already started to change. Terms once borrowed from engineering and finance are being replaced with descriptions from the social and humanist vocabulary. Thus the "efficient company" has become a "learning organization." Language is not the only thing changing. The perspective is shifting steadily and surely from labor to knowledge; from management to leadership; from product to consumers and service; from routine operation to inspired creativity; and from task repetition to marketing innovation. As technology and automation shift the boredom of work from people to machines, the human world of work that remains challenges our intellect, not our muscle.

Fast-paced competition means that businesses can no longer afford to reward the routine repetition embedded in the all-too-rigid "management" model. A new culture, one that prizes sensible action and appropriate adaptability, is challenging as well as complementing written strategic plans. These vast tomes were invariably out of date on the day they were published, and contained too many untested or generalized assumptions to be workable in practice. Long delays in the planning cycle allowed the organization to meander aimlessly while waiting for the control loop to close. It is not easy to enter into dialog with a written plan. These days, competitive advantage is not to be found in written plans alone. Corporate success is now intimately related to the way in which individual executives think, act, and interact on a daily basis. To win and receive reward, executives must now do the right thing, not simply the written thing. It is not enough to take problems to others and await a response. The competition simply will not stand back and wait. Today's successful executives do not "need the meetings," instead they "meet the needs."

The change in the nature of work is not only radical, it is also deeply pervasive as leaders continue to shift operations into the global arena. Worldwide, a realization that a key source of competitive advantage is to be found rooted in the social fabric of the company is opening up new vistas of opportunity. Whereas the technical business process was only recently seen as the dominant lever of change, we have come to recognize the human "etiquette" of the organization as a potent value driver. If we get the formula right, the currently emerging leadership culture offers leaders a genuine opportunity to make the world a better place.

Coaching offers us a unique response to help address that challenge at every level.

The Learning Executive

A complete overhaul is taking place in the way we see the relationship between education and work. In the traditional model, predicated on executing a single professional function over an entire lifetime, learning was confined to a single burst of training followed by years of practice. This sequence has now become less relevant for many. Today, "Education for Life" is rapidly replacing "A Job for Life" as the dominant career model. No longer does a specific job last for a lifetime; several jobs fragment a career, while learning has become continuous, rather than a one-time affair.

Executive skills must match the situation. Modern business is too dynamic to allow executives to succeed with the old rigid and simplistic assumptions. On a personal level, all executives face a recurring challenge in pragmatically responding to revolutionary trends and pressures in the world of work. A fresh dexterity is now demanded. Simply "painting-by-the-numbers" no longer works in a world that demands so much more than a single prescribed answer. So today's successful executives must embrace self-development and learning. At a time when organizations can no longer guarantee work for life, individuals have taken on "Learning for Life" as the paradigm model.

Fortunately, such an approach also helps to meet pressing organizational needs. Everywhere we find cycles becoming shorter, with businesses in a never-ending race to find a quicker way to reach a globally expanding market. The trend is also for work to make increasing demands on employees' time. In such a frenetic climate, executives cannot undertake learning as a separate activity. To keep technical knowledge up-to-date, an executive may have no alternative but to spend time off-site, but leadership skills are best learned in the workplace and on the job. Learning must be applied immediately, responding to issues of the moment. This "just-in-time" teaching of skills is another form of executive coaching.

Executives need knowledge and skills to cope with situations as they come up. Often the circumstances are ambiguous. An executive may need to deal with a troublesome colleague; start a new assignment; present a difficult business argument; become more "visible"; or communicate more effectively with direct reports. The coach fits into the new learning model perfectly by allowing the executive to learn, modify, and apply a suitable approach in a particular business situation. Coaching allows executives to learn while at work, while keeping up the pace.

Striving for Success

Executives are invariably concerned with issues of corporate, team, and individual success. Because they face new rules of competition and new definitions of success, modern executives must find ways to align and balance these components. They must choose activities that truly add value over efforts that merely appear effective. This may seem little more than common sense, yet it reflects a genuine attitudinal shift in the workplace. It is another important area in which a coach can challenge and validate the client's perspective. This can also engender a sense of empowerment in that the executive wants to "do the right thing."

Within the broad category of "knowledge work," mundane and passive stewardship continues to lose ground to creativity and innovation. In addition, the basis of reward is shifting from an emphasis on effort to a focus on results. Arriving at the office well before the official start time and regularly working late into the night and on weekends are no longer automatically seen as characteristics of an effective executive.

Technology has allowed working styles to be more open and flexible, while at the same time allowing work and life to impinge on each other, making both more stressful. Coaches can help executives to negotiate this delicate interface without being intrusive. Once again, the coach needs an ethical position and rules of engagement or terms of reference within which to operate. As we embrace information technology, giving ourselves more freedom in choice of lifestyle, we usually prefer—and even insist—that the value of our work contribution be measured in terms of outcomes or results. For knowledge workers in particular, the time of day or the geographic location of their efforts has become irrelevant. Outcome, not input, now attracts reward.

In yesterday's business world, the "numbers" and the routine mechanics of operations lulled organizations and their executives into believing that they were fulfilling a purpose simply by repeating traditional formulas. Certainly, repetition worked well in the factory model, but repetition is no longer a guarantee for success in a service and knowledge economy. A new style of leadership is called for. This shift from management to leadership is primarily one of outlook and attitude. Leadership moves us from rigidity to flexibility; leadership allows us to adapt in a more uncertain environment; leadership urges people to take responsibility, to take the initiative, to do the right thing, and thereby to excel.

It is not surprising to find that dynamic leadership is overthrowing the familiar and traditional "social norms" established in the era of stable hierarchical management. The successful executive today must follow this trend in order to achieve desired outcomes in a business world that is becoming more volatile.

Leadership has become crucial in creating value and achieving competitive advantage in the modern work organization. Leadership is not exclusive to a few "top executives"; it is class-free and pervasive. A leader treats people as responsible adults and encourages all to act in the interest of mutual success. A leader promotes a sense of individual worth and community and diligently directs activity toward the business ambitions of the organization. The "culture" and leadership style of an organization are not a consequence of doing work in a certain way. Instead, they are a healthy context within which excellent work is done. Managers motivate, whereas leaders inspire. Inspired companies are winners. Corporations need far fewer managers and far more leaders, and coaching offers a direct and practical way to instill this new culture into corporate life.

Coaching provides a route to leadership. Coaching can unlock the latent leadership potential in managers and reinforce leadership where it already exists. A culture of coaching can nurture leadership. And when coaching aligns the development of the individual, the team, and the organization toward a mutual definition of success, then coaching becomes leadership. Leadership through coaching offers a strategic and practical direction for all.

Coaching in Practice

It can be as lonely at the periphery of a modern networked organization as it is at the top of a traditional pyramid. Problems can come from talking too freely inside an organization, however flat or virtual it may be. Work colleagues become tomorrow's interested parties. Truly innovative concepts can sound like crazy ideas in the early stages, and few executives want to take the risk of appearing foolish. Even private discussions can contain political topics that when touched on, even tentatively, can establish a position from which it is difficult to reverse. Leaders need a safe and supportive theater or laboratory in which to rehearse and refine their ideas. Coaching meets this need.

Coaches present executives with an opportunity to engage in a dialogue of development. Where there is no coach, the chance for this reflective dialogue may be missed. When executives have no one to talk to, there is no tested or evolved dialogue, there is no attitude formation, and so an important part of executive thinking—thinking through—is missing. In all these ways, coaching is supportive of executive and organizational learning. Coaching provides a platform for practical action directed toward intelligent and strategic intent.

Every organization is different; each has its unique definition of success. In whatever way the dimensions of success are articulated by each board, team, or individual executive, coaches are charged with finding a developmental path to progress. In striving for success, leaders must find ways to advance the business, while respecting core organizational values and fundamental beliefs. These must be understood by coaches at a visceral level. To deliver quality, a coach needs to see far beyond the superficial level, at which all corporate value statements look similar, and discover in detail the actual values in play. And, then again, as the world progresses to continuously repaint an ever-emerging strategic organizational context, these values are destined to develop and change over time.

External and Internal Agents

Most leaders acknowledge that in order to remain healthy an organization must reach out to its stakeholders and into the environment. Indeed, a modern organization will actively extend its social fabric through dialogue with coaches, consultants, and others. Yet, it is a source of astonishment to many that an organization's maintenance functions require any interaction from outside.

The traditional or legal definition of a corporation can fool us into believing that it will remain forever self-sufficient. The need for external nurturing agents may seem to fly in the face of this belief. However, the "outside" or external aspect of the organization has been long recognized in "systems theory" as extremely important. In today's organizations, interaction with the environment is being rediscovered as a vital activity required to reduce business risk. Here again, the coaching opportunity supports another crucial facet of leadership—the need to be in touch with the reality beyond the formal boundary of the organization.

Yet, an organization that regards executive coaching as a service provided entirely by external suppliers can never attain a true climate of leadership. Modern corporations must be capable of maintaining cohesion in the newly evolving, flatter, and networked workplaces. Today's leaders do not seek to set themselves apart, but instead are determined to replicate their best leadership behaviors in those around them. They are also open to absorbing, as well as propagating, such exemplary behaviors. Thus, internal coaching—or internalized coaching—is vital to working in the modern, cross-functional network in which all participants find it natural to coach.

However flat an organization may be, executives will always need to interact with their direct reports. Here again, coaching provides the executive with a foundation for dialogue that is well-suited to leading "free agents," who are less likely to respect positional power as a legitimate motivator.

The term "mentoring" is widely used to describe an activity closely related to coaching. A mentor is likely to have had a successful personal track record in a role similar to that of the client. Thus, the nature of this relationship may tend to contain relatively more content than process. Reputation and trust towards the mentor are powerful determinants in making the chemistry work. A senior mentor can be a great asset who is likely to be able to tap into to an otherwise inaccessible range of useful business contacts.

When working in the same organization, a mentor requires no learning curve to absorb culture. Steps should be taken—and periodic checks should be made—to ensure the internal mentor does not inadvertently become a compromised interested party in the day-to-day operations of the person being mentored. There is only one other essential qualification: a good mentor simply needs to be a good coach.

The coaching approach is also spilling into all kinds of work relationships. For example, some organizations have instituted an informal "buddy" system, which can be little more that sharing contact information at training events. Some larger divisions of Fortune 500 companies are now putting coaches on the payroll as full-time employees. It is not uncommon for senior executives to take their coaches with them when switching companies. This becomes part of the hiring negotiation process, along with share options and other benefits. The sheer pervasiveness of the coaching relationship in organizations today—whether inside, outside, or between organizations—confirms that coaching is seen as an effective style of working with the blurring boundaries in and around organizations.

Future Directions

In its modern form, coaching is a young and evolving field whose definition has yet to be determined and within which good practice is still being understood and developed. Yet, coaching has been able to draw from many established fields, including consultancy and counseling. In addition to being integrative in the theoretical sense, coaches have to be highly accommodating and adaptive in practice.

One important challenge for the coaching profession in the future will be the ability of its practitioners to maintain the links between the personal development of individual clients and the attainment of solid business results for their organizations. Only when this can be achieved consistently can a coaching program hope to justify the investment that it demands. The formula for success will display a number of characteristics. Coaches must be able to address issues that are individual, team, and organization-wide; they must act in a way congruent with the organization's style of leadership; they must promote and facilitate positive organizational development; they must be practical; and they must help in the achievement of business results.

In combining these elements, the Strategic Coaching Model (see Figure 1.1) provides a modern blueprint for business success. Couched in a culture of modern leadership and based on the powerful dynamics of human interaction, the model simply asserts that coaching is at its best when located at the heart of strategy.

About the Contributor

Laurence S. Lyons is a senior vice president of Executive Coaching Network, Inc. He is an accomplished coach, consultant, public speaker, and author, as well as an authority on organizational transformation. His twenty-five years' experience includes senior line and staff management positions in organizations of all sizes.

Larry provides consultancy in business strategy and organizational development to clients in all sectors. Larry's executive coaching and consulting career extends over several years and includes many blue-chip and multinational clients, such as British Airways, Unilever, Pricewaterhouse Coopers, British Broadcasting Corporation, WH Smith, MediaOne, Bank of England, Oracle, Dresser Industries, EDS, and Deutsche Bank. While leading consultant relations at Digital Equipment in the U.K., Larry has worked at partner level with all the major consultancies. Many of Larry's personal coaching clients are to be found in *Who's Who*. He has chaired and presented at conferences on consulting and coaching at the Institute of Directors, the Confederation of British Industry, and the Strategic Planning Society. In the early 1990s, Larry pioneered the "strategic cell development," an approach that rapidly accelerates the development of managers and leaders.

Laurence Lyons holds a Ph.D. in organizational analysis and an MSc in management from Brunel University. He is a member of serveral professional bodies and a member of associate faculty at Henley Management College, Oxfordshire, England, where he is Director of Research of the Future Work Forum and teaches senior management courses. He is also an equity partner in The Learning Partnership, an international speakers bureau.

Together with Professor David Birchall, Larry is co-author of the highly acclaimed book *Creating Tomorrow's Organization* published by Pearson Professional. He has also been published in the *U.K.'s Institute of Directors (IoD) Director Guide Series;* the Peter F. Drucker Foundation *Leader-to-Leader* journal; and the *Financial Times Handbook of Management.*

Larry is frequently quoted in the media. He has appeared in such diverse publications as *The Times, Computing,* the *Los Angeles Times,* the *Journal of the Institution of Chartered Surveyors,* and *Practical Training.* He has appeared in *British Airways Business Life* magazine and has been interviewed on BBC National Radio 4.

CHAPTER TWO

COACHING FOR BEHAVIORAL CHANGE

Marshall Goldsmith

As leaders, we preach teamwork, but often excuse ourselves from its practice—and even more often fail to hold people in our organizations accountable for demonstrating the behavior associated with living this value (Goldsmith, 1996). If everyone, including senior executives, acknowledges this challenge, why is it so difficult for leaders to promote change among those whose behavior they can most readily influence—their direct reports?

One reason is that leaders, like most people, want to be liked. Leaders are often afraid that confronting people about poor teamwork or other behavioral shortcomings (as opposed to performance problems) will cause them to be disliked. The paradox is, leaders would be respected *more,* not less, for delivering the bad news. Outside consultants often provide behavioral coaching to leaders, and leaders usually appreciate the help. Surveys show that people highly value honest feedback—whether or not the feedback itself is positive.

The nature of the performance-review process itself accounts for much of the problem. Historically, when assessing others, most managers were forced to play the role of judge—and, potentially, executioner. The consultant, by contrast, is usually seen as an objective third party who is providing analysis, suggestions, and feedback gathered from multiple sources. A person receiving bad news from a consultant is more likely to separate the message from the messenger than a person hearing the same news from the manager.

Fortunately, leaders have at their disposal a valuable aid already in place at many leading companies—360° feedback. Carefully designed processes that include 360° feedback can allow a leader to practice consultative behavioral coaching, as opposed to merely exercising personal judgment. The results can be profound—and not just for department heads evaluating their front-line employees. The executive coaching process can help any manager whose work involves personal interaction. In fact, senior management teams at some of the world's leading companies—American Express, Avon, GE, Netscape, Nortel, and Texaco—use 360° feedback as part of an overall process to help align corporate values and individual behavior.

Before You Begin

Although this process can improve behavior, it will definitely not solve all performance problems. The behavioral coaching process described in this chapter will focus only on coaching for behavioral change, not on strategic coaching, career coaching, or any of the other types of coaching described in this book. Before you start, ask yourself whether any of the following conditions prevail. If so, behavioral coaching may be a waste of time.

- *The person you're coaching is not willing to make a sincere effort to change.* Behavioral coaching will only work if the manager you are coaching is willing to make the needed commitment.
- *The person has been written off by the company.* Sometimes, organizations are really just documenting a case to get rid of someone. If that's the case, don't bother going through this process.
- *The person lacks the intelligence or functional skills to do the job.* If a manager does not have the capacity or experience required, don't expect behavioral coaching to help.

- *The organization has the wrong mission.* Behavioral coaching is a "how to get there" process, not a "where to go" process. If the organization is headed in the wrong direction, behavioral coaching will not make it change course.

Getting Started

On the other hand, if you're dealing with people who have the will and capacity to change their behavior, are operating in an environment that gives them a chance to change, and work for an organization that is headed in the right direction, this process will work; the nature of the process itself assures its success. The approach I recommend involves eight steps:

1. *Identify attributes for the manager you are coaching.* You should not have to start from scratch. I generally work with my clients to develop custom leadership profiles, but there are many useful inventories on the market (from the Andersen Consulting Global Leader of the Future, Jim Kouzes and Barry Posner, the Center for Creative Leadership, and others) that can be a big help. Once you've determined the behavioral characteristics of a successful manager in a given position—such things as accessibility to colleagues, recognition of others, and listening—ask that manager if he or she agrees that these are the right kinds of behaviors. Securing agreement will boost commitment to the process.

2. *Determine who can provide meaningful feedback.* Key stakeholders may include direct reports, peers, customers, suppliers, or members of the management team. Strive for a balanced mix that does not stack the deck for or against the manager, and gain agreement that these are the appropriate reviewers.

3. *Collect feedback.* Assessment is often best handled in a written, anonymous survey, compiled by an outside party into a summary report and given directly to the manager being coached.

4. *Analyze results.* Talk with the manager about the results of his or her peers' feedback. The manager may choose not to disclose individual stakeholders' comments or numerical scores. The point is simply to discuss the manager's key strengths and areas for improvement.

5. *Develop an action plan.* The most helpful—and appreciated—outcome of any assessment is specific advice. Developing "alternatives to consider" (rather than mandates) should not be difficult. If, for example, you asked the manager to suggest things you could do to be a better listener, you would probably receive a pretty good list, such as:

- Don't interrupt people;
- Paraphrase what they say;
- Make eye contact;
- Pause five seconds before responding to their remarks;
- Recognize that the problem isn't figuring out what to do; the problem is doing it; and
- Focus on one or two key behaviors and develop a few action steps to improve each.

6. *Have the manager respond to stakeholders.* The manager being reviewed should talk with each member of the review team and collect additional suggestions on how to improve on the key areas targeted for improvement.
7. *Develop an ongoing follow-up process.* Within three or four months conduct a two- to six-item mini-survey with the original review team. Respondents should be asked whether the manager has become more or less effective in the areas targeted for improvement.
8. *Review results and start again.* If the manager has taken the process seriously, stakeholders almost invariably report improvement. Build on that success by repeating the process quarterly for the next twelve to eighteen months. This type of follow-up will assure continued progress on initial goals and uncover additional areas for improvement. Stakeholders will appreciate the follow-up—people don't mind filling out a focused, two- to six-item mini-survey when they see positive results. The manager will benefit from ongoing, targeted feedback to improve performance.

Moving Beyond the Basics

You may want some coaching yourself from a trusted colleague, friend, or family member on how to approach the task, but this is not a mysterious process. It requires more discipline than talent, more integrity and commitment than behavioral science expertise. Simply by sitting down with the manager and analyzing perceptions of his or her colleagues, you will be able to change your relationship with that person. And the person will change too. Managers who want to improve, talk to people about ways to improve, solicit feedback, and develop a rigorous follow-up plan will almost always improve. (Certainly they won't get worse.) And when people improve, their self-confidence goes up. They keep doing what works, and they keep getting better.

By becoming an effective coach, you can become a more credible leader and an active agent of change. You help people develop an essential habit for personal or organizational success—follow-through. By delivering what you promise—that is, measuring others on the behaviors and attributes you say you value—you cement the bonds of leadership with your constituents. And by having others follow through on their own progress toward agreed-on goals, you can help create a more responsive, positive, and cohesive organization.

It may be difficult for leaders to give and receive honest feedback—and to make the time for genuine dialogue. Behavioral coaching is simple, but not easy. It is just one tool in a total strategy of performance appraisal, compensation, and promotion that can reinforce positive behavioral change. But, if you're serious about your espoused values, shouldn't you ensure that the managers in your organization demonstrate the behaviors you promote?

About the Contributor

Marshall Goldsmith is one of the world's foremost authorities on helping leaders achieve positive, measurable change in behavior for themselves, their people, and their teams. In 2000, Marshall was listed in *Forbes* magazine as one of five top executive coaches and in *Human Resources* magazine as one of the world's leading human resource consultants. He has also been ranked in the *Wall Street Journal* as one of the top ten consultants in the field of executive development. His work has received national recognition from the Institute for Management Studies, the American Management Association, the American Society for Training and Development, and the Human Resource Planning Society.

Marshall's coaching process has been positively described in both the *New York Times* and the *Financial Times* (U.K.). He is one of a select few consultants who has been asked to provide leadership development or coaching to over fifty of the world's leading CEOs. Marshall's work is focused specifically on coaching for behavioral change.

Twenty years ago, Marshall co-founded Keilty, Goldsmith & Company (KGC). A recent study by Penn State University listed KGC as one of seven key providers of customized leadership development in the U.S. KGC's coaching, leadership development, and feedback processes have impacted over one million people in seventy organizations around the world. KGC consultants have a unique approach to behavioral coaching. They typically are not paid for one year, and they are not paid unless positive, measurable change in behavior occurs. In the process, behavioral change is not measured by the person being coached, but by the key stakeholders of their coaching client.

Clients have included many of the world's leading corporations, such as Agilent, American Express, Andersen Consulting, AT&T, BellSouth, Coca-Cola, Dow Chemical, Enron, Goldman-Sachs, General Electric, GTE, John Hancock, IBM, Johnson & Johnson, Kodak, KPMG, Lucent, McKinsey, Merck, Motorola, Nortel, Northrop Grumman, Pfizer, Pitney Bowes, SmithKline Beecham, Southern Company, Square D, Sun Microsystems, Texaco, Thomson Corporation, Titleist, UBS, Union Pacific, Warner-Lambert, and Weyerhaeuser.

Marshall has an MBA from Indiana University and a Ph.D. from UCLA. In the past year, he has taught in executive education programs for both Dartmouth and Cambridge Universities.

Marshall co-edited (with Frances Hesselbein and Dick Beckhard) the books, *The Leader of the Future* (a *Business Week* "Top 15" bestseller), *The Organization of the Future,* and *The Community of the Future* (ranked number one in its field by Amazon.com), which have sold over 600,000 copies in fourteen languages. He has also co-edited the recently released books *Leading Beyond the Walls, Learning Journeys, Leaders Are Our Most Important Product,* and Linkage's *Best Practices in Leadership Development.*

Marshall is a member of the PROVANT advisory board and a member of the board of the Peter Drucker Foundation. "Coaching for Behavioral Change" is an adaptation of one of the many articles that he has written for the Foundation's journal *Leader to Leader.*

CHAPTER THREE

COACHING EXECUTIVES FOR BUSINESS RESULTS

Alyssa M. Freas

Improving Business Results

From the point of view of corporate leaders and shareholders, the ultimate reason for running an executive coaching program is to improve business results. This means increasing profits, reducing costs, or achieving both within a defined time frame. Executive coaching can yield quantifiable, positive output: improved business performance and increased competitive advantage.

Executive coaching is the fastest growing "consulting" practice, with no slowdown in sight. For example, in the United States today the estimated number of executive coaches is in the tens of thousands. This rapid growth of executive coaching may reflect its bottom-line benefits. One of the biggest of which is that it is delivered on the job in real time, so it can be tailored to the executive's individual needs.

In the past, many senior executives who were committed to personal and staff development would sink considerable resources into often haphazard training programs, only to see that investment vanish into a black hole from which neither people nor company gained much benefit.

Coaching promises to avoid the pitfalls of—and offer far more than—the traditional training approach.

What, then, makes modern executive coaching so radically different, and what are the criteria to achieve a results-driven executive coaching process?

Strategic Executive Coaching

Coaching can be approached from a number of different viewpoints. Selecting the right approach is vital to realizing the desired outcome.

Modern effective executive coaching has to be strategic and individualized. A balance has to be struck between the organization and the individuals. In order to engage and to motivate, coaching must be individually tailored to the needs and aspirations of each particular individual. To deliver business results, the approach must also be organizationally tailored to the strategy, vision, and values of the organization. The inclusion of business factors—as well as individual factors—is the key to achieving business results.

Strategic Executive Coaching (SEC) sets out to align the development of each executive with the business challenges in the total organizational context. This is accomplished through an ongoing process of learning, during which executives are given the tools for learning that will enhance their ability to achieve enduring business results. Additionally, SEC ensures that executives develop their leadership capability to deliver the business results the organization wants. To facilitate this, an integral part of the coach's work is to help the executive introduce feedback, action planning, active learning, and follow-up into their regular work life.

Benefits of Effective SEC

The benefits of SEC flow directly from its focus on achieving real business results. This is in contrast to other approaches that might concentrate on solving a specific problem with an individual or within an organization. These alternatives might involve an attempt to change personalities or merely to follow the "charm school" approach of making individuals more affable and approachable. SEC keeps the spotlight on effecting business results; other benefits are important but subordinate to achieving business benefits.

SEC has been applied in a number of contexts, and the bottom-line benefits frequently recur. Examples include improved customer loyalty; development of future leaders; retention of high-impact people; and successful management of change.

Improving Customer Loyalty

SEC helps executives become more effective; effective executives create more satisfied employees; satisfied employees create more satisfied customers; satisfied customers create higher profits. A research study conducted by Anthony J. Rucci, Steven P. Kirn, and Richard T. Quinn and published in *Harvard Business Review* (January–February, 1998) referred to an eight-hundred-store study by Sears Roebuck, and Co., in which Sears' executives concluded that:

> "Employees' attitudes about their workload, treatment by bosses, and eight other matters have a measurable effect on customer satisfaction and revenue. If employee attitudes on ten essential counts improve by 5 percent, Sears found customer satisfaction will jump 1.3 percent, driving a 0.5 percentage-point rise in revenue. If we knew nothing about a store except that employee attitude had improved 5 percent, we could predict that its revenue would rise 0.5 percent above what it otherwise would have been."

This finding links well with our experience in developing future leaders. In one Fortune 500 company, we found that leaders who effectively coach their account managers have more satisfied client accounts than those managers who do not effectively coach. SEC leads to more effective leaders and coaches, who create the employee satisfaction, competence, and customer loyalty necessary to drive profit.

Developing Future Leaders

Winning organizations of the future know that their long-term success will be built on the capability and commitment of their employees. According to Noel Tichy, author of *The Leadership Engine* (1997), "the scarcest resource in the world today is leadership talent capable of continuously transforming organizations to win in tomorrow's world."

Today's successful organizations know that hiring and retaining talented people will be even more difficult in the future. They also know that developing leadership talent will become more critical. Executive coaching can help build bench strength within the organization by providing and developing executives with such vital coaching skills as giving and receiving feedback; varying their leadership style to meet the needs of their direct reports; and demonstrating that it is acceptable to ask for help. Many executives feel uncomfortable when delivering candid feedback. The executive coaching process teaches them how to overcome this obstacle. Consequently, more people in the organization receive the quality feedback they need and want. In this way executive coaching helps to develop employees into more effective contributors.

Retaining High-Impact People

Retaining key, competent people is a competitive strategy in today's global market. Many organizations find themselves fighting the "talent war," in which highly talented and scarce people depart their current organizations for new opportunities in companies that are viewed as better places to work. Many cost factors are to be considered here. In addition to the immediate loss of the employee's work contribution and organizational knowledge, there is also an impact on the ability of the organization to produce business results.

For example, during the first three months on the job, a new hire can accomplish only sixty percent as much as an experienced worker can accomplish in the same amount of time. Additionally, a new hire who is learning the business will tend to serve customers less well. Even a five percent drop in overall employee efficiency cuts annual revenue in a large corporation by "a couple of hundred million dollars." There are also the cost and effort of advertising for and selecting candidates. Losing an exempt employee costs an organization, on average, between one and two times that person's annual salary and benefits. Not to mention the opportunity cost of using management time in interviewing and administration or the time lag before the incumbent is up to speed (Business Issues Research Group, 1999). One Fortune 500 organization has recently calculated these costs at well in excess of $500 million per annum. That figure does not even take into account the effects on projects for which "time to market" is critical. In concentrating efforts on maintaining high employee performance, an SEC initiative helps corporations avoid incurring such massive, enduring, and crushing costs.

Managing Change

Successful executive coaching is about moving individuals into behaviors that sustain the business, in both the short and long term. When individuals and teams can work effectively together, then so will the organization as a whole.

SEC is a powerful tool for managing change because it involves key decision makers. When the coordinated, consistent actions of executives combine harmoniously, an entire organization can become more in tune with itself, thus improving its market position in a changing environment. SEC is grounded in understanding where an organization wants to go and how its people must perform in order to achieve their mutual goals; it is based on the belief that in order to achieve sustained growth in revenues and profits, company leaders must take its employees "with them."

How to Realize the Benefit

The Tenet of Strategic Executive Coaching

—A Mission of Transfer, Not Dependence—
"Give a man a fish—feed him for a day;
Teach a man to fish—feed him for a lifetime."

An effective executive coaching model has to be built on a platform of independence—not dependence on the coach. The coach's prime goal must be to help each executive learn how to learn. An intended consequence of executive coaching is transferring the coaching tools to the executive and helping them learn how to learn. This chain reaction of learning must eventually shift the power of coaching from outside the organization to within. The ultimate goal must be a transfer of learning skills—not the fostering of dependence from the outside.

A well-constructed executive coaching approach will ensure that attention is paid to strategic factors as well as to the more obvious process components that deliver the executive coaching (see Figure 3.1).

FIGURE 3.1.   GUIDELINES THAT ENSURE EXPECTED RESULTS

A. Strategic Components

- Understand the business context and challenges;
- Define success factors—current, transitional, and for the potential future;
- Identify whether there is a clear need and support for executive coaching;
- Clarify key stakeholder roles and responsibilities; and
- Ensure that the climate is ready for development (at the organizational and individual levels).

B. Process Design

- Select, match, and orient executive coaches;
- Establish an effective executive coaching process; and
- Plan for follow-up to engage effective behavioral change.

Strategic Components

At the onset of SEC, the organizational challenges and desired business results are identified and the key executive capabilities necessary to achieve those results are established. Once this has been done, the coach works with the executive sponsor (typically a chief learning officer or vice president of executive development) to understand the necessary leadership attributes and success factors. From this set of attributes, an effective leader profile is constructed that reflects the company's values and leadership principles.

See Figure 3.2 for questions to consider in this strategic and preparatory phase:

FIGURE 3.2. SOME QUESTIONS TO ASK IN STRATEGIC PREPARATION

- What are the key business challenges facing your organization today? In the next two to five years?
- Given those challenges, what leadership skills, knowledge, and abilities are required to succeed?
- Does your organization have an agreed-on profile of the characteristics required of the successful leader of the future?
- What core values (set of principles) best define a common framework for how business results are achieved?
- How does your organization determine whether you have the necessary bench strength to compete?
- What is your organization's strategy for developing leaders of the future?
- Does your organization have proven methods to attract, develop, and retain required talent?

Process Design

From the point of view of the executive being coached, by far the more personal component is experienced within the individual or team coaching between the coach and coachee. This aspect of SEC is presented in full in the following section.

A Framework for the Strategic Executive Coaching Process^{SM}

This section describes the process component of executive coaching by breaking it down into five key steps. The exact determination of dividing lines between the individual steps is less important than the approach to issues that arise during the process as a whole.

Step One: Careful Contracting

It takes skill to create a trusting environment in which open dialogue can occur and underlying issues can be brought to light. A great deal of honest communication and feedback will set the parameters of the executive coaching process.

In addition to information that responds to the questions above, the objectives of the "contracting dialogue" should include the following:

1. Identified success factors for a specific executive's (or team's) current and potential role;
2. Agreement on confidentiality boundaries;
3. Identification of specific expected business results (that is, what business results differentiate an adequate performer from a top performer in this particular role?); and
4. Confirmation that the "chemistry" is right to build trust and rapport.

Addressing these and other questions will help to define the organizational and individual expectations and support the business objectives.

It is imperative that a contracting meeting for the purpose of defining expectations take place before the individual coaching begins. Those attending should typically include a senior-level human resources representative, the executive coach, and the executive receiving coaching.

At the conclusion of step one, the following points must be accomplished:

1. Business context defined;
2. Strategic issues defined;
3. Leader profile and job success defined;
4. Clear roles and responsibilities determined;
5. Agreement regarding who is "the client";
6. Milestones and timelines clarified;
7. Confidentiality boundaries established;
8. Outcomes and expected results agreed on; and
9. Financial terms signed off.

Step Two: Comprehensive Assessment

The second step in the executive coaching process is an assessment of each individual executive. Through interviews and formal assessment tools, gaps between the current and expected performance of each executive are identified to measure how the coaching client stacks up against the business context, expected leadership attributes, and expected business results.

The preferred assessment is done through face-to-face interviews with key stakeholders, such as direct reports, peers, bosses, and customers, and by shadowing the executive during his or her daily life. The main advantage of the face-to-face approach is that it enables the coach to probe the client, and thus provide feedback that is both quantitative and qualitative. The ultimate value of the assessment process is that the results clearly illustrate areas of strength as well as those requiring attention. This paints a clear picture for the executive in terms of strengths and development opportunities, and thus focuses and informs the process.

The face-to-face interview method has been described by several executives as a 360° survey that comes to life—a much deeper and more meaningful picture then a written 360° report.

Step Three: Feedback Dialogue and Action Planning

Feedback Dialogue. The first order of business in an effective feedback session is to revisit the agreed-on objectives and to review the ground rules. Properly preparing executives for feedback is key to ensuring their willingness to listen, accept, open up, and move into action planning. Sessions should occur outside the normal office environment to ensure a more relaxed experience, free of interruptions or ready escape routes. A neutral site helps the executive manage feedback that may contradict his or her current self-perceptions. The coach must facilitate the feedback flow process; help the executive understand the data; and moderate any negative reactions.

During the feedback dialogue session, the coach will continue to refer to the business requirements, leader attributes, and expected business results and compare them to current performance. The aim is to work within a framework that directs feedback toward the key objectives of the business.

The feedback session typically follows these stages:

1. Reaffirm ground rules and establish rapport;
2. Review coaching objectives and business context;
3. Describe how to interpret results;
4. Give the executive opportunity to review results;
5. Discuss surprises or frustrations;
6. Highlight strengths;
7. Identify developmental needs;
8. Agree on areas for improvement; and
9. Begin developmental planning process.

Action Planning.   The action plan must focus on behaviors that contribute to specific business outcomes. A typical action plan includes:

1. Strengths and why they are important in the executive's current role;
2. Developmental areas;
3. Action steps required or interventions needed in areas requiring improvement, as well as leveraging strengths;
4. The type of coaching style that will best suit the development process;
5. Active learning or experiential learning suggestions;
6. Ways in which direct reports, bosses, peers, and others can help;
7. A process for following up with key stakeholders; and
8. Key milestones.

Once the action plan is complete, key stakeholders are invited to validate it. These stakeholders typically comprise the same group involved in the initial assessment interviews. By sharing the action plan with those who were initially interviewed, the executive can be assured that the planned improvements are consistent with expectations. The other benefit of closed-loop validation is that it involves those most likely to benefit from positive change in the executive's behavior. As a result, this process fosters their commitment to help the executive develop.

Step Four: Active Learning

Once the key stakeholders agree with the action plan, a variety of development strategies are implemented. The executive coach guides and reinforces the development strategies, which can include techniques such as action learning, role play, case study, simulation, video feedback, shadowing, and journaling (in other words, writing down the work carried out by the executive). Special developmental courses and team activities are often recommended to support the executive coaching process.

The coaching process is usually supported by a series of monthly meetings between the coach, executive, and key stakeholders. These dialogues help to ensure that the milestones are being met, the ground rules are being followed, and the coaching process continues to be focused on the organization's business needs.

Step Five: Reviewing and Sustaining Success

Approximately six months after the feedback session, an abridged version of the initial assessment is conducted to determine the impact of the process on the individual and the organization. The results of the assessment give credit for progress and address areas in which changes are still required or bring attention to necessary mid-course corrections. The results of the abridged assessment are shared with key stakeholders to further the development of the executive and ensure alignment to organizational goals.

Our research shows that follow-up is a critical success indicator of the entire executive coaching process. Additionally, to ensure overall quality, assessment of the coach is essential.

The following case studies illustrate the SEC process.

EXHIBIT 3.1. ALABAMA POWER MAKES EXECUTIVE COACHING PART OF STRATEGIC CHANGE AND LEADERSHIP RETENTION PROGRAMS

Alabama Power Company (APCO), part of Southern Company, is the primary electric company for the state of Alabama. As with all such utility companies, it is facing major changes, primarily through deregulation of the power market.

Like many long-established organizations, APCO went through a long and painful period of downsizing. In less than ten years, its work force was cut from over 10,000 employees to just 6,500. Its pool of managers was dramatically reduced. From 1995 to 1998 the number of managers dropped from twelve hundred to just eight hundred, and it continues to drop. As with many other companies in a similar position, many staff people whom the company would have preferred to keep left of their own accord.

Jacki Lowe, chief information officer, says: "We had taken our eyes off the employees through eight years of rigorous downsizing, and focused on everyone else—customers especially, but also shareholders—everybody but our own employees. Managers were hired for their technical expertise rather than their leadership qualities."

Executive coaching was adopted at the most senior level to shift the culture of the whole organization. The president of the company, his senior management team, and their direct reports (about forty people) went through the developmental program.

Starting in December 1997 and ongoing, the results so far have recorded improvements in team leadership, collaboration, coaching effectiveness, and leadership skills. After going through the SEC process nearly 90 percent of all APCO officers were rated by their peers and direct reports as more effective leaders and coaches. According to Lowe, "The SEC process has been a primary contributing factor to APCO having one of its best years ever." She also states, "We understood that the change of behavior would not happen overnight, and we were not looking for a 'quick fix.'" It took from six to twelve months for results to become apparent.

An essential part of the SEC process within APCO was to institutionalize the coaching process by "training the trainers," so that the effects would cascade through the organization. Each participant was essentially coached into becoming a coach. A key focus of the executive coaching was to ensure that the executive team members were role models for other executives and for all employees of the company.

Why did APCO decide on an executive coaching program? Because the human resources group had been through an internal program, and the human resources director had seen positive changes in leadership styles.

Lowe says: "High performers always want feedback on how they are doing and how they might improve. This was not being done, and it is essential if you wish to retain those executives with the potential to become future leaders of the business." The executive coaching process was highly satisfying—the officers rated their overall satisfaction 4.7 on a maximum five-point scale. The vast majority of officers stated that coaching from an external source is a valuable part of the SEC process.

EXHIBIT 3.2.   FORD LEADERSHIP DEVELOPMENT PROGRAM PRODUCES IMMEDIATE BENEFITS FOR EXECUTIVE COACHING PARTICIPANTS

Ford Motor Company has also undertaken a major leadership development program. During the 1970s and 1980s, Ford, like APCO and other companies, went through downsizing and re-engineering programs. As a consequence, many middle managers left the company.

The automobile business has changed dramatically. Product development used to take about five years. Today it takes as little as twenty-four months and will likely have to be reduced further. The pressure for continued change is very much market-driven. Previously, consumers might have been content with products lasting five or even ten years. Now they change their wants within a matter of months. This is greatly impacting the motor industry. For example, in recreational vehicles the market-leading model remains the leader for only a few months.

Ford senior management realized that the company was facing a potential shortfall of senior managers to replace those heading toward retirement. In response, they introduced a company-wide leadership development program called Capstone, plus a number of initiatives to improve the quality of management. These include an internally run 360° feedback program involving the top 10 percent of the company, as well as a company-wide attitude survey.

The Capstone Program was initially introduced in 1997 to the Human Resources Division by Harry Jones, director of human resources for Ford product development. Like the rest of the company, Jones' division was facing the prospect of too few suitable leaders in the near future. Also, the division had a secondary challenge to face in that its successful managers had, by definition, all come from highly technical backgrounds.

According to Jones, "What made these people successful earlier in their careers kept them from being successful as they moved up. At the lower levels, they needed a deep understanding of technical issues, but as they moved into more senior roles, they needed influencing skills, the ability to partner with people. We needed leadership skills, for that's how you get things done."

People who have participated in Capstone include vehicle line directors, chief product developers, and program managers. These participants also have the option to partake in executive coaching.

Nancy Gioia, Ford Motor Company's chief program engineer for the Thunderbird says, "I talked to several colleagues who had gone through the coaching with ExCN, Inc. They all agreed that it was very, very positive. While internal coaching is available at Ford, it tends to concentrate much more on specific skill building." Says Gioia, "I liked the 360° face-to-face interview approach. In any case, I prefer to have an external coach, someone from outside the company and even outside the industry. ExCN's approach was effective and personal."

The results exceeded her expectations. Much of the benefit came about through the people who were involved in her 360° interview process. The ExCN, Inc. coach personally interviewed each person, and their statements were compiled and anonymously shown to Gioia. An action plan was agreed on and discussed with everybody who took part in the interviews. Feedback to Gioia frequently included the comment that she was brave and that another person might not have gone through with the program. Such admiration for the person who has gone through the process very often becomes the basis for mutual respect and a willingness to listen better, which Gioia found was an extremely positive grounding for networking.

"It makes you into a better leader," she said. "'Manager' and 'leader' are not the same." Each executive coachee is essentially coached into becoming a coach. According to Gioia, the Thunderbird project benefited in other ways, "through getting the support of other people and being able to negotiate through tough issues with my whole management team." She believes that as a result the product has been improved, which has also improved profitability and sales forecasts, and hence yielded higher shareholder value.[1]

The Ultimate Value of Executive Coaching

The prime objective of SEC is always to improve the business results of a company. This is achieved by increasing profits or cutting costs. The business of executive coaching is neither simply intuitive nor merely the application of mechanized process. It must, at all times, be rooted in the business strategies of the individual client organization, justifying itself by delivering real and tangible business results. Executive coaches themselves must understand how businesses operate and what internal and external pressures are being faced.

Executive coaching can show improved performance in a client almost immediately and support within six months via an interim assessment.

The real advantage of a properly implemented coaching program is that it becomes self-sustaining, delivering results indefinitely. The process of coaching must not end the moment the executive coaching firm walks out the door. A strategic coaching approach offers a supporting work context that is totally in tune with delivering significant, valuable, and enduring business results.

About the Contributor

Alyssa M. Freas is one of the leading authorities on executive coaching. She is the president and CEO of Executive Coaching Network, Inc. (ExCN), a global company whose primary mission is to help organizations

---

[1] Case studies completed by Ron Ardell of Executive Coaching Network, Inc. 1999.

achieve results by improving the effectiveness of their executives. ExCN, Inc., specializes in Strategic Executive Coaching Process, a powerful results-oriented approach designed to align an executive's development with the strategy of the corporation, thereby helping individuals and teams deliver what is expected from them by their shareholder-business results. The company operates worldwide and has attracted a stellar group of coaches, including authorities on team building, strategic planning, e-business, change management, succession planning, crisis management, retaining talent, and the customer-employee-profit chain.

Through ExCN, Inc.'s Strategic Executive Coaching Process, Alyssa has helped executives translate their vision into action, strategically align corporate values, improve employee competence and commitment, manage transitions, improve executive's abilities to coach emerging leaders, and implement lasting improvements in executives' performance. Alyssa's coaching approach has been described by clients as "transformational," "life changing," and "pivotal to our companies best business year ever." Alyssa has delivered highly sustainable results for Fortune 100 companies around the world. Her clients include senior executives from many of the world's leading organizations, such as Andersen Consulting, Citibank, Coca-Cola, ExxonMobil, Ford Motor Company, Motorola, Nortel Networks, Oracle, Royal Bank of Canada, Southern Company, and United Airlines.

Prior to founding ExCN, Inc., Alyssa served as a Senior Consultant in Coopers & Lybrand's Change Management Practice in Washington, D.C., where she provided leadership development to the Army, Navy, and Coast Guard. She maintains a strategic business alliance with Keilty, Goldsmith & Company, where she acted as Practice Leader for eight years. She has a Ph.D. in Organizational Development.

Alyssa is an accomplished speaker and facilitator. She has authored and co-authored several articles, including "Increasing Customer Satisfaction," published in *Leader to Leader*, Winter, 1997. She partnered with Marshall Goldsmith, Frances Hesselbein, Gifford Pinchot, and Richard Leider to create a leadership development product published by Jones Internet Channel, Inc. 1997, Leadership Online™.

CHAPTER FOUR

ROOTS AND BOUNDARIES OF EXECUTIVE COACHING

Elizabeth and Gifford Pinchot

Develop through Coaching

Executive coaching with clients from business, government, and non-profit workplaces is a young professional practice that is still forming its identity. Coaches and coaching practices are just now cataloging the benefits and limitations of the profession and working out the professional guidelines for the delicate boundary between the individual and the employer.

Executive coaching was born out of the leadership training movement, yet it shares the viewpoints of the adult development and human potential movements. The coach is a teacher, but the subject is the development of the whole person and, in turn, the development of the whole system.

Dilemma One: For the Individual and for the Organization

Executive coaching, like most of psychotherapy, confers the privilege (and responsibility) of helping people develop on their own terms. Additionally, coaching operates within the constraint of contributing to business. There is a fine economic line to straddle in workplace coaching, as we must focus on the needs and wants of the individual while being accountable to the health of the overall system. Because it is the organization that contracts with and compensates the coach, the organization needs to realize some form of benefit.

The benefits and necessary boundaries in executive coaching more closely match those normally found in client-centered psychotherapy than in familiar leadership training programs. As in athletic coaching, the primary responsibility of a leadership training intervention is to create a leadership team that performs as well as possible in the competitive marketplace. While the organization paying for the coaching intervention still expects the performance result, the executive's coaching goals are more personal and more diffuse. To make the best contribution to the overall success of the client's workplace, the coach focuses on the growth, well-being, and happiness of each client.

A typical workplace coaching program begins with the client's goals—within and without the workplace. Next is figuring out how to achieve them with this employer, if possible, and within the reality of the rest of the client's personal life. This is an area of personal futurist work. Working together, the coach helps the client construct a realistic and satisfying picture of the future, one that is rooted in the full panoply of the client's life story and the surrounding world.

What could possibly justify the corporation putting assets into such a project? Doesn't work like this belong at home, or in church, or in some "new age" self-improvement workshop? The only possible justification for the corporate expenditure in both time and money is that personal performance improvement turns into improved performance within the company. Fortunately, people perform better when they act in harmony with their authentic selves, and it is this realization that opens up a real opportunity for a win-win outcome.

Many companies have become wise enough to see their people as their prime resource. It is common practice to focus time and money on ways to help employees function more effectively. But we have begun to "hit the wall" in responding to the demands of the modern workplace for superhuman contributions from senior executives. Pushing people to ever greater effectiveness can result in unhealthy stress and disaffection and lead to burnout. Coaching takes into account a wider view of the support needs of key people and adds further ingredients into the developmental mix. Improved effectiveness and lowered stress become part of a wider transformation of the person's work life. The individual becomes more congruent by putting in to action goals and dreams and values, both in the world of work and beyond.

In our own practice, we see that the companies with the best performance do indeed support the development of the whole person. As people grow to become more creative and well-integrated, they are able to support the development of a better workplace. (See Figure 4.1.)

FIGURE 4.1. CONGRUENT DEVELOPMENT

Company View	*Successful Coaching View*	*Successful Outcome*
Reduce stress	Derived from values and personal goals	Work life and personal life become congruent
Remove dysfunctional behaviors	Increase behavioral options	Client tries new roles, behaviors, and tasks
Train in new skills and improve performance	Client takes on system-wide responsibility and influence	Leading/innovating from personal passion and widespread caring

Boosting the individual's personal development, by coaching employees toward congruence and creativity, can accrue to the bottom-line health of the company as a whole. Fortunately, examples of personal growth contributing to corporate success abound.

One of our clients in a training function was suddenly thrown in over his head by a major change in responsibility. Instead of training middle managers in project management and supervisory skills, he rather suddenly found himself training executives in leadership, which demanded of him new skills in participatory design, working with senior leaders, and teamwork in a highly political context. Dealing with the senior management team required a broader repertoire of insights, stories, and wisdom.

In this case, as in so many others, the biggest developmental boost came not from the coaching our client received on workplace issues, but from his internal growth that spanned both the workplace and his private life.

Our client had been making significant progress in reframing issues in his intimate relationships. He was practicing inclusion of his wife and children in making family decisions. He had come to see his children's bids for independence as positive signs of growth. He had come to see his wife's very different and somewhat softer management style as highly effective and appropriate in many of the situations he and his leadership training participants were facing at work. He had learned to use the power of gratitude to dissolve conflict. He had discovered that he didn't have to play the hero around the home in order to be loved and appreciated—that in fact playing the hero often demotivated and disempowered others.

When he brought these lessons back to his work with the leadership team, he found the lessons very relevant. With his help, several members of the leadership team developed a more participative style. Better leadership began to spread. "Gratitude is the attitude" became a company mantra. The reward- and succession-planning process began to focus less on the heroes who saved the company's bacon and more on those leaders whose people were most creative and effective. The result was a significantly more effective organization.

Dilemma Two: Way Up from Already Good

The essence of executive coaching is in helping the client move "way up from already good." The people who come to executive coaches are highly functional, often star performers; yet they have room for growth. Growth often begins with dissatisfaction with what is. So, how do you mix the right degree of admiration for what the client can do with enough encouragement to help them see what needs to be changed?

Society often perceives therapists as working in the arena of the dysfunctional; therapists try to fix that which is not functioning. Such a view can lead to a belief that the client is "sick." But in coaching we are not therapists; we are peers working with admirable people who are often highly advanced in their understanding of themselves and how to get the most out of who they are. Our clients are certainly not sick; instead they are exceptional people eagerly striving to continually develop themselves—way up from already good. And the coach is there to facilitate and help.

Coaches aim to significantly increase the executive's intelligent control and responsibility. Our work helps to realize the expression of our clients' highest talents and bring to the surface their deepest strength of character. At the core of our work is a desire for clients to become more congruent, more true to self, and thus more engaged and effective in both their work and personal lives. Our task is not to add knowledge. We are not obsessed with fixing something that is wrong. So it is better to regard coaches more as providers of personalized positive training—where the product is a precise, tailor-made, fulfilling intervention.

Dilemma Three: Changing the Individual, Changing the System

In addition to our background as executive coaches, trainers, consultants, psychotherapists, and entrepreneurs (a typical sort of résumé for coaches), we are also unabashed systems theorists. So, many ideas from systems theory permeate our work. Thus, we work from two perspectives in coaching: that of the individual client and that of workplace environment or business system. We see each client both as an individual and as a part of a particular context, immersed in a particular set of relationships. *Is our executive coaching client shaped by the character of his or her workplace, or is the organization shaped by the character of the executive?* Both perspectives are useful, and the interplay of individual and system is the dynamic the individual is struggling to resolve.

The next story shows how the need to deal with barriers that were in the way of our client's success caused us to expand the boundaries within which an executive coach normally operates. For our assignment to be successful, we found we had to bring in another person whose role was complementary to that of the coach—a facilitator with a distinctly different set of boundaries and operating procedures. One of us retained the role of primary coach, while the other acted as facilitator of the larger system. In large organizational transformations, it is often necessary to work at the micro or individual level and at the macro or system level at the same time.

Our client was the CEO of an unusually structured service organization. Several members of the board of directors had formerly held the CEO post in the organization, and all of them felt an unusually strong sense of involvement with the idealistic goals and fate of the business. Members of the board—and even other shareholders—

frequently meddled in the business, often bypassing the CEO by telling her staff what to do and how to do it. The CEO disliked their inappropriate meddling in the business, but she needed their support, their continuing investment, and ultimately their continued support.

We came to this coaching assignment through the president of the board, because he was dissatisfied with both the CEO's leadership and the structure of the organization. He was concerned that the organization was losing money. He also noted that the staff seemed to have low morale and a world view that he coined "downtrodden worker-victim."

He asked one of us to coach the CEO and see what could be done to improve her leadership style. He wanted her to encourage more employee participation, urge initiative, and develop a responsive entrepreneurial focus.

The CEO had been hired to control costs and turn around a business that had been losing money for several years. She had excellent financial and business management skills and a deep spiritual path that aligned with the idealistic nature of the business and its owners. She was most comfortable with the owners and directors, spending time with them at retreats and socially. Conversely, she had not spent much time with the staff outside of formal meetings.

The CEO was not pleased with her own performance or the performance of the organization. People were not responding well to rather obvious cost control necessities. She faced a growing dissatisfaction from her staff and often felt frustrated and lonely.

The board blamed the staff as lackadaisical or uncommitted. When the CEO was with the board, rather than protecting her staff and asking for help in developing them, she often reinforced the board's prejudices by complaining about her employees. As the employees sensed that the board and the CEO blamed them for the organization's problems, morale dropped to the point that the quality of customer service was seriously affected.

The CEO knew the coach had been sent in because things were not going well. At first she presented the situation to us as one of poor organizational design. She claimed to be receiving confused directions from the board. Both were undoubtedly true. She also felt let down by her employees—both in their general responsibility level and in their specific lack of support for her efforts on their behalf. And indeed, they were disillusioned of all management.

Gradually our client became trusting enough to talk less about external causes and more about the opportunities she had for learning and improvement. She learned that we could be on her side even when we saw gaps in her effectiveness. Our client clearly had the necessary analytical skills in business management, but came to see that she needed to work on deepening her engagement with employees. She started to see her potential role as their inspirational leader and defender.

With coaching support she began to create her own clear and inspiringly fresh picture of where the organization could be headed—a courageous idea given the strength of the board's involvement in every detail of the operation. Board members would bypass her and go directly to individual employees and tell them what to do. Often, these instructions caused her employees to start well-meaning projects that sabotaged her strategic plans; they were at variance with her coherent vision and put unexpected and unbudgeted pressure on the whole organization.

She desperately needed a tactic to put a stop to this behavior by board members. So when faced with this situation in the future, she primed all her employees to say, "Good idea. I'll suggest it at the next management meeting." Although apparently a simple device, this method of maintaining control carried significant risks for the CEO. She was afraid to offend board members—a justified concern given the short tenures of those CEOs who had preceded her.

Two things became clear to us. First, the CEO had a lot to learn about implementing the kind of participative leadership that actually suited her deep commitment to her spiritual path. Second, the organizational dysfunction was largely the consequence of factors beyond her control. We discussed the option of her quitting. Here we put to good use part of the ethical boundaries inherent in client-centered therapy. What the client wishes to achieve in the areas of worldly success, emotional experience, and spiritual growth is up to the client. Our job is merely to help them to see that there may be more productive options for approaching their goals. The hiring organization must accept that if the client's best interest is to leave, the coach will not stand in the way.

The client decided that she could learn more by staying on the job and trying to handle the situation, rather than by leaving during a crisis. She knew her job would continue to be painful, but she felt she was growing new capabilities and acuity at a rapid pace.

As we pondered how to proceed, boundary conflicts arose. As the CEO's coach, we could no longer talk with the board chair about the CEO's fitness to serve. Our coaching conversations had created a privileged communication that superceded our role as organizational consultants to the board. Fortunately, our work took us in a direction in which the client's interests and the organization's interests coincided: finding a way to restore employee morale. If we focused the reborn employee energy on creating enough new business to establish profitability, the company's interests would also be served.

In this case, as in many situations in family therapy, coaching the client to change was inadequate to change the situation. We applied a basic boundary precept from fields as diverse as family therapy and organizational change: "Get the whole system in the room!"

Each member of the groups making up the system, including the owners and directors, needed to learn about the larger system, so they could channel their good intentions into effective action for the benefit of the whole. With coaching help, the CEO orchestrated a series of small- and large-group interventions that built understanding and respect between the groups and also established common visions and goals for the organization as a whole. She became the synthesizer of a challenging and unwieldy organization, improved the nature of the board's contributions, and grew to meet the challenges of effective leadership in a very difficult situation.

The best coaches we know have business consulting or organizational leadership experience, as well as experience in psychotherapy and human development. They move seamlessly between asking good questions about the business issues and delving into issues of the leadership style and the psychological impact of their client's actions on others.

Coaches in the workplace must serve the larger system while serving the individual who is presented for help. Family therapy has decades of experience walking this line between the individual, their family, and society. Practitioners have developed the skills to protect the freedom and dignity and personal development of the individual (even the fragile dignity of adolescents!), while supporting the other members in having better lives.

In family systems jargon, the client who arrives for help is referred to as the "identified patient," that is, identified by the family or group as needing help; the term implies that the entire family is the group to be helped, whether directly or indirectly through the identified patient. In many instances, whatever failings brought the identified patient into therapy can be looked at as a symptom of the group, rather than of the individual, whose behavior is, for better or worse, a response to the situation or even a backhanded attempt to change it.

For the coaching profession, the reminder of shared responsibility must be sterner: there is no identified *patient*—just good people, doing their best, encountering their growth needs, and trying to contribute in a system that somehow is not bringing out all they could be.

Dilemma Four: Integrating Work and the Rest of Life

Today's organizations can no longer be run by the tough workaholic individualists of yesterday's executive pantheon. Workaholics, for instance, have not usually learned the gentler skills needed to motivate people to work across boundaries. Rapid change and the takeover of many routine tasks by computers has left a workplace in which much of what people do is innovate, integrate, motivate, and care. We desperately need executives who can liberate and lead people. Rather than being threatened by their best subordinates, leaders must be role models who relish liberated people bringing their full commitment and abilities into a more collaborative and democratic workplace. By having success and happiness in their lives as a whole, executives are better equipped to help their employees develop their own wholeness.

One classic example of a development opportunity and challenge for the coach is to be found in the high achiever—a young executive whose strengths suggest grooming for very senior leadership. This highly productive and talented person is often hampered by weaknesses in personal communication style or human relationship skills. The corporation would like to see such weaknesses surgically removed and necessary relationship skills grafted on.

These individuals are often described as "driven." They are determined to do whatever is necessary to contribute and to succeed, regardless of personal cost. It is believed that with the right evaluations, training, or mentoring they will be motivated to make whatever changes are necessary to be a more mature manager and human being. The obvious approach is to teach them skills such as communication and to develop their sensitivity to others. But this approach may run into a brick wall. The fact is that they are driven, already controlling themselves—often with elaborate sets of rules and beliefs about what kind of behaviors will win them approval. Even when conceptually well-grounded, more rules on how to behave may not produce a warmer, more empathetic, and broadly creative manager.

Often in these cases, the executive is expressing readiness for a deeper change. After a rapid series of promotions and outward successes he or she may say, "Is this all there is to it?" Hear this as the beginning of a perceptual shift from "How do I change myself to win the next rung on the ladder?" to "How do I get in touch with my deeper self and express the power of my values and my whole self in my work?"

When a client is reaching out for deeper meaning, an opportunity exists to release more of the "true self" that has been papered over by the demands of the "false self," which was created to please others. Our true selves, in fact, have the built-in compassion and ability to see others, and so will naturally guide us toward developing better human relationship skills. When our words and music go together, when we can bring our hearts and heads and values to work, when we can be ourselves in all aspects of our lives, then we are congruent. (For more on this framework, read Alice Miller's *The Drama of the Gifted Child.*)

The Cost of Not Coaching

One of our clients, the vice president of human resources at a large computer company, told us a story about George, one of their most effective intrapreneurs. George had launched an impressive string of successful new products. Both his technical and his business judgment were excellent. He was marked at an early age for succession to very senior management positions and became their youngest vice president.

As George took on responsibility as part of the team guiding the entire company, his eager beaver "just do it" personality became a liability. He was impatient with consensual processes and sometimes tactless in his defense of good ideas. Of course, this was just the flip side of the intrapreneurial personality that made him so valuable.

A mutual frustration developed. George was frustrated by what he saw as the agonizingly slow pace and lack of courage displayed by the leadership team. The rest of the team was frustrated by George's impulsiveness and emotionalism when he did not get his way. By mutual agreement, George left to pursue other opportunities.

The vice president of human resources put it this way:

"It is clear to me now that if George had had a coach then, he would be a very senior member of our leadership team today. A coach could have helped him see how to be more effective by presenting himself in a way that didn't rub other members of the team the wrong way. And we could use his impeccable business judgment and strategic vision working for us instead of the start-ups that have made him and his new investors very rich."

As this story demonstrates, the cost of not coaching promising talent can be immense.

Tools and Limits for Coaching

Although coaching is not psychotherapy, psychological counselors have learned many lessons that can be of great help to coaches. The progressive branches of psychotherapy have long been working on tools for bringing the whole person, with their heart, into their life and work. They have moved from fixing what is wrong to bringing out the extraordinary. "Whole people" bring a kind of magic into the systems they are leading. A challenge for the profession of coaching is to continue to find better ways to inspire personal development and to improve performance in individuals, and thus their organizations, while respecting the individual's freedom and right to direct and control his or her own destiny.

Coaches without extensive training in psychotherapy may not be prepared to intervene in a client's deep personality issues, nor is the workplace necessarily the proper venue to do so. Coaches help people to see how they can be more effective and to have the courage to go through the practice period when new behaviors are awkward. They are not delivering deep therapy, nor are they offering friendship or romance. Coaches must be vigilant in limiting work with the client to appropriate coaching objectives and interventions. The coaching profession is particularly in need of professional guidelines and limits to stay within the bounds of appropriate workplace support, while still addressing the client's personal development. The discussions we hold to create and improve these guidelines will open inquiries into how our work promotes and embodies basic civil rights in the workplace, for instance, and how each member of an organization can combine more democratic ways of working with collaborative responsibility.

Collaborative Change Model

The most important contribution of the psychotherapy model to coaching is the fact that people can cause their own positive change, in their inner worlds as well as outer worlds, and often can do better with a little help. George Kelly, a great teacher of clinical psychology and personality theory, talks about psychotherapy as a collaborative venture that begins with finding where the individual's quest has bogged down and getting it going again. Given the rather short time frames and greater space between meetings that often characterize some phases in executive coaching, it is fortunate that people do most of the work themselves.

Secure Base for Change

Because it can reach a deep level of a person's being, good executive coaching, like psychotherapy, begins with creating a safe space in which the client can begin to direct the change process. This involves a discovery of his or her own goals and better ways to achieve them.

It is unfortunate but true that coaches are sometimes brought in as a last resort, just before a high-potential employee is regretfully fired. This is a particularly difficult situation, because it does not fit the "making the better the best they can be" paradigm that defines coaching. If there is any hint that the employee is on the way out, we carefully check that we are not being called in as part of an attrition process, as this is definitely outside our scope of work. Sometimes we need to educate our client's boss. The boss must understand that we will never reveal to them what we learn in sessions, no matter how useful our knowledge might be in any decision to retain or fire.

In one such case, the client's employment was so near the edge that we refused to begin without a guarantee that the client had at least six months to show improved performance. In this climate of comparative security, at least free to learn and grow, the client opened himself to a wide feedback request that included thoughtful write-ups and conversations with former staff as well as current employees. He began making changes, learning to delegate more fully and to listen before offering his solutions.

Our client's explanation for his freedom to grow and change was the supportive character of all the interventions and help he received. He knew from the beginning that the coach was on his side, and he and the coach made a point of seeing that his key colleagues supported his new actions and initiatives. In this safe context, he first succeeded in his existing job and then in moving on to what he really wanted to do.

Let Others Possess Their Experience

For clients to let go of their current patterns of behavior, someone needs to confirm the truth of their perceptions and feelings. Someone must acknowledge what it looks and feels like from the client's perspective. Only when they feel heard can clients stop defending their viewpoints for long enough to see the larger picture in which their situations are embedded. Only when the truths inherent in the client's current perception are fully acknowledged can the client relax enough to see alternative viewpoints and alternative courses of action.

A clear example of this phenomenon is the executive of color who needs confirmation that discrimination exists in order to let go of excessive concern about it and get on with succeeding despite the existence of unfair obstacles. Someone needs to acknowledge the client's discomfort or humiliation so he or she can get beyond feelings and improve the situation. Often the first task of the coach is confirmation of the client's experience and predicament. This shared understanding of the client's painful experience is the first step toward creating a safe base from which to explore new options.

As helping professionals, we need to outgrow a deep, natural compulsion to fiddle with others' experiences. Coaching—in common with good psychotherapy or good parenting—must have at its foundation a trust in the client's experience, a willingness to witness it and accept it rather than change it.

In coaching, as in therapy, the act of confirmation returns control to the client. When we create a safe relationship in which the client can discuss and take ownership of his or her experience, we create an open system. As clients come to understand that they are not imagining their suffering—and that it is in fact reasonable to be discontented in their current situation—they gain the certainty they need to make changes in themselves and their situation. Here are some maxims we use to remember this kind of client respect:

- Never diminish clients—help them to grow.
- Don't invalidate their view of reality—help them to expand it.
- Be wary of telling the client what to think—ask good questions that leave room for self-respect.

Optimal Challenge

Development for young and old is enhanced by the appropriate level of challenge and contradiction, especially in a relatively safe and supportive context such as a good coach and good company can foster. Sometimes the client situation has plenty of challenge and "optimal frustration" to spur the learning without much help from the coach. Other times the coach must inject some artful challenge, a bit riskier intervention for the coach than just confirming the client's view of the world.

With an optimal level of challenge, clients will widen their perspectives, leave their comfort zones, learn new things, try new things, listen with open minds, admit and learn from mistakes and successes alike, become more comfortable with change, learn to be more open, and become authentic. Clients can gradually see the opportunities and ingest learnings from the challenge, a big step toward taking effective action.

Who Is Setting the Goals?

The client—not the coach, not the boss—controls the goals for the change process. One of our mentors, Robert Kegan, stated this best in his book *The Evolving Self:* "Among the many things from which a practitioner's clients need protection is the practitioner's hopes for the client's future, however benign and sympathetic these hopes may be." This is a harsh specific in the general rule that we strive to recognize and honor our clients' distinctness. It is the client's own hopes and goals that provide the ongoing boundaries around our collaborative endeavor.

It is difficult to protect our clients from our hopes for them, when we hope so much for the people we want to help. It is inconvenient when we have been given specific areas of improvement from an outside evaluation of the client. Nonetheless, to paraphrase Robert Kegan, In a world where people will increasingly put themselves in the hands of "coaches," it is the coaches above all who must understand that much of human personality is none of their business.

The Involuntary Client

A truism in psychotherapy, and in fact in any creative learning endeavor, is that the client has to want to be there and engage fully in the process. When an employee is "offered" a coach to correct deficiencies, perhaps after a negative appraisal, it is a question whether the coaching is really voluntary. Yet, it is possible to engage a client who did not desire coaching by keeping his or her interests foremost in mind, and then gradually yet vigilantly returning autonomy and control to him or her.

Check Client and Company Intent

As mentioned above, before we coaches start an assignment, we need to know whether coaching is merely a procedural step in a process leading to an almost inevitable firing. In some cases, management wants the emotional protection of knowing they "did everything possible" before letting someone go, or even to take testimony from us to support a firing on which they have already decided. This work we always refuse. We need to know the company's full intent and how much support they can give to the client. Then we can decide if coaching is appropriate and if the situation is safe enough for it to be successful.

In our coaching we also try to identify the individual's needs, wants, and underlying values to compare with those of the organization. It may feel bold at first to examine the fit of the coaching client and his or her particular workplace role, as though it would be disloyal to the company, but it serves to highlight the voluntary nature of the employee/employer relationship. Does the client have a good basis for commitment, the seed of contributions, to their work and their workplace? Is the fit with the workplace strong enough for a creative and productive interaction? Does the client want to stay for the long term, or at least try to stay for awhile? In our coaching, we often do a light evaluation on this issue in introductory conversations with the coaching client and the party who hired us, if different, before we agree to launch into a larger block of coaching.

Properties in the Relationships, Not Just the People

A major contribution of psychotherapy to coaching is adding to our meager language of relationships. The philosopher Bertrand Russell reminded us not to confuse the language of objects with that of relationships. Object language dominates much of science (including psychology) and traditional business thinking. For instance, "Jane is a manager" is *object* language, giving a property of a person or thing. "Jane and Joe are colleagues" is *relational* language, telling us nothing about the people considered separately, but telling us about something that exists between the people.

Problems arise when we are taken in by the myth that properties that in fact exist between people are properties of the individual considered separately. "John is my boss" can imply a lot about John and a lot about me that may or may not be true. For instance, "boss" may mean to me someone who has all the answers (or none) or someone I should defer to (or undercut). It is easy in any relationship to presume qualities in another that may or may not exist, rather than taking responsibility for finding out what the other person is really up to, and what I am contributing to the quality of the relationship. If things are not going well, I can always ask, without blame, "What am I co-creating in this relationship?" rather than, "What's wrong with me?" or "What's wrong with that other person?"

Although pathology and even evil are out there, it is both educational and effective to assume that the qualities of one's relationships are mutually determined for both the coach and his or her clients. Strengthening this understanding for our clients can give them fresh perspectives and new opportunities.

Open Listening

Every coach's (in fact, every professional helper's) most important task is to be a good listener, for the obvious reason that there is a gap to be bridged between the reality held by the client and what we hear through our inevitable filters. If we listen sensitively, we can begin to piece together how our client constructs him or herself and his or her world.

It is a wonder we communicate at all, given our different personal realities and the human proclivity for letting habit and prejudice filter our view of others. Establishing deep communication between two people with two distinct models of reality is a bit of a miracle, requiring that we expand the intersection of our minds, at the same time maintaining our inevitable separateness of self. To the extent we carry it off, communication is an evolutionary triumph. As coaches, we continually remind ourselves of the power we can give to another by just listening, both directly (as our clients benefit from being heard) and as a model for them to use with others.

Thinking the Best of Others

As professional helpers we must model responsibility for listening and learning about what is really going on with our clients, so that they will bring more wisdom to their own relationships. For instance, each of us, from time to time, will misconstrue another's actions as rejection. Many hurts and arguments begin this way. I may feel slighted when I enter a room and an important colleague doesn't look up. I can feel slighted and hurt, even though the other person is simply engrossed in a good novel or pondering his or her own problem of the moment. Differing expectations and assumptions of meaning are particularly difficult in cross-cultural relationships, a problem in our polyglot society and increasingly a problem in our mobile and global work world. Often our task is to lead our clients in finding a kinder understanding of others' behavior.

Giving Meaning to the Facts

In the end, meanings determine the facts as much as vice versa. The core technique of coaching is creating a setting in which the client can change the meanings they and others put on the facts. Coaches conduct processes that encourage people to see more options for viewing reality and then discover which ways of seeing things will lead to a happier and more productive life.

George Kelly gave coaching a maxim of hope: "Whatever exists can be reconstrued." To the extent this is true, we have great opportunities for change, and a coach is able to help others create more constructive ways of construing the facts. However, lest this sound like "Think and grow rich," it is important to note that we are not alone in creating the meaning of our lives, for our lives are created in the spaces between us and others, as well as in our relationships to physical reality. Meaning, culture, our accomplishments, and even in some sense our talents, are co-created with others.

Working at the Edge of Politics

Remembering the importance of each client's context or environment and understanding the quality of external conditions can humanize us and politicize us. Any coach knows this. Say a person is having trouble at work being the best he can be. Yes, it is his problem, and he has to improve his approach to it, but what is impinging on him? Health? Nutrition? Family stresses? Money problems? Poor sleep? A negative co-worker? An unhealthy office? We, like the client, can begin to see the world as unfair when we add to these the workplace culture issues that may devalue the client's style or talents. However, our assignment can only be to help change those things that can be changed. When whatever is unfair seems too big to be changed or endured, we must help the person either to become better at playing the game or to summon the courage to seek opportunity elsewhere.

Helping Everyone Balance Status and Power

Managing status and power is another basic issue in coaching. Coaches must address both the perception and the reality of inequalities of status and power. One of our mentors, the family therapist Virginia Satir, brought these issues into her consulting practice. She pointed out the obvious, that we are all born small and fully dependent. From this unavoidable beginning, we are, in all cultures, vulnerable to establishing relationships of excessive and fixed dominance and submission. Satir taught her tens of thousands of students in the helping professions this: helping people change their relationships toward greater equality offers a direct way to reduce pain and suffering—no matter how seemingly psychological the suffering may be. Over the long term, people can outgrow their tendencies to expect and create relationships of dominance and submission.

It is ironic that people at every organizational level feel powerless before those in the levels above. Coaching can help clients to see that they are not as powerless as they feel. Then they can also let go of their own dominating behaviors.

Limits of Individualism, Benefits of Service and Altruism

Coaching has this built-in liability: focus on the individual client can threaten the common good in the workplace. Rampant individualism without commitment to the common good, says Martin Seligman, produces widespread depression and meaninglessness: "Our society cannot tolerate for long these painful by-products of its obsession with self." Our workplaces cannot tolerate too much obsession with self, or the depression and meaninglessness it engenders. Fortunately, workplaces with worthy missions provide the context for individuals to find purpose and meaning. It is the responsibility of the coach to help the client achieve personal meaning and more worthwhile purposes at work—and even in life. At the same time, the client can gradually take on the responsibility for raising the level of worthwhile purposes available to everyone in the workplace.

Conclusion

The profession of executive coaching is built on new concepts of human potential at work. The goal of coaching is not in fixing what is broken, but in discovering new talents and new ways to use old talents that lead to far greater effectiveness. The goal is to help people bring their whole selves to work because their authentic self, an integration of a wonderful collection of parts, has more capability than any part or acted out role.

More "fully human" people are necessary to realize the potential of the more democratic, more intrapreneurial learning organizations demanded by today's rapidly changing marketplace. Indeed, the geometric increase in organizational productivity and innovation that is occurring today rests on the convergence of these two streams, organizational and human development: organizational innovations favoring freedom, teamwork, and shared mission are converging with modern ideas of adult development (freedom to "grow," high-quality relationships, and worthwhile purposes). These more liberated organizations are the setting that maximizes the continuous learning and development of their members.

Executive coaching is both person-centered and system-centered. We are not training or "fixing" people, but freeing and focusing them to be their very best. Successful coaching achieves positive change for both the individual and the system.

About the Contributors

Elizabeth Pinchot is an executive coach, consultant and author with thirty years of experience. As founding and current president of Pinchot & Company, she has coached and trained senior executives in large organizations as diverse as the U.S. Forest Service, Canadian National Railroad, a large computer company, and the New York Stock Exchange. Elizabeth has coached entrepreneurs in startups, such as high-tech and social service companies in Moscow, Silicon Valley startups, and consulting companies, and has advised the executive directors and senior staff of many nonprofit companies in a consulting capacity. She has also chaired three boards of directors.

The Intelligent Organization, co-authored with Gifford Pinchot, shows how to liberate the full talents of employees through a self-organizing combination of free intraprise and organizational community.

In earlier years Elizabeth was a staff clinician in an out-patient clinic delivering psychological services to individuals, groups, and families. She also maintained a private practice of counseling individuals. Prior to forming Pinchot & Company, Elizabeth co-founded and ran several businesses, including a manufacturing business and a teacher training center, and was a founding staff member of the first computer-assisted education project, a joint venture of IBM and Stanford University.

Elizabeth attended Wellesley College, graduated from Stanford University in philosophy and psychology, received a master's degree from the University of Oregon in education and child development and another from Goddard College in counseling psychology.

Gifford Pinchot is an author, speaker, coach, and consultant on innovation management and related topics. He has coached teams launching over five hundred new products and services, entrepreneurs, intrapreneurs, and leaders of large firms wishing to create a better climate for innovation. His particular specialty is working the interface between difficult business problems and personal growth.

Gifford's best-selling book, *INTRAPRENEURING: Why You Don't Have to Leave the Corporation to Become an Entrepreneur*, has been published in fifteen languages. The word "intrapreneur," coined by Gifford to describe the intra-corporate entrepreneur, has been included in the *American Heritage Dictionary* and *Webster's Encyclopedic Unabridged Dictionary*.

In his second book, *The Intelligent Organization*, co-authored with Elizabeth Pinchot, this vision is broadened to include a revolutionary way of organizing all work, from the most innovative to the most mundane. Gifford approaches the subject of innovation from personal experience, ranging from a role as CEO of a Silicon Valley software firm, a partner in a venture capital firm, and the licensing of two of his patents.

After graduating with honors from Harvard University in 1965 with an A.B. degree in economics, Gifford studied neurophysiology at Johns Hopkins University. In April 1999, he co-authored *Intrapreneuring in Action: A Handbook for Business Innovation*.

CHAPTER FIVE

COACHING AND CONSULTATION: ARE THEY THE SAME?

Edgar H. Schein

Consultants often find themselves in situations that would best be described as "coaching." A client defines the situation as one in which he or she wants individual help to work on a personal issue, or a manager asks the consultant to work with an individual to improve job performance or to overcome some developmental deficiencies. From this point of view, the consultant's job can be much broader than the coach's, in that the *client system* is defined as more than the sum of the individual coaching projects in which members may be engaged. For example, I have often found myself in an individual coaching role with several members of the client system, while, at the same time, working with broader group and organizational issues that would not be described as coaching.

If coaching is defined as working with an individual, can one imagine coaching a group or an organizational unit or even a whole organization? Yes, if one considers who is being coached and on what issues. If the CEO is being coached on how to improve his or her relationship to the board or on matters of company strategy, one could argue that any behavioral change on his or her part influences the entire organization. But, if a middle manager is being coached on how to make himself or herself more effective and promotable, the connection to organizational effectiveness is more remote. This suggests that the degree of overlap between coaching and consulting depends on (1) who initiated the request for coaching, (2) who is being coached, (3) the role for which they are being coached, and (4) the issues for which they are being coached.

In my previous analyses of consulting, I emphasized the need to distinguish three fundamentally different roles that the consultant can play in any client relationship: (1) the provider of expert information, (2) the diagnostician and prescriber of remedies, and (3) the process consultant whose focus is on helping the client to help himself or herself (Schein, 1969, 1987, 1988, 1999). In all of these roles, and that would include coaching, the overarching goal is to be *helpful* to the immediate client and to be mindful of the impact of interventions on the larger client system and on the community.

The consultant must have the ability to move among these roles freely, but he or she must begin in the process mode. In order to find out in what way expertise or diagnosis and prescription are relevant to the client's needs, the consultant must establish a "helping relationship" with the client, in which the client can safely reveal the real problem. It is only by establishing such a relationship that the consultant can determine what kind of help is really needed.

In the case of organizational consulting, a further complication is that the consultant will never understand the culture of the client system well enough to make accurate diagnoses or provide workable prescriptions. Therefore, in organizational consulting, the consultant and client must become a team that jointly "owns" the consequences of all diagnostic and remedial interventions. But it must be made clear that it is the client who owns the problem and is ultimately responsible for the solution. Thereby, the consultant enters into a therapeutic relationship with the client system and can facilitate the improvement of the situation as the client defines it.

Clearly, coaching can then be thought of as one kind of intervention that may be helpful to clients under certain circumstances. In this context, I think of coaching as establishing a set of behaviors that helps the client to develop a new way of seeing, feeling about, and behaving in problematic situations. In this setting, the following issues surface:

- When should the coach be an expert who simply shows the client how to see, feel, or behave in a situation?
- When should the coach be a diagnostician and prescriber who figures out why the client is having a given problem and suggests various remedies?
- When should the coach be a process-oriented "therapist" who helps the client gain insight into his or her situation and figure out how to improve his or her own behavior?

The balance and timing of these depends on whether the coaching was requested by the client or suggested by others in the organization, what organizational role the client is in, and the nature of the problem that the client reveals. Let us look at the initiating source first.

Who Initiated the Coaching Relationship?

Initiated by the "Boss"

One major source of initiation is when someone higher in an organization suggests that someone lower use coaching to overcome a deficiency that is perceived to limit the person's effectiveness or career potential. A common version of this is a mandated 360° performance appraisal in which feedback is collected from superiors, peers, and subordinates. An outside coach then reviews the data with the person, because the discussion may be too face-threatening if conducted by the boss. If the problem is primarily defined by the boss, the issue then arises of whether the coach is expected to report back to the boss, or whether the coaching is a private matter between coach and client (Flaherty, 1999).

If the coach is expected to report back, the situation may be closer to training or indoctrination and may fit either the consultation or the coaching model. In such a case the coach is working for the boss, even though he or she may claim to be trying to help the individual. In this situation, the coach should probably function as expert, diagnostician, and prescriber, because the desired behavioral outcome is defined by someone other than the client being coached. The client's choice is whether or not to enter the relationship at all, and whether or not to make an effort to change his or her outlook and learn the new behavior. The outcome of this effort will be beneficial for both the organization and the individual if it fits the client's own developmental potentials. All too often, however, what the client is expected to learn does not fit his or her personality, resulting in failure or short-run adaptations without long-run changes. From a consulting point of view, this scenario is risky. There are too many ways it can fail: the boss may not have seen the initial situation accurately; the boss may not have communicated the need for coaching clearly; the consultant may not have understood what is really wanted; or the individual may not be willing or able to be "trained."

However, there is an alternative way that the boss can initiate the process that is more likely to be successful. In this scenario, the boss outlines to the coach (consultant) what the problem is as he or she sees it, but does not expect the coach to report back. The boss is prepared for the coaching to result in an outcome that might not have been expected. For example, through coaching, the individual may recognize a mismatch and subsequently leave the organization. If the boss accepts this as a possible outcome, then the coach can make developmental interventions to help the individual help himself or herself. In this instance, the boss is, in effect, playing a consulting role as well by trying to help the individual. As we will see below, this issue interacts with understanding what the coaching is about. Does the boss want to help the individual develop in a broad sense, or does the boss want the individual to learn a particular point of view or set of competencies that are organizationally relevant, for example, learn to use a new computerized budgeting system?

Initiated by the Individual

Any time a member of an organization goes to an outsider or staff insider for some kind of help, there is the potential relationship of coaching or individual consultation. The two roles merge to a considerable degree, and helping the individual becomes the primary agenda. In this situation, the outcome is not prescribed by the organization, and the issues may have little to do with organizational problems. This kind of coaching/consulting merges with what many of us face when someone seeks our help. Do we tell the person what to do, do we privately diagnose the situation and come up with prescriptions, or do we engage in a period of building the relationship in order to find out how best to be helpful? (Schein, 1999). This issue occurs within the family all the time. It occurs between friends, between parents and children, and between teachers and students, and it is, therefore, a generic human process that needs to be learned by all of us; individual coaching/consulting should be part of any adult's repertory of skills.

Who Is Being Coached?

How the coaching/consulting relationship evolves will depend on the rank and position of the person being coached. If coaching the CEO or a high-ranking executive, the coach must be in a peer or superior relationship to the client. Otherwise, the executive may simply not listen or may even be offended by the idea of engaging in the relationship. Also, given the potential sensitivities of high-ranking executives, it becomes especially important for the coach to begin in the process mode to ensure that a helping relationship is built before any guidance, advice, or prescriptions are offered.

If the coach is clearly superior in rank or status, a different dynamic will be active—the client may actively seek and expect expert advice. The risk in giving advice is that it may not fit the client's personality or situation and it will therefore be ignored or unconsciously subverted. The subordinate cannot really say to the higher-ranking or higher-status coach that he or she does not understand or agree with the advice offered, or that he or she has already tried it and it didn't work. So even though the temptation to become an instant expert is tremendous in this situation, it must be resisted. The coach, to be effective, must engage in open-ended inquiry to establish an equal helping relationship before he or she can determine what kind of help is needed.

If the coach is a peer in status, there still remains the problem that the client may feel "one down" for having a problem, that is, for having been singled out for coaching. In Western cultures it is not okay to need help; it implies some lack, some inability to help oneself, to solve one's own problems. Here too, the helper coach must build the relationship first, especially if the coaching involves fairly face-threatening personal issues.

In What Role Is the Client Being Coached?

The key distinction here is whether the client is dealing with a problem that is personal or is seeking help in his or her role as an executive. A personal issue might be to learn new skills, such as becoming computer competent or developing a more strategic outlook in order to be promotable to a higher level. An organizational issue might be how to manage the executive team better in order to improve the organization's strategy process, how to think more like a marketer because the future of the organization lies in better marketing, or how to learn the new computerized budgeting and accounting system on which the future of the organization depends.

If the person is in an individual development role, the same ideas apply as those mentioned above. A helping relationship must be built first, and then the coaching can proceed. If the person is in an organizational role, the issue is more complex. Suppose, for example, that the CEO wants to be coached on how to get more out of a team; he or she wants them to compete more for higher-level jobs and drive their subordinates harder. How does the coach/consultant decide whether this is an appropriate goal, given that it might hurt others lower down in the organization? How does the coach/consultant deal with the situation if he or she feels that this would be the wrong strategy for the organization to pursue? If the coach is outside the organization, he or she can walk away from such conflicts, but if he or she is part of an internal staff or human resource (HR) organization, this is not possible. It is at points such as these that coaching and consulting part ways. As a *coach*, the person might have to go along with what the client wants; as a *consultant*, even as an internal consultant, he or she must consider the needs of the larger client system and, if necessary, challenge the CEO's goals.

One might suppose that a similar issue could come up in personal coaching. The coach might disagree with the learning goals that the client articulates, but if others in the organization have set those goals, then the coach is bound to them, even if the client is not. That is again the indoctrination or "coercive persuasion" scenario that many coaches de facto find themselves in. Here again, as a consultant, the helper can "push back," but as a coach the implication is that the organization decides what is needed and the coach's job is help individuals attain it (Schein, 1999b).

What Is the Actual Issue or Goal of the Coaching?

Coaching covers everything from helping people learn a new computer system to helping people broaden their outlook on what the company is doing. Our most familiar version of coaching is, of course, athletics, where the coach helps a person to improve a golf or tennis stroke by observing, diagnosing, providing feedback, demonstrating, and setting training routines and targets. At the other extreme is the previously cited case of having a coach go over the results of a 360° feedback process with the client. In his book, Flaherty (1999) cites a case in which the issue is how to broaden an executive's outlook so that he or she can become promotable to a higher level in the company.

My assumption is that for any of these goals, from the most concrete skill development to the most abstract reshaping of basic mental models, coaches will not succeed without first establishing a helping relationship. This is relatively obvious in the more abstract personal arenas, but is often overlooked in the skill-development type of coaching. I notice, especially in coaching people on the use of computers, that the coach quickly falls into the expert or doctor mode and instructs without any sensitivity to the problems the learner is experiencing. I don't think such a coach has ever asked what my problems were in dealing with the computer or what my learning style is. Coaches jump right in with instructions, and the client finds himself or herself struggling, resisting, and not learning.

On the organizational side, this distinction has an important counterpart. Are we talking about coaching on mission, strategy, and goals, or are we talking about coaching on the means, measurement, and remedial processes the organization uses to accomplish its goals? I think coaches are much more sensitive to the needs of the client in the mission and goals area, because those are more abstract. When it comes to coaching on the means and processes, coaches quickly become trainers, forgetting to build helping relationships. This tendency to become experts may account for the poor implementation of many programs, such as new computer systems, re-engineering, quality circles, total quality programs, 360° feedback programs, and the like. If the learners are not involved in designing their own learning, and if they do not have a relationship with the coach in which they are comfortable, they will not learn at the level that the organization expects and needs. To avoid this, coaches must become skilled process consultants as well.

Conclusion

Coaching is a subset of consultation. If coaching is to be successful, the coach must be able, like a consultant, to create a helping relationship with his or her client. To create such a helping relationship, it is necessary to start in a process mode, which involves the learner/client, identifies the real problems, and builds a team in which both the coach and the client take responsibility for the outcomes. How the coaching relationship develops varies according to who initiated the process, the status differential between coach and client, whether the client is working an individual or organizational problem, and whether the content of the coaching concerns organizational mission and goals or organizational process and means. In each of these situations, the coach should have the ability to move easily among the roles of process consultant, content expert, and diagnostician/prescriber. The ultimate skill of the coach, then, is to assess the moment-to-moment reality that will enable him or her to be in the appropriate role.

About the Contributor

Edgar H. Schein is Sloan Fellows Professor of Management Emeritus and senior lecturer at the MIT Sloan School of Management. He is interested in organizational culture, process consultation, organizational learning and change, the research process, and career dynamics. His main research activities have taken him through many subjects, from a study of the brainwashing of Korean and Chinese POWs, to a study of management development and organizational socialization, and on to a deeper look at managerial careers. His interest in culture grew primarily out of clinical work with organizations in which culture became highly visible.

Ed is co-editor of the highly acclaimed Addison-Wesley series on organizational development, and he has consulted with a range of organizations around the world on culture, organizational development, and careers. He is considered one of the founders of the field of organizational psychology.

A partial list of his writing includes: *Human Resource Practices in Organizational Transformation: Are They Culture Specific?*; *Organizational and Managerial Culture as a Facilitator or Inhibitor of Organizational Transformation*; *The Leader of the Future*; *Process Consultation, Action Research, and Clinical Inquiry: Are They the Same?*; *Kurt Lewin in the Classroom, in the Field, and in Change Theory: Notes Toward a Model of Managed Learning*; *Building the Learning Consortium*; *Career Survival: Strategy Job and Role Planning*; *Organizational and Managerial Culture as a Facilitator or Inhibitor of Organizational Learning*; *The Clinical Perspective on Field Work*; *Career Anchors: Discovering Your Real Values*; *Organizational Culture and Leadership*; *Organizational Psychology*; *Career Dynamics*; *Professional Education: Some New Directions*; *Process Consultation: Its Role on Organizational Development*; *Organizational Socialization and the Profession of Management*; and *Personal and Organizational Change Through Group Methods.*

PART TWO

ROLE AND IDENTITY

Part Two is all about people. Here we identify and describe differing roles of those who engage in the coaching activity. The section opens with Richard Beckhard, who picks up the theme of the coach as a helper of people and provides a sketch of an ideal coach—who a coach should be and what a coach should strive to become. In following the theme of this book, "helping leaders learn," Dick argues that coaches might themselves consider seeking the kind of personal development that they provide to other professionals. If coaches are to be leaders, where should we start? Richard Leider picks up the leadership theme and reminds us that in order to engage others—and certainly prior to planning or acting—we must start by looking inward and first understanding ourselves. Jim Kouzes and Barry Posner make the link between leaders and coaching through the idea of "relationship" and highlight the key areas to consider and practical steps that are necessary to make this work well. Marshall Goldsmith and Howard Morgan expand the idea of coaching as a leadership relationship by introducing the idea of coaching whole teams. They share a highly practical and extremely effective coaching technique that motivates and builds almost spontaneously. Thomas Crane takes the theme of "positive regard" for others and develops an inventory of key areas for consideration by any boss who wants to become a coach. The central focus in all coaching activity must be "the person being coached." Don Grayson and Kerry Larson take their viewpoint from this role, describe six common pitfalls, and explain how to avoid them by knowing what to look for in a coach and in oneself. In returning to the essential theme of helping leaders learn, Chip Bell introduces the *mentor* role and the concept of mentoring as coaching with a learning objective. Deepak Sethi reminds us that, with the right approach, the gift of candid, caring feedback may be available to us from unexpected sources—those who are close to us on a daily basis at work and at home. Bruce Lloyd discusses the coach's role in managing the relationships between responsibility, leadership, and learning, and shows how the nature and role of power and its abuse can change the dynamics of these relationships within a situation or organization. Robert Witherspoon closes this part of the book by presenting four specific coaching roles that fit along a continuum—task, job, career, and business results. He argues the case for clear goals and roles, and shows how to apply the model to spot openings and to help in contracting a coaching relationship.

CHAPTER SIX

COACHING COACHES

Richard Beckhard

Coaching is an important and often central part of most organizational development (OD) and organizational consultants' practice. In the past five years it has become the activity that, for many, produces the basic relationship they have with clients and their "bread and butter" income.

Professional networks of coaches have sprung up in a number of areas, particularly on the West and East Coasts. Several websites and Internet conferences have been developed on the subject. At least three books on coaching are currently being written and will be published soon.

In the past year, I have personally been contacted by internal consultants who are starting individual practices based primarily on coaching. Two of the major management consulting firms with change practices are billing a significant amount of hours for executive coaching.

The subtitle of the collection of articles presented here defines a universal goal of the coaching relationship: *Helping Leaders Learn*. Within this universal goal, there are many types of specific goals that require different competencies from the coach.

The most popular type of relationship is aimed at giving the client feedback, often from a number of sources, as a basis for developing a plan for *improving his or her individual performance on the job*. Other goals may be *increasing skills in interpersonal relationships* or *communication*. Sometimes the process is used for *career planning*, and occasionally the contract is for *life planning*.

Because coaching is so obviously helpful to clients, there tends to be no rigorous criteria for defining the professional competence required of coaches. There is also no clear differentiation between professional coaching, coaching from the boss, or coaching from friends and colleagues.

Thus the range of consultants who define their professional work as "coaching" varies tremendously. On the high end there are consultancies such as Keilty, Goldsmith and Company, who use sophisticated mechanisms and well-trained practitioners in their work. At the other end of the spectrum, there are those who have been internal OD consultants and have done some advising with internal clients, who decide to form an individual practice or partnership.

Although, as I have said, there are a few networks developing, at this time there are no professional standards. Anyone can "hang out a shingle" that says *COACH*. Given the lack of standards in the field, it becomes an individual issue for practitioners to develop a basis for judging their competence and their need to improve and grow. Fortunately, more and more consultants are being made aware of this issue and are seeking help.

Several years ago, David Nadler, CEO of Delta Consulting, asked me to provide some coaching for individual consultants in his firm who wanted to be coached. Nadler is committed to the continuing development of his people, and this request fit into his values.

I began spending one day per month at Delta; people who wanted to book time with me could do so. All discussions were confidential, and Delta paid me a retainer so there was no connection between payment and who was being coached.

Several consultants began meeting with me, and I was contacted by other consultants who had heard of the mutually satisfactory arrangement. I then started a formal practice. I saw people in my office or we consulted over the telephone.

Initial expectations were that I would shadow consult on cases that they would bring from their own practices. It soon became apparent that their needs were both professional and personal. In addition to testing examples of their work, they had issues about their professional lives and careers, and in some cases their personal lives. Sessions became a combination of coaching and counseling. From the first, I demanded high confidentiality. Sessions were never reported or discussed with anyone but the client. In the past few years, the number of clients has grown slowly so that there are now enough clients to support a small practice.

I have had several significant insights from this work. One is that it is extremely difficult for people who identify their persona as a *helper* to receive help. My clients can basically be divided into two types:

The first type is experienced, usually successful, consultants who want to talk with someone older and more experienced about issues they cannot easily share with anyone. (This condition was similar to that of CEOs who told me how lonely they felt and how very difficult it was to confide in anyone in their organizations. An outside, trusted consultant could fill this role, and thus add value.)

The second type is people who are starting or have recently started coaching. They have shared that in working with their clients, they have felt less than secure about their coaching strategy. They needed to check with a more experienced mentor before implementing their plans.

I knew from earlier experience that professionals, such as ballet stars, top singers, and actors, no matter how successful, need to have a coach—a person who can help them keep fit, practice their scales, test a new opera, or do basic ballet exercises. I reasoned that consultants might need the same thing. The good coaches in the entertainment world usually have been successful performers—they've "been there" and are credible. Although they are no longer performing themselves, they are able to be helpful to current performers.

I am pleased and thankful that in the consulting world I am considered a "wise person." My commitment is to use that gift to help other practitioners continue to develop their impact on their clients and on the world.

About the Contributor

Richard Beckhard was an organization consultant, author, and professor of management and organization behavior at the Sloan School of

Management at MIT, where he served on the faculty for twenty-one years. His practice consisted primarily in working with managing complexity and change and in organizational and institutional development. He is considered a "father" in the field of organization development.

Dick authored eight books and numerous articles. His most recent book, *Agent of Change: My Life, My Practice,* was finished in 1997 and is published by Jossey-Bass. Along with Edgar Schein, he is the creator and editor of the Addison-Wesley OD Series. Dick was the co-editor of the best-selling Drucker Foundation Future Series (which has sold over 600,000 copies in fourteen languages). This series included *The Leader of the Future* (a *Business Week* "Top 15" bestseller), *The Organization of the Future,* and *The Community of the Future* (Amazon.com ranked number one in its field).

Dick's most recent teaching activities included workshops for national management associations in Ireland, Finland, Australia, Canada, Denmark, and Venezuela, and leadership conferences for organizations in both public and private sectors.

In 1984, the Sloan School created in his honor the Richard Beckhard Prize, awarded annually for the best article on his subject in The Sloan Management Review. In 1992, the Richard Beckhard Prize was created by the Family Firm Institute, an annual award honoring an outstanding practitioner in the field. In 1994, The Richard Beckhard Prize in Organization Development, an annual award from the Office of Public Management in the U.K. was initiated. The award is given to an organization or agency in the public area deemed to have done the most outstanding program in institutional development in the U.K.

Recent business and industry clients included the top managers of Imperial Chemical Industries (U.K.), Norsk Hydro (Norway), and Mastercard International (U.S.). In the health field, he worked with the leaders of several academic health centers in the U.S. and with the National Health Service in the U.K. He also consulted with several foundations, including the MacArthur Foundation and the Commonwealth Fund. He had a long-term interest in family businesses; in the early 1980s he created a research program at the Sloan School, MIT, from which came the Family Firm Institute, with a quarterly journal and a network of research institutes in the U.S. and Europe.

Dick served on a number of boards, including the Drucker Foundation, the Organization Learning Center at MIT, and the Institute for Development Research. In the U.K., he was a senior fellow of the Office of Public Management; a member of the Academy of Management, the OD Network, and the Society of Human Resource Planners; and a life member of the NTL Institute.

Dick was a personal coach, mentor, and inspiration to many of the co-authors of this book.

CHAPTER SEVEN

THE LEADERSHIP MIRROR: WHY SHOULD I FOLLOW YOU?

Richard J. Leider

It's no revelation that many leaders today are overwhelmed with change. They are being challenged from every direction. So, why do some leaders prosper whereas others do not?

We can speculate at length why some falter or fail due to *external* reasons—failure to anticipate market needs or failure to innovate. Yet the real difference between success and failure today can be traced to *internal* reasons—to how well leaders engage the hearts and souls of their followers. One sure test of leadership today is whether a leader has engaged followers.

Do People Follow You Willingly?

What does it take to engage people today? What does it take to inspire people to rally around a common purpose? First, it takes self-leadership. One big difference between the success or the failure of leaders can be traced to their character—how effectively they lead themselves. "Authentic" character usually accompanies greatness in anything, and it is largely responsible for the energy and unity found in high-performing organizations.

So a primary role of leaders in the new work world is to know the answers to the questions many followers ask: "Why should I follow you?" and "Why should I trust my livelihood to you?" Leaders must first look in the mirror to answer this question for themselves. They must understand that leadership is earned from the inside out. Real commitment and engaged followers come through asking oneself the tough character questions first.

Hold Up the Leadership Mirror

During my more than thirty years as a coach, I have been continually impressed with the courage that great leaders have for holding up the mirror to look inside themselves. They understand that the soft aspects of leading are as important as the hard ones. The prophets of the "Knowledge Age" have long pointed out that to lead the new work force, it will be necessary to lead in new ways.

While many leaders are energized by the prospects of this new era, others are hostile to what they perceive as a major change. These latter leaders had previously dismissed the early visions of the futurists as idealistic. Now that this revolutionary future has arrived, their denial has turned to fear and anger.

Where Are the New Maps and Guides?

Back in the good old days of predictable economic and market patterns, a leader could say, "That soft stuff's not for me; I'm going to keep on doing what's always worked." This choice no longer exists for the vast majority of leaders, as they are caught in a war to attract and keep talented workers. Many leaders who have enjoyed years of predictable growth are now struggling to attract and retain great people.

All leaders are going to have to be *discoverers* in the twenty-first century. The discoverers who created this nation had no maps, no guides. It was just their ambition and the potential opportunity. Some made it, but many did not. If the futurists are right, this means that for the foreseeable future we'll be continually discovering too. We'll have to take on greater career and business risks without maps and with few guides. We'll have to learn to *create trust as we lead people into new territories.*

Why Should I Follow You?

Today's knowledge employees don't blindly follow. They are educated, street smart, globally wise, and aware of their options. Their engagement on the job is dependent on the trust they have in their leaders.

Let's assume for a few minutes that you have been asked to interview your new boss or leader. What would *you* want to know about him or her as a leader? Assume you know the basics of the person's résumé: work history, age, family, hobbies, and so forth. What would you ask?

With today's workplace realities, most "followers" are hungry for purposeful leadership—leaders who have purpose, values, vision, and courage. Most people know their leaders do not have all the answers, but they want to participate in asking the questions anyway.

Purposeful leadership demands trust. Trust relies on character. In his book *Principle-Centered Leadership,* Stephen Covey (1990) notes that our heritage was governed by the "character ethic," which valued principles such as keeping promises, being honest, and exercising courage. Character is the "why" of "Why should I follow you?" Far too many leaders today have emphasized the "personality ethic" by focusing on projecting a certain image and using the right phrases. In doing so, they have mistakenly focused too much on the *form* and not enough on the *essence* of leadership. They have lost their character, and they have lost people's trust.

Character comes from the inside out. It can be summed up in the words of an Anglican bishop found inscribed on his tomb in Westminster Abbey:

"When I was young and free and my imagination had no limits, I dreamed of changing the world. As I grew older and wiser, I discovered the world would not change, so I shortened my sights somewhat and decided to change only my country. But, it too seemed immovable. As I grew into my twilight years, in one last desperate attempt, I settled for changing only family, those closest to me, but alas, they would have none of it. And now as I lie on my deathbed, I suddenly realize, if I had only changed myself first, then by example I would have changed my family. From their inspiration and encouragement I would then have been able to better my country and, who knows, I may have even changed the world."

Who You Are Comes Before What You Do

Form does not create trust. The response of others to one's form depends on the degree to which one's *essence* is also present.

Essence lies beneath the surface, at a leader's core. Essence is our underlying substance: our purpose, values, vision, and courage. When we discover our essence and learn to lead with it, then leading becomes a courageous discovery process into the future.

A key to courageous leadership is to address the question of "who we are" *before* the question of "what we do." When we focus on the *who* question before the *what* question, we discover our natural instincts as leaders.

Is Your Form or Your Essence in the Lead?

A critical question to ask oneself today is: "Who is leading? Is it my form or is it my essence?" When we lead from essence, trust is built. When we integrate who we are with what we do, many chronic problems of leadership drop away.

The Leadership Mirror presented later in this chapter is a first step to help us discern our leadership essence. It suggests important information about our leadership character. In filling out the questionnaire, it is important to dig below the surface and to look deeply into the mirror.

Effective leaders today have a strong sense of their essence. They have true purpose, values, and vision that guides their leadership. Robert K. Greenleaf (1977), in his book *Servant Leadership*, urged leaders to go "beyond conscious rationality" and to go into the "unchartered and unknown" to lead from within. Our *purpose* is our mission or the reason we were born; it is the central quality or essence that comes out in our leadership; and it is always larger than ourselves. It inspires us, of course, but it is also the quality that attracts and retains others.

Greenleaf said that "serving and leading are still mostly intuition-based concepts." He believed that self-insight is "the most dependable part of the true servant." By finding and fulfilling the purpose deep within us, we can meet Greenleaf's criteria for servant-leaders: "Those served grow as persons . . . and the least privileged in society . . . benefit, or at least . . . (are) not further deprived."

We cannot find our purpose in a book, although the writings of other leaders can be inspirational. To lead on purpose, we must be willing to look in the mirror—to understand our underlying substance and to lead from it.

The uncertainty of the workplace today makes us hungry for leaders who look in the mirror. We need leaders whom we can trust and who lead with an integrity that can only result from consistency between speech and actions, because in today's fast-paced organizations, it is only the leader who can foster real commitment and engaged followers, who will be able to navigate the unmapped territory to success.

FIGURE 7.1.   THE LEADERSHIP MIRROR*

When was the last time you stepped back and looked into the mirror? When was the last time you challenged your old answers and ways of doing things and looked for the underlying substance of your leadership?

Answer the following questions, and score yourself on a scale from 1 to 7. A "1" implies a definite "no" to the question. A "2" or "3" implies an infrequent articulation or use, "4" implies sometimes, "5" or "6" imply a frequent articulation or use, and "7" implies a definite "yes." Put your answers in the boxes provided.

1. Do I have clear values as a leader? ☐

2. Do my followers recognize my values through key actions that I demonstrate? ☐

3. Am I clear on my leadership strengths? ☐

4. Am I engaged in self-development efforts that focus on my strengths? ☐

5. Do I have a clear sense of my purpose as a leader? ☐

6. Do I leave my leadership legacy daily? ☐

7. Do I have a clear point of view about what it means to lead? ☐

8. Do those around me understand my point of view about leadership? ☐

9. Do I have a vision for what I'd like to accomplish as a leader? ☐

10. Do my followers know my vision because I communicate it to them? ☐

11. Do I take time for leadership reflection? ☐

12. Do I have a personal "board of directors" with whom to share reflections? ☐

13. Do I have written personal leadership goals? ☐

14. Do I take action on my leadership goals? ☐

*This exercise is used with permission from the *Leading from Within*® program. ©1998 The Inventure Group.

FIGURE 7.2. SCORING AND INTERPRETATION

Plot your scores on the following graph. First plot questions 1, 3, 5, 7, 9, 11, and 13. Then plot 2, 4, 6, 8, 10, 12, and 14.

The first set of statements (1, 3, 5, 7, 9, 11, and 13) assess how clear you are about your "essence" qualities. The second set of statements (2, 4, 6, 8, 10, 12, and 14) assess to what extent you apply and demonstrate those qualities. Statements on which your score fell below a "5" are growth areas in your journey to discover who you are and what you do as a leader. Our "essence" is who we truly are. When we discover it and learn to lead with it, we develop trust with our followers.

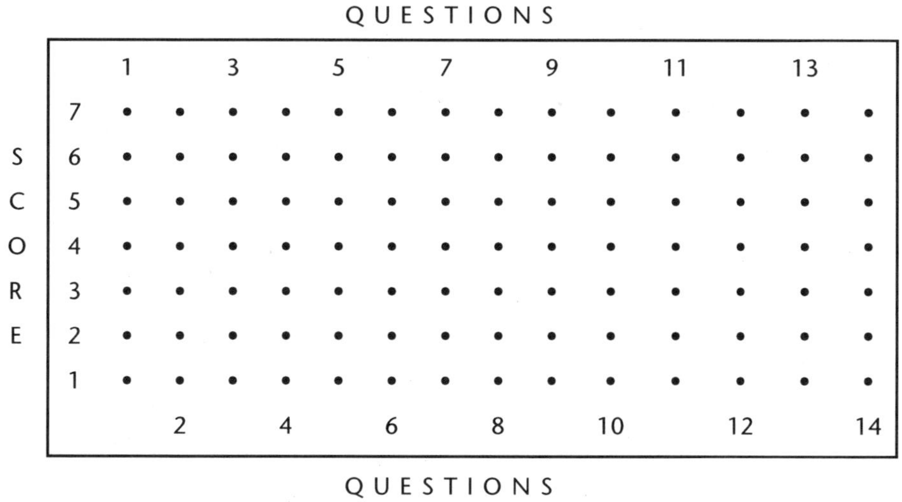

QUESTIONS

QUESTIONS

About the Contributor

Richard J. Leider is a founding partner of The Inventure Group, a firm devoted to helping individuals, leaders, and teams discover the power of purpose. As a pioneer in the field of life/work designing, Richard has become an internationally respected author, speaker, and executive coach, as well as a noted spokesman for "life skills" needed in the twenty-first century.

Richard has written or co-written four books: *The Inventurers, Life Skills, Repacking Your Bags* (an international bestseller published in fourteen languages), and *The Power of Purpose.* He has also contributed to the Peter Drucker Foundation book, *The Leader of the Future.* He was featured in *Fast Company,* the nation's fastest growing business magazine and is now an online columnist on *Fast Company's* website.

Richard has a master's degree in counseling psychology from the University of Northern Colorado and is a National Certified Career Counselor. He has a bachelor's degree in psychology from Gustavus Adolphus College, which chose him as "Distinguished Alumni in Human Services." His study received recognition from the Bush Foundation, where he was awarded a Bush Fellowship to study "mid-career renewal." His clients include leading Fortune 500 companies, such as 3M, Motorola, Pillsbury, Pfizer, Northwestern Mutual Life, American Express, and Saturn.

Yearly, Richard leads an Inventure Expedition walking safari in Tanzania, East Africa. He passionately believes that each of us is born with purpose, and his purpose is coaching individuals and leaders to discover that purpose.

CHAPTER EIGHT

WHEN LEADERS ARE COACHES

James M. Kouzes and Barry Z. Posner

Leadership is a relationship. Sometimes the relationship is one-to-many, and sometimes it is one-to-one. Regardless of whether the relationship is with one or with one thousand, leadership is a relationship between those who aspire to lead and those who choose to follow.

Evidence abounds for this point of view. For instance, in examining the critical variables for success in the top three jobs in large organizations, Jodi Taylor and her colleagues at the Center for Creative Leadership (CCL) found that the number one success factor is "relationships with subordinates" (Taylor, 1998). Earlier CCL studies have shown that the most important reason executives derail in their careers is their insensitivity and inability to understand the perspectives of others.

We're intrigued to find that even in this nanosecond world of e-everything, personal opinion is consistent with the facts. In an on-line survey, the techno-hip readers of *Fast Company* magazine (1999) were asked to indicate, among other things, "Which is more essential to business success five years from now—skills in using the Internet or social skills?" Seventy-two percent selected social skills compared to twenty-eight percent for Internet skills. Even when Internet literati complete a poll on-line, they realize that it's not the web of technology that matters the most, but the web of people.

Similar results were found in a study by Public Allies, a non-profit group dedicated to creating young leaders who can strengthen their communities. Public Allies (1998) sought the opinions of eighteen- to thirty-year-olds on the subject of leadership. Among the items was a question about the qualities that were important in a good leader. Topping the eighteen-to-thirty-year-olds' list was: "Being able to see a situation from someone else's point of view." In second place was: "Getting along well with other people." Young and old alike agree that success in leadership, success in business, and success in life have been, are now, and will be a function of how well we work and play together.

Intuitively, we all understand that when the leader is the coach, interpersonal trust and respect are significantly important. We're being asked to learn new knowledge and skills, take risks, try out unfamiliar behaviors, and, like all humans, fail a few times before we succeed. We won't do that unless we trust the person guiding and coaching us. So erase from your minds forever the image of coach as that stern-faced, chair-throwing, dirt-kicking, ass-chewing tough guy who yells orders to the players. Maybe it makes for good theater, but it certainly makes for lousy performance.

Success in the one-to-one leadership context is dependent on the ability of the leader to build a lasting relationship in which the talent sees the coach as a partner and a role model. In other words, you can't order others to perform at their best or improve what they do because of a position you hold. You can only get extraordinary things done because you have a heart.

Yes, heart. It turns out that the best leaders are caring leaders. We discovered this while researching for our book, *Encouraging the Heart* (1999), and we'd like to apply some of those lessons to the role of leader as coach.[1] Here are three of the essentials that seem to contribute most to establishing and maintaining a successful coaching relationship (Kouzes and Posner, 1999).

---

[1]Portions of this chapter are excerpted by permission from *Encouraging the Heart: A Leader's Guide to Rewarding and Recognizing Others* by James M. Kouzes and Barry Z. Posner. (San Francisco: Jossey-Bass, 1999.) Copyright © 2000 by James M. Kouzes and Barry Z. Posner. All rights reserved.

1. Set clear standards;
2. Expect the best; and
3. Set the example.

Set Clear Standards

Tony Codianni of Toshiba America explains it this way: "I have a need to be personal with my folks. To me there's no difference between work and personal life. Encouraging comes from the heart. It's heart-to-heart, not brain-to-heart. It has to be genuine."

Codianni is one of those people who loves people. He loves buying them presents; he loves inviting them out on his boat; he loves to cook for them. Codianni has nineteen first cousins, and he's taken them all to Italy. Ask anyone who works with him, and they'll all tell you they love to be around him. He makes them feel good.

But don't ever mistake Codianni's love of people for a willingness to forget about standards. Exemplary leadership is soft *and* demanding, caring *and* conscientious. As Codianni puts it, "I always tell trainers in my group that they have to master the program first, and then they're free to change it." To Codianni, having a clear set of expectations about what people will achieve is part and parcel of being caring.

The first prerequisite for encouraging the hearts of our talent is to *set clear standards.* By standards we mean both goals and values, because they both have to do with what's expected of us. Values serve as the enduring principles that enable us to maintain our bearings wherever we are throughout our lives. Goals are those shorter-term ambitions that provide us with the metrics for measuring progress.

Human beings just don't put their hearts into something they don't believe in. We won't commit with energy and intensity to something that's not a fit for us personally. It's like wearing a pair of slacks that are too tight. It's uncomfortable, we look awkward, we feel embarrassed, and we can't move around easily.

We know from the research we've been doing since the late 1970s that values make a difference in the way people behave inside organizations and how they feel about themselves, their colleagues, and their leaders. But when we take an even deeper look at the question of shared values—at the congruence between personal and organizational values—we find something quite provocative (Posner and Schmidt, 1993). We find that it's the clarity of personal values that really makes the difference in an individual's level of commitment to an organization.

Exemplary leader-coaches also make sure that work is not pointless ambling, but purposeful action. Goal setting affirms the person, and, whether we realize it or not, contributes to what people think about themselves. As University of Chicago Professor Mihaly Csikzsentmihalyi (1997) points out: "It is the goals that we pursue that will shape and determine the kind of self that we are to become. Without a consistent set of goals, it is difficult to develop a coherent self. . . . The goals one endorses also determine one's self-esteem."

People need to know whether they're making progress or marking time. Goals help to serve that function, but goals are not enough. It's not enough to know that we want to make it to the summit. We also need to know whether we're still climbing or whether we're sliding downhill. Therefore, effective leader-coaches also provide constructive, timely, and accurate feedback. Encouragement, it can be said, is a form of feedback. It is positive information that tells us that we're making progress, that we're on the right track, and that we're living up to the standards.

The wonderful thing about encouragement is that it's more personal than other forms of feedback. Encouragement requires us to get close to other people, to show that we care about other people, and to demonstrate that we're really interested in other people. When leaders provide a clear sense of direction and provide feedback along the way, they encourage people to reach inside themselves in order to do their best.

Expect the Best

Successful leaders have high expectations, both of themselves and of their constituents. These expectations aren't just fluff that leaders use to help us keep a positive outlook or psych themselves up. Another person's belief in our abilities accomplishes much more than that. The expectations that successful leaders hold provide the framework into which people fit their own realities. Both our high expectations and our low expectations influence other people's performance. Only high expectations, however, have a positive impact on both their actions and on their feelings about themselves, and only high expectations can improve performance.

Nancy Tivol, executive director of Sunnyvale Community Services (SCS) in California, is a wonderful example of this principle in action. She believes strongly in her own ability and in those of every staff member and volunteer. When Tivol first arrived at SCS in 1991, volunteers were, in her opinion, underused. Many board members and paid staff felt that volunteers didn't have the skills to handle interactions with clients, donors, and corporate contacts. Tivol believed they did. Today, SCS has volunteers doing things previously done only by staff members. Indeed, more than seven hundred volunteers run the front office, the agency's three food programs, the Community Christmas Center, the agency's computer operations, and the Volunteer Language Bank—all under one director of volunteers. Most of the lead volunteers are over sixty-five years of age, and volunteer hours have increased from 6,000 to 20,000 annually, which enabled paid staff to be reduced through attrition from twelve to eight full-time equivalents.

Not only that, but SCS became the country's only emergency assistance agency that has not turned eligible clients away because available funds have been depleted. Under Tivol's leadership, SCS has increased its funding for the emergency assistance program for low-income families during a recession and a period in which many agencies experienced significant funding cutbacks! Six years ago, SCS distributed $34,000 to prevent evictions and utility disconnections and to pay for medical care and prescriptions; last year, SCS distributed $240,000. Six years ago, SCS helped eighty families a month with food; now it helps more than 525, and the grocery bags are much more full.

Previous administrators, as well as paid staff, had made certain assumptions about volunteers. They assumed that because they were volunteers, they would be neither motivated enough nor skilled or experienced enough to take on the responsibility that the agency would require. As a result, volunteers were mostly employed at jobs that demanded little of them and they were given only minimal responsibilities. The bottom line was that they weren't given the opportunity to explore or demonstrate their own capacities beyond the performance of the most menial tasks. Their beliefs, their prophecies, so to speak, held the volunteers back; Tivol's beliefs encouraged the same group of people to excel. She placed volunteers in responsible positions, gave them the training and direction they required, and encouraged them to do their best. And they did just that!

When it became evident that SCS needed to upgrade its computer system, the assumption was that SCS did not have the money to set up the new system and train people. Tivol saw this not as an obstacle but as an opportunity. Once again, she turned to volunteers—entrusting the job to her fifteen-year-old son, a computer whiz who found the prospect a real challenge. For his Eagle Scout project, he wrote a forty-one-page manual. Then he trained ten Boy Scouts from his troop to become "coaches," who in turn taught others in the agency how to use the new computer system. Each scout adopted a staff member or volunteer and stood by those people as they learned the system.

What was the motivation that drove the volunteers? Why did the SCS picture change so radically under Tivol? The key was her high expectations of the volunteers, and her expectations literally breathed new life into the people around her. She prophesied their success.

This demonstration of belief in another's abilities comes not only in organizational settings. It can show up anywhere. A moving and powerful instance came to us from Idaho businessman Don Bennett. Bennett was the first amputee to climb to the summit of Mt. Rainier. That's 14,410 feet on one leg and two crutches!

During a difficult portion of the climb, Bennett and his team had to cross an ice field. To get across the ice, the climbers had to put crampons on their boots to prevent slipping and to dig into the ice for leverage and stability. Unfortunately, with two crutches, and only one boot with a crampon, Bennett got stuck in the ice. He determined that the only way to get across the ice field was to fall face forward onto the ice, pull himself as far forward as he could, stand up, and then fall forward again. He was going to get across the ice field by falling down.

On that particular climb, his teenage daughter, Kathy, was with him, and she saw what was happening to her dad. While the team leader cut holes in the ice so Bennett could hop onto clear snow and traverse the ice field, Bennett's daughter stayed by his side through the entire four-hour struggle. As Bennett hopped, she shouted in his ear: "You can do it, Dad. You're the best dad in the world. You can do it, Dad!"

After Bennett told us this story, he added: "There was no way that I was not going to make it across that ice field with my daughter shouting that in my ear. You want to know what leadership is? What she did is leadership." Kathy's belief in her father and her verbal encouragement touched a place deep within Bennett, strengthening his resolve and commitment.

It's no wonder, then, that when people tell us about leaders who really make a difference in their lives, they frequently tell us about people who have believed in them and encouraged them to reach beyond their own self-doubts, to more fully realize their own greatest strengths. They talk about leaders who treat them in ways that buoy their self-confidence, making it possible for them to achieve more than they themselves initially believe is possible.

The thoughts and beliefs we hold in our minds are intangible. They can't be weighed and measured like raw materials or finished products. But seen or not, measurable or not, they have an enormous impact on the people around us. Exemplary leaders know this and know how to purposefully hold in their minds high expectations for themselves and for other people.

Set the Example

Our colleague Christy Tonge and her development team at the Tom Peters Company found in their research on leader-as-coach that the factor most related to coaching effectiveness is "investing in relationship." (There's that leadership-is-a-relationship finding again!) Of all the items used to measure coaching behavior, the one most linked to success is "this person embodies character qualities and values that I admire."[*]

We keep relearning the lesson that it all starts with credibility. In our continuing research on the qualities that people look for and admire in

[*]For more information about this research on Leaders As Coach, contact Ron Crossland at the Tom Peters Company (888-221-8685) or e-mail at *roncrossland@tompeters.com*.

their leaders, time and time again we find that, more than anything, people want leaders who are credible (Kouzes and Posner, 1993, 1995). Credibility is the foundation of leadership.

Above all, people want to believe in their leaders. They want to believe that their leaders' word can be trusted, that leaders will do what they say. Our findings are so consistent over such a long period of time that we've come to refer to this as the *first law of leadership:* if you don't believe in the messenger, you won't believe the message.

Personal leadership credibility makes a huge difference in our performance and in our commitment to an organization (O'Reillly, 1984). Credibility makes a difference. Loyalty, commitment, energy, and productivity, among other things, depend on it.

So what exactly is credibility? What exactly is it *behaviorally?* How do you know it when you see it? When we ask people these questions their most frequent response is: *"They do what they say they will do"* (Kouzes and Posner, 1993).

When it comes to deciding whether a leader is believable, people first listen to the words and then watch the actions. They listen to the talk and watch the walk. Then, they measure the congruence. A judgment of "credible" is handed down when the two are consistent. If people don't see consistency, they conclude that the leader is at best not really serious about the words, and at worst, is an outright hypocrite.

Constituents are moved by deeds. Actions are the evidence of a leader's credibility. This observation leads to a straightforward prescription for leader modeling: DWYSYWD: Do What You Say You Will Do.

Over and over again, it's the same story. Wherever you find a strong culture built around strong values—whether the values are about superior quality, innovation, customer service, distinctiveness in design, respect for others, or just plain fun—you'll also find endless examples of leaders who personally live the values.

Personal involvement is what setting the example is all about. Terri Sarhatt, customer services manager of the Applied Biosystems Division of Perkin-Elmer, learned how important that is even in situations in which the rewards are tangible. Sarhatt was looking for a way to increase the amount of supportive communication she had with employees at the company, and as luck would have it, her decision to become more personally involved coincided with the annual distribution of stock options. At Applied Biosystems, as in many high-tech companies, people often receive stock options when they've had a good year, and because Applied Biosystems has been growing at around twenty percent for the last few years, it's been a regular occurrence.

In years past, Sarhatt would receive the options from her manager. She would then present options to her direct supervisors and request they do the same with their direct reports. In 1998, she decided to use a different tactic. She wanted to thank folks directly, so she asked her direct supervisors if they'd mind her meeting with each of their employees who were going to receive stock options. Her direct reports thought it was a terrific idea.

"I personally thanked them for the specific projects and the work they had done," said Sarhatt. "The employees were surprised that I would actually take the time out of my busy schedule to sit down with each of them separately, have a cup of coffee, and discuss their accomplishments. One of my supervisors informed me later that her employee appreciated the time I spent with her more than she appreciated the actual stock options!" As we have found so often in our research, the gift of personal time mattered most.

Sarhatt also told us that it's "the 'little' things that make such a BIG difference!" And that's the point. It doesn't take a grand plan to begin to set the example for encouraging the hearts of others. It doesn't take a huge budget, it doesn't take psychotherapy, and it doesn't take the boss's permission. What's most critical in all these examples is that the leaders took the initiative. Being a good role model is no exception. It has to become a conscious priority.

It's About Caring

Along the journey to developing yourself as an exemplary leader-coach, there is one truth that you absolutely must confront: *How much do you really care about the people you lead?*

Now our hunch is that you care a lot. You probably wouldn't be reading this book and this chapter if you didn't. But this question must be confronted daily, because when you care deeply the techniques that we've described will present themselves as genuine expressions of your caring. When you care little, they'll be perceived as nothing more than gimmicks, and you'll be thought of as a phony.

One of the oldest observations about human behavior is that we tend to mirror those around us. If we're around someone who's sad, for example, we pick it up. Even if we enter the room full of vim and vigor, we find that our energy starts to leak out when we're in the presence of negative emotions. Now put yourself in the position of the person being coached. Imagine spending your days with a down-in-the-mouth, negative, and pessimistic leader. What a depressing thought.

But what happens to you when you enter a room full of upbeat, supportive, appreciative, and enthusiastic people? You tend to be uplifted yourself, don't you? Human beings much prefer to be around positive people. And, by the way, researchers have also found that positive, hopeful, and optimistic people get more done in their lives and feel both personally and professionally more successful than do their more negative counterparts.

As the leader, *you* set the tone. Remember that it's the quality of the relationship *you* have with *your* constituents that matters most. When it comes to your role as leader-coach, the talent in your organization will grow and thrive only when you establish a clear set of high standards, display a strong belief that those standards can be achieved, and then demonstrate by your own actions that you practice what you preach.

When you integrate these three essentials into your daily practice, you will set a tone that loudly and clearly resonates the message: "I care about you. I care about your future. I care about your growth. I'm here to create a climate in which *you* blossom and flourish." Not only will others find great joy and success in this caring climate, so, too, will you.

About the Contributors

James M. Kouzes is chairman emeritus of the Tom Peters Company, a professional services firm that specializes in developing leaders at all levels. He is also the dean's professor of leadership in the Leavey School of

Business at Santa Clara University and an executive fellow at its Center for Innovation and Entrepreneurship.

In September 1993 the *Wall Street Journal* cited Jim as one of the twelve most requested "non-university executive-education providers" to U.S. companies. A popular seminar and conference speaker, Jim shares his insights about the leadership practices that contribute to high performance in individuals and organizations, and he leaves his audiences with practical leadership tools and tips that they can apply at work, at home, and in their communities. He has conducted leadership development programs for hundreds of organizations, including AT&T, Arthur Andersen, Sun Microsystems, and the YMCA.

Barry Z. Posner is dean of the Leavey School of Business, Santa Clara University, and professor of leadership. He served previously as managing partner of the Executive Development Center and has also served as associate dean with responsibility for leading the school's MBA and undergraduate programs. He has received the Dean's Award for Exemplary Service, the President's Distinguished Faculty Award, and several outstanding teaching and leadership honors. A frequent conference speaker and workshop facilitator, Barry has worked with such organizations as Merck, Hewlett-Packard, and Kaiser Permanente Health Care.

Jim and Barry are co-authors of the award-winning book, *The Leadership Challenge: How to Keep Getting Extraordinary Things Done in Organizations,* which is now in its second edition (1995) with over one million copies in print. *The Leadership Challenge* is available in eleven languages and has been a selection of the Macmillan Executive Book Club and the Fortune Book Club. It's the winner of the 1989 James A. Hamilton Hospital Administrators' Book Award and 1995-1996 Critics' Choice Award. Jim and Barry have also co-authored *Credibility: How Leaders Gain and Lose It, Why People Demand It,* which was chosen by *Industry Week* as one of the ten best management books of 1993. Their newest books, *Encouraging the Heart* and *The Leadership Challenge Planner,* were released in early 1999.

CHAPTER NINE

TEAM BUILDING WITHOUT TIME WASTING

Marshall Goldsmith and Howard Morgan

Teams are becoming more and more common and important. As the traditional, hierarchical school of leadership diminishes in significance, a new focus on networked team leadership is emerging to take its place. Leaders are finding themselves members of all kinds of teams, including virtual teams, autonomous teams, cross-functional teams, and action-learning teams.

Many of today's leaders face a dilemma: as the *need* to build effective teams is increasing, the *time* available to build these teams is often decreasing. A common challenge faced by today's leaders is the necessity of building teams in an environment of rapid change with limited resources. The process of re-engineering and streamlining, when coupled with increased demand for services, has led to a situation in which most leaders have more work to do and fewer staff members to help them do it.

Research involving thousands of participants has shown how focused feedback and follow-up can increase leadership and customer service effectiveness (Hesselbein, Goldsmith, and Beckhard, 1996). A parallel approach to team building has been shown to help leaders build teamwork without wasting time. While the approach described sounds simple, it will not be easy. It will require that team members have the courage to ask for input and suggestions regularly and the discipline to develop a behavioral change strategy, to follow up, and to "stick with it."

To implement the following team-building process successfully, the leader (or external coach) will need to assume the role of coach or facilitator and fight the urge to be the "boss" of the project. Greater improvement in teamwork will generally occur if the team members develop their own behavioral change strategy rather than if the leader develops the strategy and imposes it on the team. This process should not be implemented if the leader has the present intention of firing or removing a team member.

Steps in the Process

Step One. Begin by asking all members of the team to confidentially record their individual answers to two questions: (1) "On a 1 to 10 scale (with 10 being ideal), how well *are* we doing in terms of working together as a team?" and (2) "On a 1 to 10 scale, how well *do we need to be* doing in terms of working together as a team?"

Before beginning a team-building process, it is important to determine whether the team feels that team building is both important and needed. Some people may report to the same manager, but legitimately have little reason to work interactively as a team. Other groups may believe that teamwork is important, but feel that the team is already functioning smoothly and that a team-building activity would be a waste of time.

Step Two. Have a team member calculate the results. Discuss the results with the team. If the team members believe that the gap between current effectiveness and needed effectiveness indicates the need for team building, proceed to the next step in the process.

In most cases team members believe that improved teamwork is both important and needed. Recent interviews involving members from several hundred teams (in multinational corporations) showed that the "average" team member believed that his or her team was currently at a 5.8 level of effectiveness but needed to be at an 8.7 level.

Step Three.   Ask the team members, "If *every* team member could change two key behaviors that would help us close the gap between *where we are* and *where we want to be,* which two behaviors should we all try to change?" Have each team member record his or her selected behaviors on flip charts.

Step Four.   Help team members prioritize all the behaviors on the charts (many will be the same or similar) and (using consensus) determine the two most important behaviors to change (for all team members).

Step Five.   Have each team member hold a one-on-one dialogue with all other team members. During the dialogues each member will request that his or her colleague suggest two areas for personal behavioral change (other than the two already agreed on above) that will help the team close the gap between *where we are* and *where we want to be.*

These dialogues occur simultaneously and take about five minutes each. For example, if there are seven team members, each team member will participate in six brief one-on-one dialogues.

Step Six.   Let each team member review his or her list of suggested behavioral changes and choose the two that seem to be the most important. Have all team members then announce their two key behaviors for personal change to the team.

Step Seven.   Encourage all team members to ask for brief (five-minute), monthly "progress reports" from all other team members on their effectiveness in demonstrating the two key behaviors common to all team members and the two key personal behaviors. Specific suggestions for improvement can be solicited in areas in which behavior does not match desired expectations.

Step Eight.   Conduct a mini-survey, follow-up process in approximately four months. From the mini-survey each team member will receive confidential feedback from all other team members on his or her perceived change in effectiveness. This survey will include the two common items, the two personal items, and an item that assesses how much the individual has been following up with the other team members. The mini-surveys are simple enough to be put on a postcard and might look like the sample in Figure 9.1.

Step Nine. Have an outside supplier calculate the results for each individual (on all items) and calculate the summary results for all team members (on the common team items). Each team member can then receive a confidential summary report indicating the degree to which colleagues see

FIGURE 9.1. SAMPLE MINI-SURVEY

Do you believe this person has become more (or less) effective *in the past six months* in regard to the following items? (Please circle the number that best matches your estimate of any change in effectiveness.)

	Less Effective		No Perceptible Change			More Effective		No Change Needed	Not Enough Infor- mation

Team Items:

1. Clarifies roles and expectations with fellow team members	−3	−2	−1	0	1	2	3	NCN	NI
2. Supports the final decision of the team (even if it was not his or her original idea)	−3	−2	−1	0	1	2	3	NCN	NI

Individual Items:

1. Genuinely listens to others	−3	−2	−1	0	1	2	3	NCN	NI
2. Strives to see the value of differing opinions	−3	−2	−1	0	1	2	3	NCN	NI

How has this person followed up with you on areas that he or she has been trying to improve? (Check one)

____ No Perceptible Follow-Up
____ Little Follow-Up
____ Some Follow-Up
____ Frequent Follow-Up
____ Consistent (Periodic) Follow-Up

What can this individual do to become a more effective team member?

_____
_____
_____

his or her increased effectiveness in demonstrating the desired behaviors. Each member can also receive a summary report on the team's progress on the items selected for all team members.

"Before and after" studies have clearly shown that if team members have regularly followed up with their colleagues they will almost invariably be seen as increasing their effectiveness in their selected individual "areas for improvement." The group summary will also tend to show that (overall) team members will have increased in effectiveness on the common team items. The mini-survey summary report will give team members a chance to receive positive reinforcement for improvement (and to learn what has not improved) after a reasonably short period of time. The mini-survey will also help to validate the importance of "sticking with it" and "following up."

Step Ten.   In a team meeting have each team member discuss key learnings from their mini-survey results, and ask for further suggestions in a brief one-on-one dialogue with each other team member.

Step Eleven.   Review the summary results with the team. Facilitate a discussion on how the team (as a whole) is doing in terms of increasing its effectiveness in the two key behaviors that were selected for all team members. Provide the team with positive recognition for increased effectiveness in teamwork. Encourage team members to keep focused on demonstrating the behaviors that they are trying to improve.

Step Twelve.   Have every team member continue to conduct brief, monthly, "progress report" sessions with all other team members. Re-administer the mini-survey eight months after the beginning of the process and again after one year.

Step Thirteen.   Conduct a summary session with the team one year after the process has started. Review the results of the final mini-survey, and ask the team members to rate the team's effectiveness on *where we are* versus *where we need to be* in terms of working together as a team. Compare these ratings with the original ratings that were calculated one year earlier.

(If team members followed the process in a reasonably disciplined fashion, the team will almost always see a dramatic improvement in teamwork.) Give the team positive recognition for improvement in teamwork, and have each team member (in a brief one-on-one dialogue) recognize each of his or her colleagues for improvements in behavior that have occurred over the past twelve months.

Step Fourteen.   Ask the team members if they believe that more work on team building will be needed in the upcoming year. If the team believes that more work would be beneficial, continue the process. If the team believes that more work is not needed, declare victory and work on something else!

Why This Process Works

The process described above works because it is highly focused, includes disciplined feedback and follow-up, does not waste time, and causes participants to focus on self-improvement. Most survey feedback processes ask respondents to complete too many items. In such surveys most of the items do not result in any behavioral change and participants feel they are wasting time. Participants almost never object to completing four-item mini-surveys that are specifically designed to fit each team member's unique needs. The process also works because it provides ongoing feedback and reinforcement. Most survey processes provide participants with feedback every twelve to twenty-four months. Any research on behavioral change will show that feedback and reinforcement for new behavior needs to occur much more frequently than yearly or bi-yearly. A final reason that the process works is because it encourages participants to focus on self-improvement. Many team-building processes degenerate because team members are primarily focused on solving *someone else's* problems. This process works because it encourages team members to focus primarily on solving *their own* problems!

Let us close with a challenge to you (the reader) as a team leader. Try it! The "downside" is very low. The process takes little time and the first mini-survey will quickly show whether progress is being made. The "upside" can be very high. As effective teamwork becomes more and more important, the brief amount of time that you invest in this process may produce a great return for your team and an even greater return for your organization.

About the Contributors

Marshall Goldsmith is a founding director of Keilty, Goldsmith & Company (KGC). A recent study by Penn State University listed KGC as one of the seven key providers of customized leadership development in the United States. Marshall is one of the select few consultants who has been asked to work with over one hundred executive teams. Busy executive teams tend to love his approach to team building because of its simplicity and time effectiveness. He and his colleagues at KGC have helped teams from organizations around the world achieve positive, long-term, measurable change in team behavior.

Howard Morgan is a director of Keilty, Goldsmith & Company and Leadership Research Institute. Howard specializes in executive coaching as a strategic change management tool leading to improved customer and employee satisfaction and overall corporate performance. His recent achievements include the development of an internal coaching model for a large international organization and coaching executives on the art of managing managers. He continues to assist executive committees of many of the world's leading organizations.

CHAPTER TEN

BECOMING A COACH FOR THE TEAMS YOU LEAD

Thomas G. Crane

One of the core competencies of contemporary leadership is coaching. It is a field of management practice that is receiving renewed interest for the power it has to create and sustain *high performance.*

Although there are technical components to coaching, it is much more than technique. This article explores what is really required to make the transformation to *becoming* a coach—at all levels of human interaction. It's called "Transformational Coaching," and is further described in *The Heart of Coaching* (Crane, 1998).

In traditional Western organizations, most managers have been conditioned to adopt a hierarchical command-and-control mentality. Moving from this traditional mind-set into Transformational Coaching requires us to do more than learn a few new management techniques. It requires us to *change the way we think.* It requires us to discover *what* we think—about our roles and the outcomes we attempt to achieve with people—and to transform both our thinking and our behavior.

Why is it necessary to change at such a deep level? Shouldn't business stay out of the personal arena? Why can't you just learn some new methods and techniques and begin coaching?

The fact is that personal aspects of our lives do not stay out of the business arena. Everyone brings to work the entire array of his or her personality—thoughts, attitudes, behaviors, habits, needs, wants, fears, desires, roles, and conditioning. Transformational Coaching does not *bring* the personal into work situations. It simply acknowledges that the personal element is a part of work and provides a framework—the heart of the coach—for dealing effectively with the whole human being.

Becoming a Boss

Be honest. If you have had authority over others, haven't you found it compelling? At times, didn't you feel powerful and strong? It's easy to see how even well-intentioned managers can enjoy the power trip of being the boss. Most of us possess at least some of the human beliefs that make us prey to this mentality:

- Our egos become invested in the roles we play and in the trappings of our authority;
- We believe that, because we have paid our dues, it is fair to expect others to do the same;
- We fear change and letting go of control;
- We fear failing in the eyes of the world; and
- We develop habits of behaving and thinking that reinforce the correctness of the boss approach.

Add to this list the fact that most of our role models at work are bosses, and that the human system of which we are a part does not accept changes to long-established roles easily, and there you have it: a boss in the making.

Beliefs and the Results Cycle

The "Results Cycle" describes the inevitability of this mind-set. The key to stopping the cycle is in understanding it. Let's begin with beliefs.

Our beliefs have a great influence over how we interact with people. What we believe tends to determine how we behave toward others. Our behavior tends to influence the quality of the relationships we have with others, which affects *their* behavior. This, of course, influences the results we obtain with these people. In turn, the results usually reinforce our belief in the correctness of our beliefs.

For example, if you believe that it is inappropriate to share your feelings with your co-workers, you might be formal and rigid with them to keep distance between them and your feelings. If this behavior is experienced by your co-workers as aloofness or coldness, they may feel put off and intimidated and begin drawing their own (potentially negative) conclusions about your feelings. Because they do not feel comfortable communicating with you, they may do work based on inaccurate interpretations of your instructions, rather than checking back to make sure that they understood. When you see the results, you may say to yourself, "See! If I can't trust them to get the most fundamental instructions right, how can I trust them with personal information? You just can't bring personal feelings into the workplace."

Another example: If you believe that a manager is supposed to be strict and unbending with the rules, you may be tough and punish those who break the rules. In turn, your direct reports may become guarded and stop taking risks. As a result, your department may do all right, but turnover may be high and, unlike other departments, it will not win awards from top management for innovative and creative solutions to business problems. In frustration, you may hold even more tightly to your belief in the need for control and adherence to the rules. This cycle is self-reinforcing and self-perpetuating.

On the other hand, if you believe that collaboration between people leads to better results, you might be open with your thoughts and encourage others to be open in sharing their needs and ideas for solutions. Relationships become more open and trusting; the people you lead are more willing to take risks with presenting ideas; and you obtain better results.

The easiest place to break the power of the Results Cycle is in changing the beliefs. So which beliefs support bossing and which ones support coaching? Here's a list:

- Bosses believe that their job is to push people or drive them; coaches believe that they are there to lift and support people.
- Bosses believe that they should talk at people by telling, directing, and lecturing; coaches believe in engaging in dialogue with people by asking, requesting, and listening.
- Bosses believe in controlling others through the decisions they make; coaches believe in facilitating others to make decisions and empowering them to implement their own decisions.
- Bosses believe they know the answers; coaches believe they must seek the answers.
- A boss triggers insecurity through administering a healthy dose of fear as an effective way to achieve compliance; a coach believes in using purpose to inspire commitment and stimulate creativity.
- Bosses believe that their job is to point out errors; coaches believe that their job is to celebrate learning.
- A boss believes in solving problems and making decisions; a coach believes in facilitating others to solve problems and make decisions.
- A boss believes in delegating responsibility; a coach believes in modeling accountability.
- Bosses believe in creating structure and procedures for people to follow; coaches believe in creating a vision and promoting flexibility through values as guidelines for behavior.
- A boss believes in doing things right; a coach believes in doing the right things.
- Bosses believe that their power lies in their knowledge; coaches believe that their power lies in their vulnerability.
- A boss believes in focusing on the bottom line; a coach believes in focusing on the process that creates the bottom-line result.

The Challenge of Change

If we did not get something out of the roles we play, change would be easy. Traditional working roles and relationships do offer a lot that is appealing. Let's take a look at the payoffs—and the penalties—for not changing.

Payoffs and Penalties for Bosses and Subordinates

Remaining a boss has its advantages. For example, bosses feel that they are in control; are "right" a lot (at least in terms their egos understand); maintain power, position, and authority, and therefore fit in with the establishment; make efficient short-term use of their time; maintain old habits; and keep all their current thinking or beliefs.

But they pay for keeping their positions as bosses (rather than transcending the role to become coaches). The costs include: losing the optimal contribution of other people's creativity; missing others' ideas, options, and alternatives; maintaining ownership of problems; and not learning from and about others. Bosses are more likely to create resentment with employees. Furthermore, there is always the risk that they will have the *wrong* answer and create more resentment when they cannot admit it.

There are prices and payoffs for being subordinate to a boss, too. On the plus side, subordinates have it easy—they usually wait for the boss to make decisions. They do not have to think or assume responsibility; they do not have to be afraid of making waves; they are safer politically; and they can get out of many difficult situations simply by saying, "It's not my job." Subordinates are likely to be able to retire on the job.

On the flip side, subordinates must often put up with not being allowed to think; not feeling valued or trusted; and feeling discounted and diminished. They often have to deal with their resentment toward their bosses, and they usually can't expect much in the way of growth and development on the job. Their self-esteem can suffer.

Payoffs and Penalties for Coaches and Coachees

Changing to a coach-coachee relationship is not necessarily a bed of roses, however. It, too, carries compelling prices and payoffs. For example, coaches learn more about others and themselves, witness the development of other people's capacities, and build better teams. They also benefit from improved working relationships, overall performance, and watching themselves grow and improve as coaches.

But, they often find that the risks are higher (both personally and politically). They must learn to trust others more. Transformational Coaching takes more time and more personal courage than bossing. Coaches must share accountability. Coaches must become comfortable with confrontation of performance issues, and they must let go of their illusions of control.

Coachees also discover a set of positives and negatives when they make the transition. Although they have the opportunity for more growth and development, being a coachee means that more is required. Their working relationships improve, but they have more responsibility and accountability. There is usually a new pride of accomplishment, but it is uncomfortable becoming used to new ways. They feel valued, but find that the new paradigm requires that they risk more. Work is more fulfilling, but they have to change. They are performing at higher levels than before, but it is not always easy to hear their coach's feedback; sometimes they take it personally by interpreting the suggestions as if they were personal criticisms.

If you look closely, you will notice some trends here. Most of the payoffs for the boss and subordinate are short-term. The traditional boss/subordinate roles allow people to remain in their personal comfort zones. The prices paid, however, are long-term and weaken the overall capability of the individual, the team, and the organization. This transformation is not easy. Each of us tends to be governed by our belief system about how things "ought to be." These beliefs filter our incoming experience, causing us to ignore what lies outside our own system.

Beliefs that Block Transformational Coaching

It can be extremely helpful to acknowledge your own personal barriers. Do you see yourself in any of the statements below?

- "I don't know how to coach. I don't want to coach. I don't consider myself coaching material."
- "Coaching is not valued around here. There are no coaching role models here. I'll look different if I'm the only one doing it. I won't be supported."
- "The benefits are unclear to me. Look at me—I didn't have coaching and *I'm* successful. I'm doing okay; I don't need feedback."
- "It's not my job. Somebody else will do it."

- "It takes too long to learn to coach and then to do it. My immediate needs are greater than their developmental needs. Other things are more important. I'll do it later."
- "It is inconvenient. It's difficult. It's time-consuming. It's unnecessary."
- "Change is scary. I'm afraid to ask how. I'll lose control. I'll make mistakes."
- "I had a bad personal experience with coaching. It doesn't really work."
- "I don't trust others to coach me. I do not want to confront others."
- "I can't change. I don't want to change."
- "It won't make a difference. People won't change with coaching. People won't keep their agreements. People don't want to be coached. People are really lazy and won't respond. My people already know what I think about them."
- "It's just another management fad. Coaching is just a fancy word for 'bossing' people around."
- "Real work is more important."

Looking at the above list, which beliefs can you identify as your own? Are any close to your own beliefs? Are there other beliefs you may hold about coaching? If you are committed to becoming a coach, these beliefs need not be anchors around your neck. Suspend them for a moment while we look at a belief system that may support your changing your personal Results Cycle as a Transformational Coach.

Empowering Beliefs of a Coach

Just as bosses have underlying belief systems that support their Results Cycles, coaches have beliefs that support theirs. Let's explore their thinking.

- As a supervisor, manager, or leader, I am responsible for my own and others' work performance. I want to be successful in my role. I realize that all of the important work of this enterprise is done by and through people. I cannot succeed unless my teammates—above me, below me, and beside me—are also successful.
- I appreciate that I do not have all the answers. Others will become more effective if they are permitted to discover answers for themselves.

However, I have experience, wisdom, insights, and good ideas to pass along.

- I may be able to help others achieve their goals even more effectively if I share what I know and what I see. I can use coaching as the process of empowering and inspiring others to higher levels of performance.
- Therefore, I choose to be a Transformational Coach.

This leads us to a Transformational Coach's credo, which rests on the following beliefs:

- People are inherently good and they want to contribute.
- People are doing the best they can with what they know and are aware of at any given moment.
- People make mistakes, but most do not set out to make mistakes on purpose.
- Mistakes can be framed positively as learning opportunities for everybody on the team.
- Most people's limiting beliefs about their capacities and capabilities keep them from accomplishing more than they do.
- Because most work is done by, through, and with the cooperation of people, transforming their individual effectiveness will transform the performance of the team.
- People support the changes and commitments they create, not the ones forced on them.
- Unnecessary control is resented; people prefer to be "led" rather than "managed."
- Outside input from anybody is most helpful when it is really desired.
- Coaches can build strong, trusting relationships by being open and honest in owning and disclosing their thoughts and feelings.
- People's feelings must not be ignored; a holistic view of people allows one to see the whole person.
- People appreciate clear, honest feedback delivered in a straightforward manner.
- People really do want to improve.

All these beliefs can be summed up in a Transformational Coach's version of the "golden rule": a coach has *positive regard* for others. This is the attitude that typifies Transformational Coaching. The challenge is to suspend beliefs that block us from becoming coaches. When we consciously explore and replace our limiting belief systems, our energy, tone, and intention shift. It is a journey well worth the effort!

About the Contributor

Thomas G. Crane is a consultant, facilitator, author, and coach who specializes in assisting leaders in creating high-performance teams. He works with all levels of leaders and their teams to enhance their individual and team effectiveness in achieving performance objectives.

Tom's passion is also the title of his first book, *The Heart of Coaching*, which focuses on changing a leader's mind-set from "the boss" to the mind-set of "the coach." The premise of the book is that a performance-based, feedback-rich culture will more effectively support an organization's business strategy and lead to higher and more sustainable levels of performance.

Tom has worked as a consultant and engagement leader for the last fifteen years in small and large organizations going through strategic change and culture alignment. Some of the organizations with whom he has worked include AES Corporation, AEP Corporation, Anadarko Petroleum, A.T. Kearney, Baker & Botts, Bell Atlantic, CBS, Continental Airlines, Crowne Plaza Redondo Beach, Dixieline, Duty Free International, Dynegy Corporation, ENRON Corporation, Equiva Services, Florida Power & Light, GPU Nuclear, Helen Woodward Animal Center, Hilton Grand Vacations, Holiday Inn Crowne Plaza, Home Savings of America, Host Travel Division–Marriott, KFC, Micron Electronics, KPMG Peat Marwick, Los Alamos Laboratory, New York Life, NYNEX, Qualcomm, San Diego State University, Shell Oil Company, Southern California Gas, Sonat, Inc., Teledyne Ryan Aeronautical, Times Mirror, Transco Energy, United Airlines, Vastar Resources, Von's Grocery Company, and Westrend Electric, Inc.

Prior to founding Crane Consulting in 1995, Tom was vice president of Senn-Delaney Leadership and consulted with clients engaged in strategic culture change. Additionally, he worked in financial planning and project management roles with Solar Turbines, a division of Caterpillar. He has a bachelor's degree from Purdue University and an MBA from Drake University.

CHAPTER ELEVEN

HOW TO MAKE THE MOST OF THE COACHING RELATIONSHIP FOR THE PERSON BEING COACHED

Don Grayson and Kerry Larson

The person being coached is afforded a rare opportunity—the chance to be seen through the eyes of another by working with a coach. But the person being coached must have the right mind-set and skill set in order to get the most from the coaching experience.

Unfortunately, the person being coached may either consciously or subconsciously subvert the coaching process. In our experience, there are six common pitfalls that may snare the person being coached. In this article, we cover the pitfalls and ways to help the person avoid them and gain the greatest benefit from the relationship. The six most common pitfalls for the person being coached are:

1. Failure to commit;
2. Unrealistic expectations;
3. Defensiveness;
4. Passive role in the coaching process;
5. Playing it safe; and
6. Failure to involve others.

Pitfall One: Failure to Commit

Without true commitment, the coaching process may be doomed from the start.

> For example, Joe was very upset when his manager took him aside to discuss the need for coaching. Joe knew he was aggressive, but he'd always been aggressive and it had always gotten him his way or gotten him noticed by management. He actually regarded his aggressiveness as a major contributor to his success. He believed he was always the strong one. He'd show his boss that if anyone needed help, it certainly wasn't him. He'd show this "supposed coach" that he wasn't the one in need of coaching.

There are a number of possible reasons for the lack of commitment on the part of the person being coached:

1. The individual may not understand the reason for coaching.
2. Coaching may be seen as a punishment and not an opportunity. The individual may resent or rebel against the perceived accusation of being a "bad manager." Rebellion may take the form of overt aggression. Alternatively, a more subtle rebellion is when the individual makes coaching into a game, pretending to go through the motions with no intention of putting any effort into the coaching relationship.
3. The individual may not trust the boss's motives.

It is essential that the coaching relationship be a relationship of commitment. Without a true commitment the person being coached will put forth a half-hearted effort. In turn, the coach will lose interest and expend energies elsewhere, and both parties will lose out on a great potential opportunity.

Both parties must work hard to achieve the goal of improved performance. There may be many ups and downs, but commitment sustains effort when the going gets tough.

> For example, Linda saw coaching as an opportunity to learn and to prepare for future responsibilities. She was determined to improve her effectiveness. She put forth her best effort, and she devoted time and energy to thinking about and actively working to change her problem

behaviors. She took the initiative to contact her coach with questions. As a result, her coaching was successful.

Pitfall Two: Unrealistic Expectations

Many people who are coached enter a coaching relationship with the following incorrect or unrealistic expectations:

- *Behavior is easily changed.* The person being coached may believe that all behavioral problems have simple and quick solutions.

   For example, Ellen's people were in the dark and felt no opportunity to offer their opinions and concerns. Ellen oversimplified her problem behavior. Rather than trying to understand *why* she communicated sparingly, she decided to hold weekly meetings with her people. She thought this would satisfy her boss. Unfortunately, she wound up canceling most of her meetings because of "pressing priorities." Without realizing it, she further demonstrated her problem behavior; communicating with her people still remained a low priority for her.

- *It takes time.* Experts in human behavior recognize that it normally takes years of experience to shape our behavior patterns, and it is important for anyone being coached to understand that changing behavior takes a great deal of time and effort.
- *Several behaviors can be changed simultaneously.* Some people simply go overboard. They try to improve too many behaviors at once. This is too ambitious. Any skill—one's communication ability or even one's golf swing—is best improved when broken down into discreet steps and tackled one step at a time.
- *Successful coaching will be rewarded.* It is a mistake to think that, by itself, successful coaching will automatically lead to promotion or that there will be some specific reward for success.

   To avoid these problems, it is critical for the person being coached to discuss expectations with his or her coach. Outcomes may then be realistic and achievable.

Pitfall Three: Defensiveness

Our defenses serve a purpose; they protect us. The following defenses help us to cope with life:

- *Rationalization:* Helps us to explain behavior we might not otherwise understand;
- *Blaming:* Prevents us from getting overwhelmed by taking on too much responsibility; and
- *Denial:* Permits us to digest only the information that we can absorb.

However, our defenses can also harm us: they may distort our view of reality; they may cut us off from receiving useful information; and they may chase other people away from us.

For coaching to be successful, the person being coached must be brutally honest about his or her strengths and limitations. He or she must be open to a coach, to let the coach in on his or her goals, fears, concerns, thoughts, and feelings. Defenses can easily serve as a roadblock by preventing insight into oneself and others. Defenses can also lessen the coach's understanding of the person being coached, and thus diminish the coach's ability to help.

Joanne thought she was highly effective. She was bright and successful. She was given the tougher assignments. She was on the fast track for promotions. Imagine her surprise when her boss reprimanded her for a lack of team play. Her defenses went into high gear. She blamed others for not keeping pace with her, and she denied the fact that she put others off and acted like a Lone Ranger. She pointed to numerous examples of working with others (and very cooperatively, she concluded), and she put off meeting with her coach, saying she was too busy "doing her job."

As a result, Joanne convinced only herself that she was fine and not in need of any assistance. Her defensiveness shielded her in her own eyes, but condemned her further in the eyes of others.

Pitfall Four: Passive Role in the Coaching Process

Some people who are being coached do little to help themselves, but remain passive in the coaching process. A number of reasons may account for this, such as:

- They may resent being placed in this position of punishment and stubbornly make the coach do all of the work;
- They may be embarrassed about having to be coached and may wish to remind themselves of it as little as possible; or
- They may not understand the importance of playing an active role. They just go through the motions to satisfy the boss and get him or her off their backs.

The more active and involved the individual is in the process, the more the person will get out of coaching. Coaching is a highly personal and customized process; *one size does not fit all.* To the degree that the person being coached can be the architect of his or her own coaching plan, he or she will be more successful.

An active role on the part of the person being coached is helpful throughout the coaching process. It is helpful in:

- Understanding the expectations that management has for coaching outcomes;
- Identifying areas for improvement;
- Soliciting the assistance of others; and
- Raising questions to discuss with the coach.

For example, Helen sought to understand why she was being asked to be coached. She listened without interruption or defensiveness about the behaviors that her manager observed and how her behaviors were impacting others adversely. She sought to further understand what expectations her manager had of the coaching, and what would constitute success.

When Helen met with her coach, she was prepared with her own assessment of herself. She sought information about the coach's expectations and the coaching process. She identified people the coach might talk to in order to gain additional insights into her behavior and its impact.

Helen discussed her coaching opportunity with her peers and subordinates. She told them that her coach would be talking to them about her and asked them to speak freely. She thanked them in advance for their assistance. Helen then met with her coach to identify those behaviors that needed improvement. She met again with her peers and subordinates to inform them of her desired behavioral changes. She invited them to help her by providing feedback about the behaviors she was working to improve.

Pitfall Five: Failure to Risk/Playing It Safe

Coaching can be scary. Opening up to another person (a stranger in most cases) can be frightening. In order to protect our egos, many of us deceive ourselves and others, either knowingly or unknowingly.

The person being coached, perhaps fearful of failure and determined to appear successful, may select improvements that are easily achieved. On the surface, the coaching process may appear to be successful, but in reality the fundamental problem has remained unresolved.

For example, Hector was told by his manager that he needed to delegate more, that he was becoming too bogged down in detail. His own productivity was suffering. Privately, Hector was afraid to delegate. He didn't have confidence in some of his people; they consistently fell short of meeting their obligations; and he always had to clean up after them. He felt it was easier to do the work himself. He liked harmony and avoided confronting people at all costs. Some of his staff were much older than he; one of them had even hired Hector several years before. This made him particularly ill at ease confronting or disciplining them.

Fearing the discomfort of confrontation, Hector selected time management as a skill to improve. These skills were easily learned, but were not the fundamental issue, and his achievement did not affect the problem that was causing him difficulties in the first place. Had he been willing to take a risk and step outside of his comfort zone, he might have been able to truly improve his effectiveness.

Pitfall Six: Failure to Involve Others

Individuals who have been recommended for coaching by their bosses may view coaching in a negative light. The person being coached may see the boss's request as a form of punishment. He or she may feel embarrassed or may believe that he or she will be diminished in the eyes of peers and subordinates if others know about the coaching.

As a result of these fears, the person being coached may wish to keep others in the dark about the coaching.

For example, John was very unhappy when his boss recommended coaching to help him with his authoritarian management style. He feared that others would see it as a sign of weakness, so he went to great lengths to hide the coaching. He was evasive when asked about this person (the coach) with whom he was meeting. "Just some consultant," he would respond.

Such secrecy is usually unfortunate. Except in the case of a highly political, mistrustful, or vindictive organizational culture, the person being coached is better served by "going public." By informing peers and subordinates, the individual can gain support and assistance, because the majority of people respect someone who is not only willing to acknowledge shortcomings, but wants to improve.

If the person being coached lets people know he or she is working on changing dysfunctional behaviors, others tend to make allowances and offer their support. These supporters may alter their own behavior when interacting with the person being coached. A person being coached, for example, might be working on the ability to listen to suggestions. Once this developmental goal has been made public, those who have long since given up any attempt at talking to deaf ears may try again to offer suggestions. Colleagues can also assist the person being coached by providing feedback about successful and unsuccessful attempts to change.

Our research at Keilty, Goldsmith & Company reinforces the value of involving others in the coaching process. In surveys of thousands of people, the results are clear, consistent, and compelling—the more a manager involves others in the coaching process, the more that manager is perceived as having improved.

Conclusion

Coaching can be immensely rewarding for all involved. To gain the greatest benefit from a coaching relationship, the person being coached must avoid the common pitfalls to success. Suggestions offered in this article are summarized Figure 11.1.

FIGURE 11.1. HOW TO GET THE MOST OUT OF EXECUTIVE COACHING

Winning Mind-Set About Coaching	Losing Mind-Set About Coaching
A positive experience, great opportunity	A negative experience, punishment
An opportunity to develop professionally	An opportunity to get management off my back
Honesty is the best policy	This is a game to be played
Have an open mind	Have a closed mind
Desire to trust/healthy skepticism	Mistrustful
Accepting	Rejecting
Proactive (you are the architect)	Passive (you are being done to)
Vulnerability can lead to growth	Play it safe, defensive

Stage	Do's	Don'ts
Establish need for coaching	Ask questions to understand the reasons for coaching, the coaching process, and management's expectations	Assume or second-guess, adopt a negative (self fulfilling) mind-set

Stage	Do's	Don'ts
Meet with the coach	Ask questions of the coach, disclose fully about yourself, discuss expectations	Blindly "go with the program" (make sure it is your program), hold back
Data gathering and needs assessment	Think about your strengths and weaknesses, review past performance appraisals, solicit feedback from others, invite others to participate for your benefit, thank them for their help	Play a passive role (just wait and see what the coach comes up with), be closed-minded or argumentative about the coach's findings, become defensive, be passive-aggressive (agree, but don't follow through)
Develop coaching plan	Be a full participant	Pick goals that are easy or safe, don't include others, be unrealistic about what can be accomplished
Execute coaching plan	Try out new behaviors, monitor yourself, bring questions and observations to discussions with the coach	Go through the motions, try nothing different, tell coaches what "they want to hear"
Evaluate progress	Solicit feedback, revise goals as needed	Evaluate based on activity and not on results, treat it as a "check off" and move on

About the Contributors

Don Grayson has consulted with management on topics of individual and organizational effectiveness. From 1981 to 1987, he was a top producer for the firm of RHR International, a firm of management psychologists. Since 1987, he has maintained his own consulting practice and has forged partnerships with other firms. He works with Group 7 West in its family business practice and with Rembisz & Associates in its global consulting practice. He manages the team development practice for Keilty, Goldsmith & Company.

Don's areas of specialty for his clients in the public and private sectors include team building, meeting facilitation, executive coaching, 360° feedback for individuals and teams, leadership training, and the management of organizational change. As a licensed psychologist, he conducts psychological assessments to aid clients with selection and promotion decisions.

He co-developed the Professional Development Report, a computer-generated report of an individual's personality characteristics and their application in the workplace. He is currently working in the area of brand personality, pinpointing a product or brand's perceived personality characteristics.

Prior to his consulting career, Don directed the career development program at the University of Tennessee. He holds a B.A. in psychology from the University of Massachusetts and an M.A. and Ph.D. in counseling psychology from the University of Utah.

Clients commend Don for his ability to establish rapport easily, making it safe for others to quickly "open up" and get to the task of improvement. He relates well to all levels of the organization and may be called in to intervene by executive management or may be recommended by the union. Clients also find his humor to be a useful vehicle for introducing and working on potentially sensitive subjects.

Kerry Larson is a senior partner with Leadership Strategies International and is vice president of People Development at Teledesic, which includes organizational planning and development, benefits, compensation, training, and recruiting. Previously, he was senior vice president with AT&T Wireless Services, responsible for people development, which included organizational planning and development, benefits, compensation, training, and recruiting. Kerry's history with AT&T Wireless began in 1983, when he was hired to provide consulting services in organizational psychology to McCaw Cellular. Prior to that, Kerry worked for Avia International as vice president of organizational development, where he headed human resources and established international subsidiaries for the company. He was also a senior consultant with RHR International, a management psychology firm.

Kerry has taught undergraduate psychology courses at Virginia Tech and graduate courses at the University of Utah and North Texas University. He holds a bachelor's degree in psychology from Brigham Young University. He received his master's degree and doctorate in psychology from the University of Utah.

CHAPTER TWELVE

MENTORING AS PARTNERSHIP

Chip R. Bell

My mother-in-law had a five-and-dime store parakeet named Pretty Boy. Over the years she taught Pretty Boy to sing a number of songs. One day she ordered a new vacuum cleaner. It came with a tube-shaped attachment she thought perfectly suited to vacuum out Pretty Boy's cage. You know where this story is going! The phone rang one day and Pretty Boy ended up in the vacuum cleaner bag!

She panicked. Tearing open the vacuum bag, she found the poor parakeet alive, but totally covered with dust, dirt, and soot. She rushed the bird to the bathtub and turned both tub faucets wide open, almost drowning Pretty Boy! Realizing her extreme over-reaction, she grabbed the hair dryer to blow dry the poor bird!

A few days later at the church social the editor of the local newspaper heard of her catastrophe and sent a reporter around to get this unique human-interest story. At the end of his interview, the reporter asked, "By the way, how's Pretty Boy now?"

Without expression or hesitation, she answered: "Pretty Boy doesn't sing any more. He just sits and stares!"

Times of Change

We live in a time of turbulent change. Far too many employees hired to "sing a bunch of songs" are almost daily traumatized by downsizing, re-organizations, mergers, and just plain old uncertainty. Some end up "sitting and staring" like Pretty Boy, and customers experience these traumatized employees through rigid "Rules 'R Us" front-line behavior. Managers witness "sitting and staring" when they observe compliance instead of commitment; inflexibility rather than creativity; and resistance instead of responsibility.

One group of employees, however, still "sing" in the midst of turmoil. Thriving on discord, this group turns dissonance into harmony. They are the *learners* in the organization. Philosopher Eric Hoffer (1998) wrote, "In times of massive change it is the learner who will inherit the earth, while the learned stay elegantly tied to a world which no longer exists." Learners are not only happier employees, but they are less likely to jump ship at the first sign of rough seas.

An increase in the number of those who still "sing" is not likely to come about by reducing the chaos, because massive change is here to stay. Nor is it likely to come about by adding more training programs or expanding the tuition refund policy. Instead, such a change requires a fundamental alteration in the role of the leader, from "corporate parent" to "compassionate partner." It requires that all leaders must add "learning coach" or "mentor" to their existing repertoire of roles.

The Magic of Mentoring

Mentor—the word conjures up the image of a seasoned corporate sage conversing with a naive, still "wet behind the ears" young recruit. The conversation would likely be laced with informal rules, closely guarded secrets, and "I remember back in '67" stories of daredevil heroics and too-close-to-call tactics. Mentoring has had an almost heady, academic sound, solely reserved for workers in white collars whose fathers advised them, "Go get to know ol' Charlie."

But what is mentoring really? A mentor is simply someone who helps someone else learn something that he or she would have learned less well, more slowly, or not at all if left alone. Notice the power-free nature of this definition! Mentors are not power figures. *Mentors are learning coaches—sensitive, trusted advisors.*

The traditional use of the word "mentor" connotes a person outside one's usual chain of command who helps him or her to "understand this crazy organization." Not all mentors are managers. But, all—absolutely *all*—effective supervisors and managers *should be* mentors. Mentoring must become simply that part of every leader's role that has growth as its primary outcome.

Organizations cannot afford to rely on mentoring programs alone to ensure system-wide "singing." Although mentoring programs can be helpful, they are, by themselves, simply inadequate to create a learning organization. In the words of A. De Geus and P. Senge (1997), "Your ability to learn faster than your competition is your only sustainable competitive advantage." Every leader must mentor—and mentor especially those associates whose performance they influence.

Mentoring employees is never easy. There are certain inherent conflicts between the roles of mentor and manager. Mentors have to take a broad view of an individual's development over the long haul. Line managers may need to have day-to-day tasks completed immediately. How does a supervisor or manager encourage a subordinate to experiment, try new behaviors, and even make mistakes—all important to learning—when both know the inevitable performance review may be just around the corner? Overcoming this powerful obstacle to learning can only happen within a partnership relationship.

Creating a Partnership for Learning

Mentoring from a partnership perspective is fundamentally different from the classical "I'm the guru; you're the greenhorn" orientation. Mentoring from a partnership perspective means, "We are fellow travelers on this journey toward wisdom." Stated differently: the greatest gift a mentor can ultimately give his or her protégé is to position that protégé as his or her own mentor. However, a learning partnership does not simply happen. It must be created, and the mentor must take the lead in crafting it.

The main event in mentoring involves giving and receiving a series of "learning gifts": advice, feedback, focus, and support. However, such learning gifts may not be seen by the protégé as desired. A gift, no matter how generously bestowed, may not always be received with glee. Recall the last time someone said to you: "Let me *give* you some advice" or "I need to *give* you a little feedback." You probably did more resisting than rejoicing! Protégés are no different.

Smart mentors create a readiness for the main event of mentoring. Protégés are more likely to experience the benevolence of their gifts if they are delivered within a relationship of safety, advocacy, and equality. Mentoring from a partnership perspective entails four stages: (1) *leveling the learning field,* (2) *fostering acceptance and safety,* (3) *giving learning gifts,* and (4) *bolstering self-direction and independence.* The first two stages are aimed at creating a readiness for the main event—gifting. The final stage is all about weaning the protégé from any dependence on the mentor.

Stage One: Leveling the Learning Field

The first challenge a mentor faces is to help the protégé experience the relationship as a true partnership. Leveling the learning field means stripping the relationship of any nuances of mentor power or command. Such a relationship does not seek control; instead it regards the need to surrender to the *process of learning* as paramount. This requires the creation of rapport or kinship by removing the mask of managerial supremacy.

The word "rapport" comes from French, literally meaning "a bringing back" or "connection renewed." The success of a mentoring relationship can hang on the early mentor-protégé encounters; good starts impact good growth. The tone created at the first meeting can determine whether the relationship will be fruitful or fraught with fear and anxiety. Quality learning will not occur until the shield has been lowered enough for the learner to take risks in front of the mentor. Rapport building expedites shield lowering.

In the United States, the customs of bringing a gift when visiting a friend, giving flowers on the first date, telling a joke to open a speech, and introducing small talk at the beginning of a sales call, remind us that opening expressions are important. Therefore, how does a mentor build rapport?

Rapport begins with openness and authenticity. Any normal person approaching a potentially anxious encounter will raise his or her antennae in search of any clues that might give an early warning signal about the road ahead. Will this situation embarrass me? Will this person take advantage of me? Will I be able to be effective with this encounter? Is harm or risk awaiting me?

Given this pioneering search for signals by the protégé, it is crucial that the mentor be quick to transmit responses with a welcoming tone and feel. Open posture (for example, no crossed arms), warm and enthusiastic reception, eye contact, removal of physical barriers, and personalized greetings are all gestures communicating an attempt to cultivate a level learning field. Mentors who rely on the artifacts of power (peering over an imposing desk, making the protégé do all the approaching, tight and closed body language, a reserved manner, or facial expressions that telegraph distance) make a grave error in not putting the other person at ease, so important to building a relationship.

Mentors often use a gifting gesture to signal a level learning field. The perfunctory "how about a cup of coffee" is certainly a well-worn gifting gesture. However, think about how much more powerful a statement such as, "I had my assistant locate this article; I thought you might find it useful," could be as early evidence that this relationship will be power-free. I once had a mentor who kept a supply of his wife's homemade jellies for visitors, and the gift was always bestowed early in the encounter, not at the end! Strip any nuance of sovereignty from the relationship and focus on crafting a learning partnership.

Stage Two: Fostering Acceptance and Safety

Great mentors who are effective at fostering acceptance avoid testing tones, judgmental gestures, and parental positions. Great mentors show acceptance through focused and dramatic listening. When listening is their goal, they make it *the* priority. They do not let *anything* distract them. A wise leader said, "There are no individuals at work more important to your success than your employees—not your boss, not your customers, not your vendors."

When your protégé needs you to listen, pretend you just received a gift of five minutes with your greatest hero. What a great concept! Think about it! If you could have only five minutes with Moses, Mozart, or Mother Teresa, would you let a call from your boss, your customer, or *anyone* eat up part of that precious time? Treat your protégé with the same focus and priority.

Listening done well is complete absorption. Have you ever carefully watched Larry King on CNN? His success as a superb interviewer lies not in his questions, but in his terrific listening skills. He zips right past the interviewee's words, sentences, and paragraphs to get to the interviewee's message, intent, and meaning. The mission of listening is to be so crystal clear on the other person's message that it becomes a "copy and paste" execution command from one brain's computer screen to another's.

One of my biggest challenges in striving to be a good parent was simply to listen without an agenda. As my son began to catalog his concerns, convictions, or curiosity, I would usually feel the urge to make a point, teach a lesson, correct an action, or offer caution. When I finally gave up trying to be a smart daddy and worked at simply being a mirror, he began to open up and, most importantly, he felt heard.

When he asked, "How would you . . . ?," I worked to remember to have him tell me what he would do before offering my opinions. When he voiced concern, I tried to first communicate through my actions that his message got through before I delivered an answer, especially when my answer was likely to be different from the one he thought he was going to get. The ancient adage, "You are not eligible to change my view until you first demonstrate that you understand my view" serves us in two ways. First, it helps us to stay focused on being heard, not on making points. Second, it tells our listeners that they are important.

Protégés feel the relationship is safe when mentors demonstrate receptivity and validation of their feelings. The coaching goal should be a position of empathetic identification. This "I am the same as you" gesture promotes kinship and closeness, so vital to building trust. Empathy, when appropriately applied, offers a powerful and positive pathway through the coaching process.

Empathy is quite different from sympathy. The word "sympathy" comes from a Greek word meaning "shared suffering." Relationship strength within coaching cannot be productively built from a foundation of sympathy—the belief that "misery loves company." Strength comes from identifying "I have been there as well."

Reflective responses can be as simple as a personal story that lets your protégé know you appreciate her or his feelings. Mildly self-deprecating anecdotes can be particularly good, as acceptance is best earned by humility and sensitivity. If you feel awkward, say you do. If you feel excited, say so. The sooner you verbalize your own feelings, the faster your protégé will be open to expressing his or her own.

Mentors do not just listen: they listen *dramatically*. They demonstrate through their words and actions that the words of their protégés are valued and important. When people feel heard, they feel valued. Feeling valued, they are more likely to experiment and take risks. Only by trying out new steps do they grow and learn. Fundamentally, if your goal is to become a great mentor, start by using what you say to help you fully use your talents as a great listener.

Stage Three: Giving Learning Gifts

Leveling the learning field and fostering acceptance and safety lay the groundwork for the main event: giving learning gifts. Great mentors give many gifts, such as support, focus, courage, and affirmation. But the two most crucial learning gifts are *advice* and *feedback*. We will look briefly at each, starting with advice.

Someone once asked famed retired Notre Dame head football coach Lou Holtz what he considered to be the toughest part of his job. With his typical "aw shucks" charm, he finessed the question, but ultimately communicated that *one* of the hardest parts was "teaching lessons that stay taught." Mentors have a similar challenge. Protégé resistance and resentment for advice and feedback create the challenge in "teaching lessons that stay taught." As one frustrated supervisor commented, "I tell them what they ought to do, but it seems to go in one ear and out the other!"

Begin by letting the protégé know the focus or intent of your mentoring. It sounds something like this: "George, I wanted to talk with you about the fact that your last quarter call rate was up, but your sales were down 20 percent." It is vital that you be specific and clear in your statements. Ambiguity clouds the conversation and could leave the protégé more confused than assisted.

Make certain the protégé is as anxious to improve or learn as you are to see him or her improve or learn. What if the protégé either disagrees that learning is needed or is unwilling to learn what you want to teach? First, take a broader perspective. Decide whether this is your issue or actually something your protégé needs to do. If performance is a factor, be sure to have objective information available (as a tool, not as proof). If all else fails, delay the conversation to a time at which the protégé demonstrates a greater readiness to learn.

Ask permission to give advice. This is the most important step! Your goal is twofold: (1) to communicate advice without surfacing protégé resistance, and (2) to keep ownership of the challenge with the protégé. It can sound like: "I have some ideas on how you might improve, if that would be helpful to you." The goal is to communicate in a way that minimizes the protégé's feeling of being controlled. State your advice in the first person singular. Phrases such as "you *ought* to" quickly raise listener resistance! Keeping your advice in the first person singular helps eliminate the "should's." For instance, the protégé will hear "what *I've* found helpful" or "what worked for *me*," without the internal noise of resistance.

In the way that advice is about *adding information*, feedback is about *filling a blind spot*. The presence of blind spots makes giving protégés feedback a tricky gift! Think of it this way. *Advice is expertise the protégé may have or could acquire.* You (the mentor) are telling me (the protégé) something you have which, in time, I might acquire on my own. But feedback is you (the mentor) telling me (the protégé) something you have (given your perspective) that I will probably never acquire on my own (and that makes you, the mentor, irritated).

Whereas the issue with advice is potential resistance, the issue with feedback is potential resentment. How does a mentor bestow a gift that by its basic nature reminds the protégé of his or her inability to see it? How can you fill a perceptual gap and have the recipient focus on the gift, not the gap?

The mentor's goal is to assist the protégé's receptivity for feedback by creating a climate of identification. Use comments that have an underlying "I'm like you" message. This need not be a major production or overdone, just a sentence or two.

State the rationale for your feedback. Subtlety or diplomacy are not required as much as a way to create a climate of readiness to listen. Help the protégé gain a clear sense of why you want to give him or her some feedback.

Assume, for a moment, that you are giving *yourself* the feedback. We more accurately hear feedback delivered in a sensitive and unambiguous fashion. Another key dimension to effective feedback is that it possess the utmost integrity. This means it is straight and honest. Frankness is not about cruelty; it is about ensuring that the receiver does not wonder, "What is he or she *not* telling me that I need to hear?" Think of your goal this way: How would you deliver the feedback if you were giving *yourself* the feedback. Take your cue from your own preferences.

It is instructive that the word "feedback" starts with the word "feed." Truly the optimum way to see feedback is in the spirit of nurturing. It is also fitting that the word "advice" originated from the Latin word "concilium," meaning "to call together." If we blend these archaic definitions of "feedback" and "advice," we get a perfect description of a learning partnership: "to feed together."

Stage Four: Bolstering Self-Direction and Independence

All mentoring relationships must come to an end. The question is how to close with a focus on the "what next?" Effective mentoring relationships are rich, engaging, and intimate. As such, ending them is not without emotion. However, healthy mentoring relationships craft separation as a tool for growth. Effective adjournment of the relationship paves the way to move on into the next mentoring relationship.

Celebrate the relationship with fanfare and stories or in as simple a way as a special meal together, a drink after work, or a peaceful walk in a nearby park. The point of celebration is to clearly close the mentoring relationship. The rite of passage is a powerful symbol for gaining closure and moving on.

The celebration should include compliments and stories. Weave in laughter and joy. Your protégé now needs your blessing far more than your brilliance, your well wishing more than your warnings. Avoid the temptation to lay out one last caution. Your kindest contribution will be a solid send-off rendered with confidence, compassion, and consideration. Lace your final meeting or two with opportunities to remember, reflect, and refocus. Let your recollections bridge the discussion toward the future.

Let some time pass before you follow up. The easiest way to get this wrong is to follow up with a protégé too soon after departure. Let at least a week pass before calling or visiting, maybe longer. Setting your relationship free requires space and time. Should you follow up at all? Absolutely! Partners follow up on partners. The key is not to do it too quickly. Allow weaning time. Let go!

As building rapport was crucial to the successful beginning of a mentoring relationship, adjournment is equally important. Letting go is rarely comfortable, but it is necessary if the protégé is to become a self-directed learner who will flourish and grow out of the shadow of the mentor. Growth implies an upper end: "grown," which implies closure and culmination. Mark the moment by managing adjournment as a visible expression of achievement and happiness.

In golf there is an expression, "playing over your head." It means that a golfer is playing at an unexplained level of excellence in which serendipity and the extraordinary seem the momentary norm. Effective mentoring can also be seen as a relationship of a mentor and protégé who seek to honor their alliance by "learning over their heads." I've found that such an occurrence is practiced at its most harmonious level when the two "sing" as a partnership.[1]

---

[1] Portions of this chapter adapted from *Training and Development*, February, 2000.

About the Contributor

Chip R. Bell is senior partner of Performance Research Associates, Inc. (PRA), a consulting firm that specializes in helping organizations create a culture that sustains customer loyalty. He is also manager of the company's Dallas, Texas, office. Additionally, he is co-owner of Beepbeep.com.

A renowned keynote speaker, Chip has served as consultant or trainer to such major organizations as IBM, Cadillac, Microsoft, Motorola, Lucent Technologies, Marriott, State Farm, Merrill Lynch, Ritz-Carlton Hotels, Bayer, Eli Lilly, Royal Bank of Canada, First Union, Aurora Health, Harley-Davidson, and Victoria's Secret. Prior to starting a consulting firm in the late 1970s, he was vice president and director of management and organization development for NCNB (now Bank of America). In the late 1960s, he was an infantry unit commander with the 82nd Airborne Division in Viet Nam. Dr. Bell holds graduate degrees from Vanderbilt University and the George Washington University.

He is the author or co-author of fourteen books, including *Beep Beep: Competing in the Age of the Road Runner* (with Oren Harari); *Knock Your Socks Off Service Recovery* (with Ron Zemke); *Dance Lessons: Six Steps to Great Partnerships in Business and Life* (with Heather Shea); *Managers as Mentors: Building Partnerships for Learning; Customers as Partners: Building Relationships that Last*; and *Managing Knock Your Socks Off Service* (with Ron Zemke). His newest book, *Customer Love: Attracting and Keeping Customers for Life* is scheduled for release in 2000. Chip has also written over two hundred articles in such professional journals as *Management Review, Quality Digest, Training, Executive Excellence, Training & Development, Services Magazine, Advanced Management Journal, Supervisory Management,* and *Journal of Management Development* (U.K.). Additionally, he has hosted four major training films on service quality and leadership.

CHAPTER THIRTEEN

COACHING FROM BELOW

Deepak (Dick) Sethi

Even top leaders can have blind spots in some areas of their behavior, and so fail to see the true impact of their conduct on others. When this is the case, the most precious gift one person can give another is candid, caring feedback.

Most modern organizations have a 360° process that allows managers to collect feedback from multiple sources. This worthy effort needs to be encouraged, but it is not sufficient. In fact, a manager does not necessarily need company-sponsored programs, electronic forms, or even paper and pencil to receive feedback.

In my experience, the most insightful sources of feedback are often the most overlooked. Valuable sources include those people who have known us for a long time. They include those who have worked with us and for us over time and our families. All these people will have held a long-term, unadulterated, and unvarnished view of us. We often forget that these durable audiences will not be fooled by our facades; they can see through our many facets as easily as if we were a piece of glass. They can provide a wealth of feedback and coaching for us—if only we have the courage to tap into their knowledge. I call this "coaching from below."

For coaching from below to be successful, three factors (described below) must be in place. Within an organizational context, our subordinates are often able to provide us with a rich source of feedback. However, the success factors described here apply equally well to others outside the workplace setting.

Creating a Safe Climate

A safe climate for giving feedback is the most critical prerequisite for receiving candid feedback. In the past, organizations have been hierarchical, which has fostered a one-way, up-down, mode of communication that offers little opportunity for quality feedback. This command-and-control culture will be a competitive disadvantage in the future, because the success of tomorrow's organization will be based on intellectual capital and open communication between team members, employees, and managers.

With this in mind, managers must create a climate of complete safety and actively seek out feedback from key high-performing subordinates. An informal contract should be developed between manager and employee, so that feedback can be given without fear, and so that specific areas in which feedback would be most beneficial are defined.

Do not expect employees to be candid just because you ask for candor. This is probably a new experience for many subordinates and can be daunting for any number of reasons. Perhaps the person does not have full confidence in his or her ability to give feedback—but more importantly—the person may not believe that you truly want honest feedback. Let people test you. You need to win them over with patience and sincerity. Remember the cyclical nature of this process. Your subordinates will be willing to coach you when and if they trust you, and such trust will be augmented by your reactions and responses to their feedback.

Using Effective Feedback and Communication Skills

The manager receiving coaching from below must possess a cluster of excellent communication skills in order for the process to work effectively.

It is necessary to suspend all traces of judgment and defensiveness and to listen merely to learn. This can be difficult because many of us have poor listening skills, which is the problem at the root of most miscommunication. Even with all that Carl Rogers (1961) and others have taught us about the art of listening and the many volumes that have been written on the subject, the basic underlying challenge is that the ears will not listen to what the mind does not want to hear.

Listening is a mind-set issue. To gain a better understanding of the listening mind-set, I would encourage reading the many writings of Chris Argyris (1985) and others. Also, it is important to remember that most of our communication is non-verbal, so, we need to be much more aware of our body language and learn to manage it so that it is consistent with our intentions.

The receiver of coaching should also possess a healthy emotional intelligence—and a sense of humor—when receiving feedback, so as to put it into the proper perspective. Two related skills are helpful in this aspect: first, it is important to set the expectation that not all suggestions will be acted on (for any number of reasons); second, it is important to allow a short finite time for feedback, and then to make a smooth switch back to work. It is necessary to be able to swap the two hats of managing and coaching easily, remembering that coaching is learning and that learning should be fun!

Practicing Self-Discipline

Having received feedback and coaching from a junior, the ball is in the court of the senior person. It is helpful to reflect on the coaching received and then focus on one or two valid areas. Marshall Goldsmith, the feedback guru, warns his clients that any more than two issues is too many for anyone to handle at one time (Goldsmith, 1996). We might identify and use resources in the form of programs, workshops, courses, books, audio tapes, or videos. An extremely important resource is role models to help us learn new behaviors, enhance or alter existing behaviors, or unlearn old behaviors. But even with the best of intentions, change isn't easy, and old habits of thought and behavior die hard. Patience and relentless perseverance on one's own part, and also co-opting the employee (or whoever gave the feedback) to become part of a follow-up support system are important ways to ensure victory over old behaviors.

To extinguish an old behavior, it is often necessary to start practicing a new one. Start by rehearsing in a simulated safe environment. Then, before adopting it more generally, practice the behavior in a low-risk situation until it feels natural. Your efforts will be exponentially more effective if you can muster the additional self-discipline to supplement the actual practice of the new behavior with a recurring visualization of it in authentic detail. Visualization is an extremely powerful technique that cannot be overused.

Conclusions

At home and at work, we are under close scrutiny by those below us. Our subordinates have an intuitive and intimate knowledge of our strengths and weaknesses, our inconsistencies and frailties, and the gaps between our walk and our talk. If we can enroll them to partner with us in a journey of personal growth, the results can be truly amazing.

Our subordinates can help us in a wide range of areas, from fairly benign matters such as time management, prioritization, or meeting management, to much more complex areas in which we are lacking, such as presentation skills, teaming, interpersonal skills, and leadership abilities. They can help us uncover ways to enhance our effectiveness and work relations and manage our own bosses more effectively. Subordinates can help make us aware of our perceived credibility and reputation, and they can alert us to any habits or behaviors that can become potential derailers. They can help us grow personally and professionally, if only we are willing and able to think "out of the box" and embrace a coaching approach.

In such a process of collective self-development, we find a promise to create the dynamic and competitive human organization of tomorrow— a learning organization in which knowledge and self-awareness flow without boundaries. Only when we reaffirm our vulnerability and our humility do we uncover our humanity and reach toward our goals.

About the Contributor

Deepak (Dick) Sethi is a leading authority in the field of executive and leadership development. He is director of executive and leadership development for the Thomson Corporation, a $6 billion, 40,000 employee information company. Previously, he was assistant director, executive education, for AT&T. The leadership development program for high-potential middle managers and senior executives that he helped design and direct at AT&T is widely considered a leading-edge benchmark program in the country.

Dick's unique leadership development work has been extensively featured in the *Wall Street Journal, USA Today, NY Newsday, Training Directors' Forum Newsletter, Corporate University Xchange Newsletter,* and in the book, *Leadership by Design.* He has also been quoted in *Business Week,* the *New York Times,* the *Washington Post, Miami Herald,* and the *Economist.* Dick has published articles on leadership in both *The Leader of the Future* (a *Business Week* bestseller) and *The Organization of the Future.* Both books were sponsored by the Peter Drucker Foundation.

In addition to his management development experience and expertise, Dick has had successful sales experience with Mobil Oil in India and with Control Data Corporation in New York and marketing and product management experience with AT&T. He has also taught workshops on entrepreneurship, as adjunct faculty at New York University.

Dick came to the United States as a Rotary Foundation Fellow. He is listed in *Who's Who* and *Who's Who in the World,* and is a frequent speaker at management and leadership development conferences. His interactive presentations and workshops are consistently rated very high by diverse audiences.

Dick is president of the New York Human Resource Planners and is on the board of directors of the national Human Resource Planning Society. He is also on the Leadership Advisory Board of the Peter Drucker Foundation and on the board of the Institute for Management Studies.

CHAPTER FOURTEEN

LEADERSHIP AND POWER: WHERE RESPONSIBILITY MAKES THE DIFFERENCE

Bruce Lloyd

An enormous amount of sociological literature is to be found on *power*, but little relates to management issues of responsibility, leadership, or learning. Many publications exist on *leadership*, yet sadly only a few discuss the nature and role of power. Even fewer consider the relationships between power, responsibility, and learning. Writings on *learning* abound, but very few consider the nature of power and its abuse in a learning context. *Ethics* is an emerging leadership topic that promises to bridge these concepts. But a satisfactory analysis of the use and abuse of power by a responsible business leader in a learning context is only now starting to emerge.

Leaders—and those who coach them—have a duty to use power responsibly. Some common understanding of the relationships, interactions, and dynamics of power are vital prerequisites to support this high aim.

Coaching redefines the way we look at responsibility, leadership, learning, and our legitimate use of power—at a truly fundamental level. The coaching approach enables leaders to transform their organizations into ones in which personal accountability, creativity, risk-taking, and achieving business results are hallmarks. Coaching is not power-neutral. Coaching determines a complex power relationship based on openness and merit.

Coaching is the methodology for shifting a culture of "power over" people to one in which "power within" people is unleashed. It provides the vehicle for organizational learning to take place and for the honest interests of all stakeholders to be actively pursued by individuals throughout the enterprise. By applying coaching methods, we facilitate the coming of age of a new organization model; one in which responsibility, leadership, and learning, have exciting new meanings, and in which power is always released in order to enable, never to constrain.

Power

"If we are to understand organizations we must understand the nature of power and influence, for they are the means by which the people of the organization are linked to its purpose" (Handy, 1985).

But what is power?

"A has power over B to the extent that he can get B to do something that B would not otherwise do" (Dahl, 1957).
   And
   ". . . they will say anything and do almost anything to hang onto power" (Kaletsky, 1994).

These comments are typical of the management literature on power. They reinforce the prevailing concept of power as illegitimate behavior designed to benefit self-interest rather than organizational goals. Occasionally it is recognized that:

"The responsible use of power is a concern to all sectors of society. Somehow we need to marry the understanding and use of power with an appreciation of its consequences on those on the receiving end of it . . . to find new ways to understand and act on the power structures of which we are all an inevitable part" (Hardy, 1995).

It is not surprising that power has been, and still is, a highly negative force in many organizations. Employees feel intimidated because they have little recourse for what they consider to be essentially arbitrary and potentially painful decisions. This reaction has led to a greatly increased concern over issues such as bullying in the workplace.

Whether power takes a constructive or destructive course depends primarily on whether it occurs in a cooperative or competitive situation. When people feel united in a common effort, they build up each other's power and use it to achieve their common goals. When they feel competitive, they undermine each other's confidence and power. Unfortunately, it is often assumed that power inevitably involves a win-lose struggle. It should not be surprising to find that severe alienation can easily lead to the generation of conditions for radical, or revolutionary, ways of redistributing power. In essence, history is the study of the use and abuse of power, and is at the core of understanding the rise and fall of organizations, public or private.

This analysis leads us to the conclusion that power has primarily been a self-focused or ego-driven preoccupation with the ability to make things happen. Under these circumstances it usually has a short-term focus, and it will almost inevitably be abused, corrupt, corrupting, or corrupted. On the other hand, power that is concerned with accepting a wider sense of responsibility (that is, power that is essentially "others" focused) is more likely to have a long-term focus and incorporate a broader consideration of stakeholder interests in any decision-making process. In the end, power is about the ability to make choices, and its effective use requires a detailed stakeholder analysis of the potential impact of decisions on all those involved.

Responsibility

A responsibility approach has at its starting point the question, "In whose interests are the changes being made?" This question establishes a relationship between power and responsibility, in which power is defined as "the opportunity to exercise responsibility." Next, the effective exercise of power requires an answer to the question, "What is in the long-term interests of the organization for whom I am acting?"

To be effective over the long term, leaders must be concerned with issues associated with responsibility rather than issues associated with power.
Before going further, it is useful to consider some of the issues associated
with the concept of responsibility.

A considerable amount of management literature focuses on responsibility.

> "Corporate responsibility continues to mean many things to us. It is
> the fair and equitable treatment of all our stakeholders, including
> associates, shareholders, customers, and suppliers. It is our sense of
> concern for all the well-being of the public at large and for our
> environment. And it is the time and money that we contribute
> toward strengthening the communities where we do business"
> p. 11 (Brennan, 1994).

The link between rights and responsibilities is emphasized by
Brauer (1993): "When we speak of human rights, we should also speak of
human responsibilities. . . . It is no use clamoring for human rights if we
are not prepared to accept our human duties."

Companies cannot expect to operate a responsibility-driven policy unless top management is seen setting an example—reflecting two key elements of leadership: good practice and the ability to communicate that
practice effectively. "Companies are part of society and have to behave responsibly. They have to take account of the views and contributions of their
employees and customers" (Davies, 1995).

In a major report to the Royal Society of Arts, George Bull (1995),
group chief executive of Grand Metropolitan, maintained: "Increasingly,
business people are recognizing that their prosperity is directly linked to
the prosperity of the whole community. The community is the source of
their customers, their employees, their suppliers and, with the wider spread
of share ownership, their investors." The report itself emphasized the
importance of a stakeholder approach—the central idea of the "inclusive"
company that values all its stakeholders. The report concluded: "There is
clear evidence that companies which put shareholders first do less well
for them in the long run than those that recognize the claims of all their

stakeholders." In fact it can be argued that: "A failure to give due weight to important stakeholder relationships could thus constitute a failure by the directors to discharge their duty properly" (Plender, 1995).

Personal responsibility begins with self-understanding, which is essential if we are to manage our weaknesses and develop our strengths. "We all need to recognize and accept our obligations, which go with our organizational roles, and learn to resist any temptation to abuse our positions of trust or power" (Tam, 1995). Add a responsibility to customers and suppliers to this quotation, and hence provide the basis of the stakeholder analysis mentioned earlier.

Yet, as Firestone CEO John Nevin (Stewart, 1989) put it: "If you want to drive a person crazy, the easiest way to do it is to give them a deep sense of responsibility and no authority." This point is critical to effective policies relating to empowerment, and ignorance in this area is a major course of organizational stress.

The conclusion at this stage, is that the most effective concept of power over the longer term is that which is responsibility driven. The connection between power and responsibility can be made by ensuring that a thorough stakeholder analysis is undertaken within the decision-making process.

The next step is to integrate these arguments on power and responsibility to: What do we mean by "leadership"? But, before that connection is made, it must be emphasized that any stakeholder analysis must be believed in by those undertaking it. Effective results will be more dependent on the spirit of the analytical process than on whether or not the survey was undertaken technically.

Leadership

Many of the traditional, "macho" leadership views of power are revealed in the following quote from van Maurik (1994):

"The concept of power is a preoccupation for many leaders. For some it is a drug and for others it is a source of fascination. In earlier chapters, I examined the sources of a leader's power and so it may seem strange that the central focus of this chapter is 'giving it away.' However, the concept of giving away one's power is both a demand made on us if we are leaders in the work situation and a choice that is a open to us. We invent most of the constraints. . . . So it is with leadership. The leader who clings to power, who is afraid to give it to others, will in fact cease to be a leader. In business, this person will increasingly become ineffective and in the end will be ousted, while in politics it is the leader's relationship to power that makes the difference between a legitimate leader and a tyrant." (p. 1)

Put simply, some power-driven individuals (and organizations) can be defined as successful in the short term, but evidence increasingly suggests that these individuals "contain the seeds of their own destruction." Both leadership and power are best seen as a form of trusteeship; unless those who have power use it responsibly (and are seen to use it responsibly), it will be taken away from them in one way or another.

An alternative approach is that of servant-leadership, which defines leadership as: "The use of gifts and talents on behalf of all of us in a way that models what we can be and empowers us to try." This statement is an echo of Robert Greenleaf's statement: "Do those served grow as persons; do they, while being served, become healthier, wiser, freer, more autonomous, more likely themselves to become servants" (DeShano, 1995).

The link between leadership and power is made by Kets de Vries (1993):

"Those leaders who are able to combine action with reflection, who have sufficient self-knowledge to recognize the vicissitudes of power, and who will not be tempted away when the psychological sirens that accompany power are beckoning will in the end be the most powerful. They will be the ones who are remembered with respect and affection. They will also be the ones truly able to manage the ambiguities of power and lead a creative and productive life." (p. 224)

It is not difficult to see the link between power and learning organizational concepts, as Conger (1989) showed:

"Effective organizations hold leaders accountable for the development of all subordinates. . . . Empowerment is defined as the process of enabling and motivating subordinates by increasing their personal efficacy. . . . Thus it becomes the leader's responsibility to help each other subordinate reach his or her full potential." (pp. 171–172)

This positive approach to empowerment, which is at least implicitly concerned with matching power and responsibility, has a good chance of avoiding the limitations of empowerment mentioned earlier.

However, it is valuable to recognize that: "The ultimate judgment of leaders is often not about how they acquire and use power, but how they relinquish it" (Sonnenfield, 1995). Ultimately, this comment reflects how many politicians have interpreted their power. In the end, leadership is concerned with the effective and efficient management of all the stakeholder interests and interfaces in the long-term interests of the organization as a whole. It is the ability to act effectively and responsibly in the interests of those who are being lead. Essentially this reflects the servant-leadership/trusteeship approach.

At the core of the philosophy of servant-leadership are the following basic tenets:

- *It takes people and their work seriously.* The servant leader says human beings have a value in their own right. In Greenleaf's view, valuing people requires a new business ethic: "Business exists as much to provide meaningful work to the person as it exists to provide a product or service to the customer."
- *They listen, learn, and take their lead from their staff.* The primary mission of the servant-leader is to encapsulate the will of the group, express that will, and then develop it as effectively as possible. "Servant-leaders today don't have all the answers, but they do know how to ask the right questions."

    In practice the servant-leadership process emphasizes the importance of consensus building. It may take time to develop, but once it is established there is considerable evidence to suggest that consensus produces commitment, and that is invariably the key to improved performance.

Increasingly, it is recognized that successful strategies are critically dependent on effective implementation.

- *They heal.* Servant-leaders manage openness and a willingness to share mistakes, focusing on the critical process of learning. A learning environment is about passing on what you know. It is about empowering others, rather than being possessive about knowledge on the grounds that "knowledge is power."

- *They are self-effacing.* Servant-leaders emphasize the interests of the group as a whole and recognize the value of humility as a basis for further learning. They are certainly not interested in the pursuit of power for its own sake. Servant-leaders are more concerned with ensuring that the results are relevant and effective, rather than focusing on who receives the credit.

- *They see themselves as stewards.* Servant-leaders strongly believe they have been entrusted with authority, and that drives them to take a responsibility-based, rather than power-based, approach. It also encourages decision making within a long-term perspective.

- *Leadership is considered everyone's responsibility.* Servant-leaders reflect into themselves before they address the faults of others. Leaders must have their own visions, but they also need to realize that everyone else in the organization may have his or her own vision. If this is the case, the leader's role starts with the need to integrate that diversity. Increasingly the primary role of leadership is seen as "the management of organizational values"—using the word *management* in its inclusive interpretation. The servant-leadership approach also emphasizes the importance of the old phrase: "It's not *what* you do, but *how* you do it." Organizations and individuals who do not practice what they preach are pursuing a high-risk strategy that invariably ends in disaster.

John Rosenblum, dean of the University of Virginia Business School, sums up the discussion by saying: "Servant-leadership at its heart is an openness, an ability to listen, and an ability to speak in a way that engages people directly affected by the choices to be made. It positively encourages commitment, and there is no better way to improve organizational performance."

The link between leadership, power, responsibility, and the Greenleaf approach is also reflected by Binney and Williams (1997), who concluded their study with the comment:

"The paradox of leaders is that as they give power away, so they become more powerful! Rather than impose their will on others, they work through example and the evident authenticity of their words and actions. Their leadership becomes more compelling, and the people with whom they are working are more likely to respond because they feel more responsible, more committed, and more fulfilled in their work."

Many people also argue that we are really only rediscovering old principles. For example, the quotation of Lao Tzu from over two millennia ago (Heider, 1995): "As for the best leaders, the people do not notice their existence. The next best, the people honor and praise. The next, the people fear, and the next the people hate. When the best leader's work is done, the people say, 'We did it ourselves.'" and "The wise leader is not collecting a string of successes. The leader is helping others to find their own success. There is plenty to go around. Sharing success with others is very successful. The single principle behind all creation teaches us that true benefit blesses everyone and diminishes no one. The wise leader knows that the reward for doing the work arises naturally out of the work."

However, few people in recent years have articulated a more relevant reinterpretation of the vision of leadership than Robert Greenleaf. Not only do organizations perform better using the principles of servant-leadership, but it is no surprise that they also help the world become a better place. In the long term, this is an even more important objective and result.

Learning

Within the confines of this paper, it is necessary to recognize the increasing importance of effective learning as a critical success factor within all organizations and to emphasize the increasing role of the "learning organization" approach. As Zuboff (1988) said, "Learning is the new form of labor. It is no longer a separate activity that occurs either before one enters the workplace or in remote classroom settings . . . learning is the heart of productive activity." The more change that is going on, the greater the need to get learning attitudes and structures right. And if the rate of change is greater than the rate of effective learning, there is little chance that the changes will be defined as progress. Reflecting Reg Revan's axiom: "For any organism to survive, its rate of learning must be equal to, or greater than, the rate of change in the environment." With the amount of change in the world today, the learning process is becoming an even more critical challenge for us all, both individually and organizationally.

Continuous improvement means recognizing the need for new ideas, identifying those that are relevant to the future organization, taking them on board, and then implementing them effectively. In order to be effective, an organization must be able to learn. The great advantage of humility is that it is an effective foundation for learning, with *complacency* and *arrogance* the most powerful barriers to learning. One paradoxical challenge for today's wise leader is how to avoid becoming complacent about one's humility, a problem that has recently overcome some Japanese businesses.

Nonaka and Takeeuchi (1995) defined organizational knowledge as: "The capability of a company as a whole to create new knowledge, disseminate it throughout the organization, and embody it in products, services, and systems." This statement emphasizes the importance of the view that "The organizations that will truly excel in the future will be the organizations that discover how to tap people's commitment and capacity to learn at all levels in an organization" (Senge, 1990).

The learning company goes beyond the idea of excellence to make learning the central process. Peters and Waterman (1982), among others, were concerned with adaptability, responsibility, and learning: "The excellent companies are learning organizations." Experimenting and learning are at the heart of the Peters and Waterman vision, but the structures and strategies of a learning organization were not articulated until later.

If there is a responsibility and learning focus, there is a natural sympathy for processes such as upward appraisal—in contrast to a power culture, which often applies traditional appraisal systems bureaucratically in an attempt to exert control. It is not surprising to find that the latter approach rarely produces the results expected.

The conclusion we reach is that the ability to change is directly related to the ability to learn, and the ability to learn, both individually and organizationally, is directly related to the ability to operate a responsibility-driven culture throughout the organization.

A power-driven approach tends to be preoccupied with the short term, while a responsibility approach is more concerned with long-term issues. As a result, a responsibility-driven approach is likely to produce a more effective balance of the respective interests of all the various stakeholders so essential for the long-term success of any organization. It helps to provide a climate in which innovation is encouraged and failure is an opportunity for learning, rather than an excuse for punishment. In fact, the responsibilities will only be rewarding and positive if supported by an overall learning approach to all aspects of life and work. Unfortunately, taking responsibility, being able to live with it, and knowing how to use and develop it in others is rare.

Power cultures may well stem directly from the encouragement competition—externally with competitors and internally with colleagues. In these cultures, information is seen as power, so people often focus on building themselves up as unique marketable resources by keeping information to themselves, rather than sharing it through a team-building approach.

According to Birchall and Lyons (1995), "Power in organizations is based on what and who people know. Access to information is vital to those responsible for managing business operations. Electronic systems make it possible to distribute that information widely, cheaply, and quickly." Hence, what is done with knowledge, whether it is kept or spread, can be a valuable indicator of whether an organization or individual is driven by power or responsibility. Both new technology and more effective management approaches will require attitudes toward power and responsibility to change radically in the future.

A responsible approach to learning combined with learning to manage responsibility are essential prerequisites for any effective learning organization or learning environment. A learning environment is about passing on knowledge; it is about empowering others with knowledge, rather than being possessive on the grounds that "knowledge is power." A learning organization approach cannot be expected to work without a genuine concern for others. Hence "learning organizations" cannot be expected to operate effectively within a power-driven culture. Similar points can be made about the effort to introduce empowerment programs.

The way responsibility is shouldered in an organization can have a profound effect on the decision-making process. When facing a crisis or disaster, Western managers tend to pinpoint blame, fire the person involved, then pretend the problem is solved. The tradition in Japan is that the executive who hired or managed a person who made mistakes is let go. This approach encourages an attention to detail and a focus on the development of people, which in turn encourages loyalty and respect. Because managers in Japan are held directly responsible for the behavior of their subordinates, they take more interest in ensuring that their subordinates do not fail or make mistakes. They are motivated to maximize the learning transfer, which generates a virtuous circle. In a traditional Western environment the position is often reversed, leading to a cycle of decline.

In theory, there are grounds for expecting female managers with more "feminine" characteristics to be more responsibility driven, and, hence, more open to learning and more future-focused than their more traditionally power-driven male colleagues. However, further research is needed to establish whether or not this difference is actually significant. In addition, it will also be important to cross-check against differences in nationality.

This analysis has argued that center of the debate about leadership should be more about how and what we learn about responsibility, rather than traditional preoccupation with power. In order to make progress, we need to generate new alliances (and improve the effectiveness of old ones) in which learning for leadership helps shift the historic power-driven approach into a more positive direction in which the prime emphasis is responsibility. Within this context, it is important to recognize that "political correctness" and attempts to overcome sexism and racism are about minimizing the abuse of power and encouraging a responsibility-driven approach. Also, the role of ethics and ethical behavior by individuals and organizations must be fully rooted in the issues raised in this chapter.

In the end, the vital links between responsibility, leadership, and learning must be more widely recognized if we wish to be optimistic about the shape and nature of society in the decades ahead. But what do we do about this situation? At this stage, recognizing and emphasizing the importance of these links is a useful place to start. But it is only a beginning. As another authority perceptively put it: "The key facilitating role of directors is to create the climate in which learning is encouraged, rewarded, and allowed to flow freely around the organization" (Garratt, 1990).

Empowerment

Essentially, empowerment involves passing decision-making authority and responsibility from managers to employees. As Bowen and Lawler (1992) define it:

> "Empowerment also necessitates sharing with employees information and knowledge that enable them to understand and contribute to organizational performance, rewarding them based on the organization's performance, and giving them the authority to make decisions that influence organizational outcomes." (pp. 31–39)

Ford and Fottler (1995) say that the perhaps greatest challenge

> ". . . is for managers to carefully assess themselves, their organizations, and their employees. Are managers ready to give up decision-making authority, or are they distrustful of their subordinates? Are employees ready or willing to participate in empowerment programs or are they disinterested in the organization in general and their own job in particular? While these questions cannot be answered definitively, steps toward finding answers can be taken." (p. 27)

Many of the factors that are critical to the success of empowerment programs have already been discussed. Essentially, these factors involve a basic commitment to a learning organization approach, within a responsibility-driven leadership culture. A similar point can be made about many other management techniques, such as total quality management and re-engineering. Unless the issues relating to power and responsibility are both understood and implemented effectively, it is not surprising that a significant majority of management programs fail.

Language

One dimension that cannot be ignored is the role of language in changing culture and/or behavior. As Berlin (1994) said: "Minds are formed by the character of language, not language by the minds of those who speak it." The dynamics of the language employees use to communicate with one another and with management is a key component in helping the company decide what knowledge is legitimate and what is not. The world both reflects the language we use and is changed by it. Nowhere are these issues more apparent, important, or problematic than over the use of the words *power* and *responsibility*. A wide range of phrases incorporating the word power are in use: power politics; power dressing; abuse of power; absolute power; power to the people; corridors of power; struggle for power; lust for power; and balance of power. Would things change, would the world become a better place, if we all tried to substitute the word *responsibility*, wherever possible, for the word *power*. Perhaps it is up to us to start talking about the "corridors of responsibility" rather than "the corridors of power."

Integration

Finally, if we want to improve the quality of life in the twenty-first century, we must improve the priority given to the quality and quantity of our *learning* and emphasize the importance of the effective use of that learning. We need to incorporate the latest ideas on *knowledge management*.

How do we learn? Why do we learn? What do we learn? and, then, What do we do with what we learn? These questions should be a particular focus for policy issues related to the learning and leadership development of the next generation. It is essential that we move away from our traditional preoccupation with power toward a responsibility-driven approach to decision making and change. These changes would benefit organizations in the long term, as well as be a considerable benefit to individuals and society as a whole.

Unless an integrated approach is taken to the relationships between responsibility, leadership, learning, and power, organizations will be increasingly less successful over the long term. At the core of this approach is understanding and effectively managing the relationship between responsibility and power. Only when this relationship is based on a strong foundation of responsibility, can we be optimistic about the future of our organizations, individuals, and the society within which we live.

About the Contributor

Bruce Lloyd is principal lecturer in strategy at South Bank University, London, England. Over the past decade, he has been particularly concerned with writing, researching, and lecturing on a wide range of strategic issues that critically influence organizational performance.

Since joining the academic world in 1989, Bruce has provided a major input into the development of the university MBA program. Previous experience included seven years' involvement in the international venture capital industry with the Commonwealth Development Finance Company and new venture development with ICI plc, as well as earlier experience as an investment analyst in The City and as a plant manager with the British Petroleum Company, Ltd.

Bruce is the author of over one hundred papers and articles on strategy-related topics, from economies of scale to political risk management, with a recent focus on the future of office and office work; flexible working; the relationship between power, responsibility, leadership, and learning; and the role of wisdom in knowledge management. He is editor of two volumes in *The Best of Long Range Planning on Creating and Managing New Ventures* and *Creating Value Through Acquisitions, Demergers, Buyouts, and Alliances,* and has spoken widely at international conferences.

Bruce is a member of the World Future Society and World Future Studies Federation, the executive committee of the Strategic Planning Society, and the editorial board of the *Leadership and Organisational Development Journal* and *Futures.* He is also a past chairman of the editorial board of the journal *Long Range Planning,* as well as being its review editor.

CHAPTER FIFTEEN

STARTING SMART: CLARIFYING COACHING GOALS AND ROLES

Robert Witherspoon

Coaching is relatively new in the executive suite. So, clear goals and roles are especially crucial—both for getting started and for sustained success. Executives may use coaching for a number of reasons: to learn specific skills, to improve their effectiveness, to prevent derailment, or to prepare for career moves; or they may have a larger agenda, such as obtaining better business results. Most coaching is based on one-to-one relationships between executive and coach, typically behind closed doors. Each coaching situation is different. Yet, some distinctions are essential to recognize, both to establish focus and to foster informed choice.

My client and I begin coaching by assessing the situation and his or her felt needs. How we collaborate depends on key situational factors, starting with the executive's[1] coaching issues. Together, we define coaching goals and roles that respond to these needs. I distinguish four points along a continuum of executive coaching roles as follows.

[1] I use the terms "executive" and "client" interchangeably to mean the person being coached, which is distinct from the "customer" or "client system," that is, the organization that contracts for the services and pays the bills. I am also mainly concerned here with one-on-one executive coaching in organizations and with formal coaching, for which regular sessions are scheduled and tangible results are expected.

- *Coaching for skills*—to focus on a client's current project or task.
- *Coaching for performance*—to focus on a client's effectiveness in a present job.
- *Coaching for development*—to focus on a client's future job responsibilities and/or career.
- *Coaching for an executive's agenda*—to focus on a client's larger issues, including better business results.

These critical distinctions help us jointly set the coaching agenda. Unless my client and I can identify one of these coaching roles as primary, there can be confusion about expectations, the amount of time it will take, and the effort we'll put into the relationship. Unless we contract to focus on one of these four, it is hard to check progress toward our goals. My colleagues and I have found that this coaching continuum constitutes a good conceptual framework for dealing with different (and evolving) issues that come up throughout our coaching relationships.

This chapter explores these topics from the perspective of the executive coaching practice used by me and my organization. I begin with a working definition of executive coaching and a brief overview of the Coaching Continuum Model outlined above, then discuss some practical implications for coaching executives.

Beyond a Buzzword

Coaching is a current buzzword with many different meanings in business circles. Some see coaching as part of the boss's responsibility to develop subordinates, often in conjunction with an annual performance review. Others conceive of coaching as a manager's efforts to modify and reinforce employee behavior—a key part of performance management. Still others have applied coaching to a certain managerial style or connect coaching with mentoring, management development, and career development that takes place over a long period of time. Moreover, a growing management literature (Evered and Seleman, 1989), along with articles from the popular press and training materials (not to mention the use of coaches in sports, the performing arts, and other areas of life), have made coaching a household word.

The main concern here is coaching executives in organizations, in which some promising new practices have evolved, such as 360° surveys and feedback; the integration of coaching into large-scale, leadership development programs; and other new coaching applications.

A Definition of Coaching

Coaching is undertaken to bring out the best in people. The first use of the word in the English language was in reference to a particular kind of carriage. Hence, the basic meaning is to "convey a valued person from where he or she is to where he or she wants to be."

Elsewhere (Witherspoon, 1998) I have suggested the following elements of executive coaching: a professional relationship (as opposed to a managerial function) to enhance effective action and learning agility (the ability to learn from feedback and experience) through a deliberate process of observation, inquiry, dialogue, and discovery that provides—the three core values of my coaching—*valid information, informed choice,* and *internal commitment* (Argyris and Schön, 1974).

I also see executive coaching as a highly personal learning process: (1) it is individualized, as each person has a unique knowledge base, learning pace, and learning style, and (2) it can uncover blind spots and change one's personal style.

So, for purposes of this chapter, let's consider this working definition:

Executive coaching is an action-learning process to enhance effective action and learning agility. It involves a professional relationship and a deliberate, personalized process to provide an executive with valid information, free and informed choices based on that information, and internal commitment to those choices.

One outcome of this process is that the executive can accomplish more (effective action) after coaching than otherwise would have been true. Another outcome is that the executive can learn better (learning agility) after coaching—for example, by asking for feedback and reflecting before and after taking action—than otherwise would have been true.

Coaching Theory: The Coaching Continuum

A key dimension for distinguishing among coaching roles is client need. Does the executive need to learn a new skill, to perform better in the present job, or to prepare for a future leadership role? Is the executive looking for a confidential sounding board and a source of constructive feedback? Coaching executives involves one or more of the following coaching roles as defined in the Coaching Continuum Model.

Coaching for Skills

"Skill" refers to the knowledge, skills, abilities, and perspectives that enable an executive to take effective action. Coaching for skills involves a dynamic interaction between executive and coach. It is distinct from teaching, which relies on one-way telling and instruction; rather, it requires a deliberate process of observation, inquiry, dialogue, and discovery. The essence of coaching executives is helping them to learn, rather than training or tutoring them. To coach in this sense is less to instruct than to facilitate (literally, "to make easy").

When	"I need to sharpen my skills for. . . ." "I know how, but I don't always do it well."
Who	Any executive, manager, or individual contributor.
Why	Better skills. The primary coaching focus is to sharpen an executive's skills for a current project or task. Coaching sessions often address one or two key skill areas.
What	Executive works with coach to:

- Assess current skills;
- Clarify expectations for current project or tasks;
- Prioritize the executive's needs for present project or tasks;
- Plan for skill building;
- Enhance effective action; and
- Improve (to some extent) learning agility.

Coaching for skills usually occurs over a short term, such as one or more sessions over several weeks or months.

Coaching for Performance

"Performance" is used broadly to refer to the executive's competencies and his or her characteristics that contribute to a current job or role. A related coaching role is "coaching to correct performance" (or "fix its") for executives at risk. As a rule, coaching to correct performance involves interventions to remedy problems that interfere with an executive's job performance or that risk derailing a career.

When	"There's pressure to improve."
	"I need to do a better job at. . . ."
	"I'm not aware of my impact on. . . ."
	"I haven't made a commitment to doing it well."
Who	Senior executives, key performers, or executives at risk.
Why	Better performance. The primary coaching focus is to improve the executive's effectiveness in a current job or role. Coaching sessions often address one or more core competencies for the executive's current success.
What	Executive works with coach to:

- Assess current competencies for present job;
- Clarify expectations for present performance;
- Prioritize the executive's needs for present job performance;
- Plan for continuing improvement;
- Enhance effective action; and
- Improve (to a noticeable extent) learning agility.

Coaching for performance usually occurs over a longer term (several months or quarters).

Coaching for Development

"Development" is used broadly to refer to the executive's competencies and characteristics that are required for a future job or role and may entail considerable growth. Over time, an executive's personal growth and development process is one of becoming more open (able to entertain alternate perspectives), differentiated (able to draw from distinctions), and integrated (able to weave these differences into an increasingly complex whole).

When	"I'm being groomed to advance. . . ."
	"I'm being promoted to. . . ."
	"I'm considering a career move to. . . ."
	"I'm in the succession planning pool for. . . ."
Who	Promising people and high potentials.
Why	Better development. The primary coaching focus is to prepare the executive for a future position, a leadership role, or a career move. Coaching sessions often address one or more core competencies for future success.
What	Executive works with coach to:

- Assess current competencies;
- Clarify expectations for future performance;
- Prioritize the executive's need for future job performance;
- Plan for continuing development;
- Enhance effective action; and
- Improve (to a significant extent) learning agility.

Coaching for development usually occurs over a longer term (several quarters or more).

Coaching for an Executive's Agenda

"Executive's agenda" is used broadly to refer to personal, business, and/or organizational issues or concerns. Often this coaching covers important issues for executives and their organizations that are otherwise overlooked, particularly during change initiatives, layoffs, or company downsizing. Sometimes the sessions border on life coaching, as the executive considers his or her life purpose and personal challenges.

When	"It's lonely at the top."
	"I'm in over my head."

	"I need a talking partner for. . . ."
	"I'm facing a big challenge at. . . ."
Who	CEOs and heads of a business or major business function.
Why	Better business results. The primary coaching focus is on the executive's larger agenda, including better business results. Coaching sessions often address executive's agenda in the broadest sense.
What	Executive works with coach to:

- Develop more ideas and options;
- Prioritize the executive's needs;
- Plan for the executive's agenda;
- Obtain better support for the executive's agenda;
- Enhance effective action; and
- Improve (to a variable extent) learning agility.

Coaching for the executive's agenda can be ongoing and is highly variable, depending on the issue. These distinct executive coaching roles are essential to recognize for the following reasons:

Clarity. Effective problem solving requires valid information. When people share relevant information about a situation in a way that each can understand, they are more likely to make sound decisions. Drawing distinctions among coaching roles helps provide clarity and a common language about executive coaching and can be a useful way to orient all parties to the process of contracting, assessment, and feedback.

Choice. Effective decisions require free and informed choice. When people base their choices on valid information, they are more likely to make such a free and informed choice. Recognizing the distinctions among different coaching roles helps foster informed choice by the client (and possibly family members), the client's boss, the human resources officer, and the coach(es) providing the service.

Commitment. Effective implementation requires internal commitment. When people make free and informed choices based on valid information, they tend to feel personally responsible for their decisions and find their choices intrinsically compelling or satisfying. Offering parties a choice of coaching responses throughout the life of the coaching relationship helps foster internal commitment.

Roles and Behavior. Each coaching role helps to define behaviorally how coaches and clients work together. So choosing the right coaching role can make the difference between meeting or missing client expectations. An open discussion of coaching roles can also help to create ground rules and a feedback system.

Coaching Practice: Openings and Contracts

Turning from theory to practice, let's consider two specific ways the Coaching Continuum Model can be applied in executive coaching situations: (1) to spot openings for coaching and (2) to contract for working together. I will explore how to spot openings and how to contract under each of the four points on the continuum: skills, performance, development, and an executive's agenda.

Three skills are essential for any person taking a situational approach to executive coaching. They are (1) *flexibility,* the ability to use more than a single coaching style and to turn down work outside of one's professional competence; (2) *diagnostic ability,* needed to determine the primary need(s) the client has for coaching (and therefore decide the most appropriate coaching response); and (3) *knowledge of contracting,* the negotiation process with an executive in a face-to-face meeting, involving both a discussion of client needs and of the coaching role most appropriate for the situation.

The following sections show how the coaching continuum can be used to diagnose coaching situations correctly and contract effectively. As Harold Hill said in *The Music Man,* "You've got to know the territory," before you decide which of your styles to use.

A general principle is to begin with the client's interests and concerns. As Herbert Shepard (1985) has said, "start where the system is." When a client is focused on a particular issue, he or she may not be able to fully attend to other issues. Another assumption I make is that my client usually understands the situation better than I do, or at least has important insights, so my choice of an appropriate coaching response is guided directly by the client's manifest needs, not by any preconceived agenda.

One way to identify the client's interests and concerns is to ask. Does the executive need to learn a new skill to perform better in the present job or to prepare for a future leadership role? Does the executive understand and acknowledge these needs? Is he or she willing to seek and accept feedback and coaching? These questions suggest client need—the focus for the coaching continuum—as a key aspect of any coaching situation.

Seeing Openings for Coaching

An opening for coaching is that critical moment at which one or more relevant people notice a need for coaching and believe that change can occur. As a rule, openings result from a significant situation or event. Everyone involved should learn to recognize a coaching opening and carefully evaluate where it falls on the coaching continuum—including executives, managers, and human resource officers.

What constitutes an opening for coaching? A request for coaching by any executive is an obvious example. Other openings come during the situations that arise daily in any organization. Some are built into the time cycles of business activities (for example, annual performance reviews or the beginning of a new budget period). Some are presented by a particular circumstance (for example, difficult performance issues, complaints from customers, a new possibility in sales or marketing, or a crisis in the enterprise). Others occur around important firsts (for example, before a customer's first visit or a first board meeting).

Still other openings occur randomly. For example, openings occur when an executive decides it is time to improve performance in an important area, or the boss sees business results that are below expectations or key working relationships that are strained. Openings could be for any of the four types of coaching on the continuum.

Given an opening for coaching, the key factors to assess are goal clarity, consensus, commitment, and control, as shown in Exhibit 15.1. For each of the factors listed, I may probe for specifics. For example, to assess goal clarity I ask about the primary focus for coaching. I may also question the parties involved in the coaching (especially the client, but also the boss and relevant others) about the extent to which:

- Coaching goals are clear and specific;
- Parties understand what is expected of them; and
- Coaching activities are well-planned and organized.

Of these four factors, goal clarity—the primary purpose of coaching—is the key to sizing up coaching needs: how to approach an opening for coaching, where to start, what to emphasize, and what to leave alone for the time being. High goal clarity may also contribute to high consensus (people agree about the need for coaching), high commitment (people are strongly committed to coaching), and high control (people believe they have a good chance of achieving their goals).

To illustrate, let's look at situations that are well-matched to each coaching role along the continuum.

EXHIBIT 15.1. SITUATIONAL FACTORS TO SIZE UP COACHING NEEDS

Clarity

The extent to which relevant parties (the executive, boss, others) understand the business reasons for coaching, the primary coaching focus, specific coaching goals, success measures, and so on.

Consensus

The extent to which relevant parties agree about the business reasons for coaching, the primary coaching focus, success measures, and so on.

Commitment

The extent to which relevant parties are committed to goal achievement and continually evaluate their own performance against these goals.

Control

The extent to which relevant parties consider the coaching goals to be realistic and achievable.

Openings for Skills Coaching

Coaching for skills helps people learn specific skills, abilities, and perspectives, often over several weeks or months. Openings well-suited to this coaching role are summarized in the list below. A coach can infer these openings from something seen or heard in organizations, such as an executive saying, "I need to learn on-the-job. . . ." In this case, it is fairly easy to see an opening because of a close match with the executive's statement. I like to clarify such needs statements, then confirm an opening for coaching through further conversation.

Openings for Skills Coaching

1. To enhance learning on the job (for example, before or after a key "first," such as a customer's first visit or a first board meeting);
2. To enhance training (for example, by reinforcing learning and practical applications back on the job);
3. To enhance performance after job redesign (for example, when re-engineering introduces new or different roles and responsibilities); or
4. At key project milestones (for example, when starting with new equipment).

In these cases, coaching can be used to help an executive build skills needed for a current task or project. Sometimes, the executive's statements indicate a need for conceptual clarity: "I'm not familiar with the basic principles" or "I don't understand why these skills are needed or when to apply them." Other times, the executive's statements indicate a need to acquire a skill: "I never learned how to do it" or "I know how, but I don't always do it well." In these cases, coach for skills and/or recommend learning resources that are tailored to these needs. Because the needs are clear and specific, executives can start applying their new skills and behaviors promptly.

In openings to coach for skills, there is often high clarity about the skills to be learned. Executives know what is expected of them. The business reasons for coaching are clear and thoroughly understood by all.

Consequently, coaching for skills can often occur over a relatively short period of time.

Openings for Performance Coaching

By comparison, consider coaching for performance. In openings to coach for performance, there is often less clarity by key parties. The executive may have one coaching agenda and the boss another. For example, there may be a presenting issue ("He's not getting the results we expected"), but little clear definition of actual behavior or root causes. People may be expected to improve their effectiveness, but don't know how. In the same way, the business reasons for coaching may be less clear. Consequently, coaching for performance tends to involve more time, if only to reach clarity and consensus about the need for coaching and the desired outcomes.

Coaching for performance helps people improve their effectiveness on the job, often over several quarters or a year or more. This coaching role applies to openings such as those listed below.

Openings for Performance Coaching

1. To enhance effective action and capabilities for a current job (for example, by practicing new behaviors);
2. To clarify performance goals, when expectations about behavior are unclear or when business goals, roles, or conditions change; or
3. To orient and support a newly appointed executive or someone with significant new responsibilities in making a smooth transition.

Coaching to correct performance ("fix its") also can help to change individual behaviors and correct problems such as these:

Openings for Performance Coaching (for "Fix Its")

1. To confront ineffective attitudes or other motivational issues;
2. To alleviate performance problems (for example, when deficiencies jeopardize a person's productivity, job, or career);

3. To increase confidence and commitment (for example, when seasoned players have experienced career setbacks and disappointments); or
4. To deal with blind spots that detract from otherwise satisfactory performance.

In these cases, I can act as a performance coach by helping clients assess their performance, obtain feedback on individual strengths and weaknesses, and enhance their effectiveness. The coaching sessions typically focus on performance in the present job, although continued improvement may lead to coaching for competencies that are needed for future advancement.

To diagnose these coaching openings, I start with a client's felt needs and consider the same situational factors as before: goal clarity, consensus about the need for coaching, commitment, and control. Then, I listen for a close match between the executive's statement and one or more characteristic wordings from the coaching continuum. Assuming the opening calls for performance coaching, I also strive for a clear understanding of what is meant by "performance" in my client's current job or role.

Few words in the management lexicon are as important as *performance*, but the word has two quite different meanings in practice:

- *Product:* What gets accomplished? Have individuals, teams, and organizations achieved their goals? Are standards being met? Are projects completed on time? Are products and services delighting customers? Have business goals been achieved? What were the business results?
- *Process:* How well do people do their work? Are they knowledgeable and skilled? How effectively do they use their skills? How well do employees interact with each other? How do people treat their customers? Are procedures effective? How is the work getting done?

Coaching for performance may involve both process and product, and in fact there is a connection between how the work is done and what gets done. However, the two meanings of performance are separate and distinct, and it's important to understand that competence—knowledge, skills, abilities, perspectives, and so forth—is only one factor among many that influences results. Strategy, structure, and culture are also at play.

Given these different meanings, it's often essential to probe further, especially in complex situations. In coaching conversations, one way to do this is to reflect on a client's action[2] (Argyris and Schön, 1974). I often start by asking a series of questions such as the following:[3]

1. Start by asking, "What's the result that concerns you? Describe concretely what is happening. What is working? What is problematic?"
2. Then ask, "What actions produced this result?" It is crucial to obtain concrete descriptions of what key players say and do.
3. Then ask, "How have you and others been framing the situations such that you acted the way you did? How do you see your task? Yourself and others? Key themes?"
4. Then ask, "What are the contextual factors that influence the behavior of you and other key players? What are your goals and roles? How are you measured? What are your loyalties?"

Coaching for Development

Coaching for development helps people prepare for advancement, often over an extended period of a year or more. In openings to coach for development, there is usually less clarity by key parties compared with when coaching for skills or performance. Because coaching for the future is involved, shared agreement about the need for development coaching can be difficult to obtain and can vary from high in some organizations with well-honed succession plans to low in organizations without them. Clear and specific goals for coaching may be lacking, or at best limited, and predicting future requirements is difficult at best. Consequently, coaching for development tends to involve considerable time, both to reach clarity and consensus and to realize potentially far-ranging changes. The business

---

[2] *Reflecting-in-action* is a core competency for executive coaching. It refers to the paradoxical ability to step outside immediate events while still in them through a process of on-the-spot reflection and experimentation. The skill is instrumental for helping clients in the moment to produce valid information, informed choice, and internal commitment.

[3] Adapted from Action Design, with permission. © Action Design, 1998.

examples of coaching for development include preparing an executive for a career move, often as part of succession planning, and providing support for possible promotions, lateral transfers, and so on. This coaching role applies to such openings as these:

Openings for Development Coaching

1. To enhance effective action and capabilities for a future job, sometimes after coaching for performance;
2. To clarify shared goals about success when executives and their organizations are at odds about the skills and perspectives needed for success in a future position; or
3. To encourage the long-term development of promising people by facilitating learning from challenging career experiences.

In these cases, I act as a development coach by helping clients discover their potential to advance and addressing their long-term development needs, often over several years or more. The coaching sessions typically focus on development for future jobs by helping an executive discover strengths and weaknesses, determine where growth is needed, and how to fill the gaps.

To diagnose these openings, start with a client's felt needs and consider the same factors as above: clarity, consensus, commitment, and control. Then listen for a close match between the executive's statement and one or more characteristic wordings from the coaching continuum. Assuming the opening calls for development coaching, also strive for a clear understanding of what is meant by development for a client's future jobs or roles. For example, an early step in coaching for development is often to help executives and their organizations clarify the skills and competencies for success in a future executive job or leadership role. The resulting success profile (also known as a competency model) defines the skills, abilities, and perspectives that are required for effective performance in these future situations. However, the competencies for future jobs or roles are always changing, so the foundation for future competence is to increase one's capacity to learn how to learn (that is, learning agility).

Coaching for the Executive's Agenda

Coaching for the executive's agenda helps that person realize broader purposes, such as better business results and/or well-being in life, often on an ongoing basis. In openings to coach for an executive's agenda, goal clarity is often highly variable, broad, or open-ended. In other cases, the coaching may be tied to an organization's priorities, such as to help key people implement major change initiatives successfully. Consequently, the time involved for this coaching role can be highly variable. Depending on the executive's agenda, the actual coaching sessions may take place at regular intervals over a specific time period or on an on-call basis.

The scope for this type of coaching can range considerably and often goes beyond a single person or situation. Business examples include: mergers and acquisitions, productivity and quality improvement, executive leadership transitions, turnarounds, and coping with explosive growth. Among the situations well-suited to this coaching role are these:

Openings for Agenda Coaching

1. To support better decisions when insight and perspective are needed on an executive's ideas;
2. To open up more options when creative suggestions could improve the chances for sound decisions;
3. To enhance change management by preparing an executive to implement specific change initiatives successfully; or
4. To guide an executive through unknown or unexplored areas or when the executive feels overwhelmed.

In such cases, I can act as a sounding board by offering feedback and suggestions to support or supplement a client's ideas. As the coach I am free to offer suggestions, but the coaching process ensures that executives address the issues and concerns that matter most to them.[4]

---

[4]Depending on the executive's agenda and the scope of the project, you may act in other capacities, such as facilitating strategic retreats or planning sessions, which are logical extensions of executive coaching.

To diagnose these coaching openings, I start with a client's felt needs and consider the same factors as above: clarity, consensus, commitment, and control. I listen for a close match between the executive's statement and one or more characteristic wordings from the coaching continuum. Because agenda coaching is typically the most open-ended coaching role, many ongoing conversations may be required to diagnose a client's need and design an appropriate intervention.

Contracting for Coaching

At the start of any coaching engagement, the coaching continuum is helpful for fostering informed choices and contracting for coaching services. Contracting is typically the first step in formal coaching. As in most relationships, the parties tend to make implicit, critical assumptions about the relationship, chiefly about its purpose, roles and responsibilities, coaching methods, the willingness of others, and so on. When these assumptions are not clarified, trouble can ensue.

Contracting for a formal coaching relationship is a way to make these assumptions explicit, and it provides three important functions:

1. Contracting establishes focus on one or more of the primary coaching roles and agreement on the desired results, as well as a common language for coaching and development activities.
2. Contracting addresses structure: the steps for realizing goals, the coaching methods employed, time frames, progress measures, and related matters.
3. Contracting models the action-learning process at the heart of coaching, including disclosure, inquiry, and commitment to one another's success.

Contracting is especially useful in determining *blended* coaching engagements—those that entail more than one coaching role. The following two cases will help to show how I determine the right mix of roles on the coaching continuum when contracting.

An executive had just received a negative performance review from her new boss, delivered as part of the organization's annual appraisal process. As her coach, I first served as a sounding board and we discussed how to "read" her new boss and interpret the results of this first review. (This work was coaching for the executive's agenda.) After the executive decided to develop better relations with the boss, she worked with me on how to repair strained working relations, starting with practice sessions to develop active listening and communication skills and to practice for her next meetings with the boss. (This was coaching for skills.)

A newly appointed leader had just received a promotion and significant added responsibilities. In this case, we started meeting frequently to help the executive address his urgent new agenda. During the first part of each four-hour coaching session, we worked on his choice of topics. Next, we focused on developing his charter for the new position: key roles, responsibilities, and relationships for a successful transition. (In this case, we agreed that both parts of these coaching sessions were for the executive's agenda.) Several months later, the focus shifted to coaching this same executive in implementing his development plan, based on 360° feedback about his effectiveness as an executive and the key success factors for his new position. (We called this coaching for development.)

In these engagements, the right mix of coaching roles was essential. And in both cases the blended coaching was successful, because key differences among coaching roles were clarified and contracted for early in each engagement.

To recap, actual coaching engagements (and sessions) can entail more than one coaching role, but I strive to maintain these distinctions (and role clarity), as it helps in the coaching process. To this end, I find the coaching continuum especially helpful when contracting (or re-contracting). This model is also helpful in situations in which executive coaching is relatively new to the client and/or organization being served and in which clear definitions and shared expectations are lacking.

A Final Word

For decades, top athletes, public speakers, and performing artists have turned to coaches to help them perform better. For these individuals already atop their fields, the next level of performance cannot be taught, but it can be learned. Now this approach has taken hold in organizations, in which top executives are turning to coaches to help them to reach their business and personal best. Coaching executives entails a highly personalized learning process to enhance both effective action and learning agility.

I offer these distinctions and the coaching continuum as a contribution to a common language about executive coaching and to foster informed choice and internal commitment by everyone involved. Beyond informed choice and improved coaching practice, I hope that these distinctions can foster a dialogue about the roles coaches play. I see a future in which coaching is widely available in organizations and in which coaching practice is formed by insights from an evolving practice theory for coaching executives.

Earlier I distinguished between the Coaching Continuum Model (the "what") and a larger practice theory for executive coaching (the "why"). The coaching continuum can be seen as only one element of an evolving practice theory for executive coaching (Witherspoon and White, 1997).

My approach to coaching practice theory draws on a theory of action perspective developed by Chris Argyris and Donald Schön (1974). This conceptual framework, with its emphasis on valid information, free and informed choice, and internal commitment, provides a foundation for understanding and explaining human action in my work with executives. Short-term, I believe that a useful practice theory (Argyris, Putnam, and Smith, 1985; Argyris and Schön, 1974; Weisbord, 1987) should answer at least two questions for a professional coach: "What do I say and do in this situation?" and "What are the underlying principles that explain why I do and say this?" Long-term, I believe a coaching practice theory should seek to integrate a comprehensive theory and sound practice for executive coaching, such as Schwarz (1994) proposes for group facilitation.

Looking ahead, the challenge of integrating thought with action in executive coaching is exciting! Effective action requires the generation of knowledge that crosses the traditional disciplines with as much competence and rigor as possible. From my perspective, a useful practice theory would serve two aims: to enhance the effectiveness of those who practice it and to improve their ability to learn about their own behavior. Thus, the purpose of useful practice theory reinforces the purpose of executive coaching itself.

In closing, I look forward to a productive dialogue around an evolving practice theory for executive coaching—focused on making the premises explicit, making the inferences from the premises explicit, and having the conclusions tested by logic independent of the logic used to create the conclusions in the first place. This is difficult work, but well worth the effort.

About the Contributor

Robert Witherspoon is a coach, speaker, and author on executive coaching and development. In 1990, he founded Performance & Leadership Development Ltd. (P&L) after successful careers in business and consulting. At P&L, he helps executives and their organizations to improve their business results by developing the performance and leadership of key people. P&L clients include senior executives, professionals, middle managers, and those with high potentials in Fortune 500, professional service, and public sector organizations.

Robert assists executives and their organizations, including CEOs, boards, and senior managers, in business, government, and institutions. His primary areas of expertise include coaching and developing executives; facilitating strategic retreats, problem-solving sessions, and team building meetings; and planning and executing organizational change.

His main interest is in helping executives to lead more effective organizations and live better lives. The success of his practice is built on three strengths: his business background and orientation, his organizational change expertise, and his years of experience in helping executives confront their most difficult challenges and realize their highest potential.

Robert is the lead author of *Four Essential Ways That Coaching Can Help Executives,* a bestseller about executive coaching from the Center for Creative Leadership. A regular speaker and recognized authority on executive coaching and development, Robert has had work appear in professional publications by the American Society for Training and Development (*Training & Development*) and the American Psychological Association (*Consulting Psychology Journal*). As a leading practitioner, he has also been quoted in *Across the Board, Fast Company, Investors' Business Daily, The Human Resource Executive,* and elsewhere.

Prior to founding Performance & Leadership, based in Washington, D.C., Robert was a partner at Arthur Andersen & Co. He began his professional career in 1969 with the Institute of Public Administration of New York, then served the Organization for Economic Cooperation and Development in Paris. Subsequently, he was a founder and principal of a national consulting firm.

Robert earned a B.A. from the University of Rochester, and advanced degrees from Princeton University and the University of Paris. He has also completed the Organization Development program at Georgetown University, as well as workshops at the Action Design Institute, the NTL Institute for Applied Behavioral Sciences, the Center for Creative Leadership, and elsewhere.

PART THREE

MOMENTS AND TRANSITIONS

I n this part, we take a view of coaching having time as its baseline. Time can be thought of as something that is durable and flowing, which allows an entire process to roll out to achieve a long-term planned result. In contrast, the opportunity contained in a single instant or moment of time might cause us to reflect on our role or on our behavior. Then again, we ourselves may instigate—or unwittingly become the subject of—a step transition or situational discontinuity. All these aspects of *time*—process, moment, opportunity, and transition—allow for reflection and development. Moments and transitions make us take stock, persuade us to undertake behavioral exploration, and give us the chance to consider, review, or adjust our behavior. Dave Ulrich considers that unique and critical moment of CEO transition and shows how coaching can help that life-changing situation by making it smoother and more likely to succeed. James Belasco focuses in on the coach-leadership moment in a team setting and suggests how to react. Newly appointed leaders provide the transitional moment in Julie Johnson's chapter—a valuable chapter for anyone coming into leadership, in which "soft skills" are all-important. Liz Thach and Tom Heinselman show how coaching is being used in different professions in which a learning process is replacing traditional training programs. David Allen discusses that critical moment when a leader recognizes a need to change behavior and why a coach may be a critical factor. Beverly Kaye takes a broad view over an entire career and shows the vital link between informal, spontaneous "coachable moments" and alleviating employee frustrations about development on and beyond their current jobs.

CHAPTER SIXTEEN

COACHING CEO TRANSITIONS

Dave Ulrich

In the best of cases, successful coaching is difficult, and it often resembles teaching. For example, my high-school son, when receiving an A takes credit for his hard work, but on receiving a C or D, he blames the teacher. In the same way, teams or individuals who win often claim to do so because of their talent and skills; those who lose often blame the coach. This may be why coaches are more likely to be replaced than players.

Ultimately, the difficulty of coaching comes from assuming someone can change someone else's behavior or attitude. Psychologists tell us that many attitudes and behaviors derive from genetics, others form in early developmental years, and others come from peer groups and associations over time. If coaches have the goal of changing ingrained behaviors or attitudes, why would we be surprised that successful coaching is so difficult?

Increasing opportunities for coaching success may come by focusing on *transition moments*, times at which individuals experience major change and thus are more open to new ideas and willing to experiment with new behaviors. A significant transition moment occurs when an individual assumes a new role in the organization. New roles often bring excitement, enthusiasm, and energy. At these times individuals are willing to try new ideas. Perhaps the most visible transition moment within an organization comes when a new chief executive officer (CEO) is appointed. A new CEO has a number of unique and paradoxical challenges: to honor the past and create a future; to set an agenda that others will follow; to manage both the institutional and symbolic role as head of the organization; and to deal with the individual and personal challenges of leadership. Recently, I have had the privilege of coaching current and future CEOs through this critical transition moment, and I have found proud and confident, and at times recalcitrant, individuals open to learning and change. In this chapter, I lay out steps for coaching CEOs through transition moments, assuming that the same coaching logic may be applied to transition moments of leaders throughout an organization.

Set the Stage

Succession represents both a real and a symbolic transition moment. Realistically, succession transfers power and authority from an old to a new regime. Symbolically, succession communicates values both in terms of who is appointed and in how the appointment is made. CEO succession creates a firm's symbolic identity: "he's from marketing," "she's had global experience," "this person is committed to technology." Each of these statements sends a signal about the organization's direction. Many firms have thoughtful, rigorous, and useful succession plans that identify potential successors, provide CEO candidates opportunities to demonstrate competence in multiple roles, and select the individual for the new role based on ingenious screening processes. However, once a candidate has been identified as CEO successor, coaching kicks in.

Coaching deals less with who the successor is and more with orienting the successor to the new role. Coaching facilitates a process whereby current and future roles are clarified and makes the transition from old to new regime as seamless as possible. Generally, the retiring CEO initiates transition coaching. Transition coaching generally occurs between the time when the new CEO is identified and the old CEO retires, often prior to the formal announcement of the new appointment. At times, coaching transitions may be accomplished by the former and incoming CEOs alone, but more often, CEO transition coaching requires an outsider respected by both the retiring and incoming CEOs. An individual outside the firm cuts through political issues, raises sensitive and difficult questions, and generally has little or no personal agenda in the transition.

The stage is set for CEO transition when the current CEO has identified a successor and has initiated a dialogue about transition, and when the current and future CEOs feel comfortable with a third-party coach who will help them through the transition. Again, this chapter focuses on CEO transition, but the logic may be transferred to other leadership transitions.

Define the Purposes

CEO transition coaching has outcomes for both the retiring and incoming CEOs. If possible, the retiring CEO should leave the office with honor and dignity. This may be difficult because of business conditions, but when a CEO leaves angry it sets a bad tone throughout the corporation. For example, recently a large computer firm grew under the direction and guidance of the founder. When the business hit a series of difficult times, the founder was ousted by the board. The founder did not leave easily or nicely, and the ruckus created through his departure echoed throughout the organization. Employees whose professional and personal lives were indebted to this founder were unable to say thank you, to shift their loyalties to the new regime, or to face new business realities. The new CEO could never fully engage employees as had the firm's founder, ultimately resulting in the demise of the firm.

In addition, retiring CEOs need to transfer their *relationship equity* to the incoming CEO. Relationship equity refers to the network of personal contacts and alliances formed by the current CEO. These relationships may be defined as the shareholders with whom a CEO forms relationships, including: peers (other CEOs), the board, top team members, all employees, customers, suppliers, regulatory agencies, investors (shareholders and bond holders), and other unique circumstances (for example, family members in a family held firm). CEOs, through their tenure, build relationship equity with each of these stakeholders. Through coaching, the retiring CEO must transfer this equity to the incoming CEO.

Incoming CEOs have two purposes in coaching. First, they need to develop a point of view about how they will interact with each of the stakeholders—a theory or perspective about what he or she wants from each stakeholder and how he or she will work to accomplish those goals. Coaching helps the incoming CEO explore alternatives, define desired future states, and establish an agenda for each stakeholder.

Second, coaching helps incoming CEOs explore behaviors to enact their points of view. A critical challenge of every new leader is to figure out where to spend the most precious resource—time. How much time the incoming CEO spends with each stakeholder and what he or she spends time on sets the tone for his or her term.

Coaching the outgoing and incoming CEO through this critical transition allows an ending to occur and a beginning to be initiated. Coaching helps this transition, because a coach might have insights and observations unbiased by either the retiring or incoming CEO.

Create a Stakeholder Map

Each retiring CEO has a set of stakeholders with whom relationships have been formed. A coach working in a CEO transition moment identifies these stakeholders and raises questions the old and new CEO need to address for each.

Some of these stakeholders outside the firm might include: customers (target customers now and in the future), investors (the source of capital to fund the firm's growth, either key shareholder or lenders), suppliers (sources of supply now and in the future), regulators (key regulations facing the firm and key lobby groups), trade associations and professional groups (leaders in the industry), community leaders (the community leaders that the new CEO needs to know), and media relations (key observers of the firm in the local and national press). A coach helps the current CEO identify specific individuals in each stakeholder group who have been important, makes observations about future relationships for the new CEO, and plans to transition relationship equity to the new CEO.

Internal stakeholders and pertinent questions might include: *board of directors* (who is on the board, how does the board work together, and what board issues should the new CEO pay attention to), *top management team* (what is the quality of the top management team, who will be leaving with the current CEO, and how should the new CEO think about this team), *corporate governance* (how should the new CEO go about making decisions, structuring the organization, setting an agenda), *the retiring CEO* (how should the CEO manage the symbolic, timing, and other aspects of the transition), and *all employees* (how did the old CEO relate to employees). Again, a coach helps the retiring CEO reflect on specific experiences and relationships. In this case, the new CEO likely knows many of the people already, but having a candid dialogue about people and governance helps the new CEO reflect on the internal stakeholders.

Some other stakeholders who must be considered are those in one's personal life. CEO transitions have an impact on personal life, as CEOs often become public figures. The new CEO must remember to include himself or herself as a stakeholder. Because the decision has already been made about who the new CEO will be, the former CEO is in a unique position to share personal observations about strengths and weaknesses of the incoming CEO. Often these discussions alert the new CEO to style challenges required in the new job (for example, "be more patient in demanding results," and "be willing to delegate and focus on the big picture"). No incoming CEO has all the attributes required to succeed, so feedback from the retiring CEO, who likely played a role in selected him or her, helps in preparing for upcoming challenges. Because the retiring CEO has already demonstrated confidence and trust in the new CEO through the selection itself, feedback is often less threatening and more instructive.

At a personal level, the new CEO also has to deal with how the job will affect lifestyle. Scheduling private time, managing his or her calendar, and thinking through personal issues (for example, health, hobbies, community image, and so forth) fall within the coach's purview. In addition, a coach helps him or her think about the family demands of the new role. CEOs become visible embodiments of the firm in social settings, so helping him or her consider the responsibilities required of other members of the family in this role is important. In a couple of cases in my practice, the retiring CEO and spouse hosted the incoming CEO and spouse, talking through the changing roles as a couple. This dialogue helped the incoming CEO and spouse understand the implications of the new position.

Again, many of the stakeholders listed above should not be new to the incoming CEO; however, relationship equity must be identified and transferred from old to new CEO, and the new ways to deal with those stakeholders must be determined. In this type of coaching setting, I have seen stakeholder maps drawn on which individuals are identified. In most cases, I have found that, although one would assume that the new CEO has already built these relationships, opening the dialogue leads to new insights and issues for him or her.

Articulate a Point of View for Each Stakeholder

As the stakeholder map is generated and relationships are identified, the incoming CEO needs to create a point of view for each stakeholder. This generally is done in two steps. First, the new CEO determines which stakeholders require the most attention and when. If there are ten stakeholders and each requires ten units of energy to be fully satisfied, but the new CEO only has sixty units of energy available, a coach may help allocate the sixty points. Some of this allocation may be sequential. For example, when the CEO transition actually occurs, the new CEO has a unique opportunity to have media coverage of the event and to go public with a direction and point of view. This may require a higher percentage of the sixty units of energy for a short period of time, but the media stakeholder may receive less attention soon after the transition. Multiple stakeholders can also be managed by sharing similar messages. For example, one new CEO prepared a clear statement about his goals and purposes, then used this as his "eighty percent talk." This "eighty percent talk" was the same for employees, customers, suppliers, board of directors, and investors. The eighty percent came from completing the statements: "I am excited about this new role because. . . ." "My agenda as CEO will likely be to . . . ." Coaches help with the reflection and responses to these questions, so that the eighty percent message is communicated vividly and clearly. Then, the new CEO tailors the final twenty percent of his or her message depending on the audience.

Second, the new CEO must develop a point of view about key stakeholders. The CEO must determine which customers and suppliers will be most critical in going forward and why. How will the CEO build credibility with the investment community? How will the CEO communicate to employees? How will the CEO manage the transition of the retiring CEO in a dignified and appropriate way? To answer these questions for each stakeholder, the new CEO must decide who the key stakeholders are with whom he or she must form relationships; what his or her goals and desired outcomes are from each relationship (for example, build trust with employees, maintain continuity with suppliers); and how he or she can communicate this agenda in ways that have the most impact. Coaches help new CEOs build an agenda for each stakeholder, and they add value by raising these issues, forcing a dialogue between the old and new CEO, and helping the new CEO craft an agenda for each stakeholder.

Specify Behaviors for Each Stakeholder

A point of view that does not result in behavior is pointless. The most challenging, valuable, and scarce asset for the incoming CEO is time. Everyone will want to be on his or her calendar. The incoming CEO must be disciplined in scheduling his or her calendar. Of course, many events, such as board meetings and shareholder meetings, are mandated. Other events must occur, but there is flexibility as to *when* they occur; customer and supplier visits, investor relations meetings, and top management team meetings fall into this category. Finally, some stakeholders might be overlooked if they are not scheduled, such as employees, personal time, and family time. Calendars must remain flexible, yet provide a disciplined method for the incoming CEO to use as he or she invests time.

For one CEO transition, we prepared a four-quarter calendar depicting which stakeholder would receive CEO attention each quarter. The first step was to identify required and expected meetings, then manage the CEO's calendar to make sure that each stakeholder received adequate attention. Using this framework, she shared with her marketing people the fact that she had fifteen days in a particular quarter to spend with customers, and she invited them to help her make sure she used the time wisely. The marketing department appreciated the opportunity to leverage the CEO's valuable time with important current and future customers.

One of the most critical and immediate issues for most new CEOs is the transition of the former CEO. The incoming CEO is the only person who can help the former CEO leave with dignity. One type of transition might include an employee or customer tour, on which the former CEO gives and receives thanks for the work performed. Although this type of event may seem perfunctory, it allows employees to experience the important endings and beginnings of the new regime. In one company, the incoming CEO founded a scholarship for the retiring CEO at his alma mater, which meant a great deal to the retiring CEO and sent a strong message to the rest of the company about how the new CEO would treat people.

Coaches of CEO transitions who advance ideas into behaviors add value. They force the new CEO to realize that he or she will have more demands on his or her time than resources; they help the new CEO prioritize and sequence activities that will have the largest impact; and they create a relationship plan that helps the new CEO set and deliver an agenda.

Conclusion

I chose CEO transition coaching as the topic of this chapter because it is a critical time for any firm, when the old melds into the new and when significant changes may be made. The stakeholder logic that is used to create the plan for the CEO transition may be applied to other management transitions, such as a new plant manager, department head, or functional director. In any case, the coach who recognizes this transition, intervenes with sound frameworks and questions, and forces honest dialogue is in a position to add enormous value. Transitions occur more quickly; former CEOs leave the firm with dignity; new CEOs have the impact they desire; and overall, the firm makes progress.

About the Contributor

Dave Ulrich, a professor at the School of Business at the University of Michigan, was named by *Business Week* as one of the world's top ten educators in management and the top educator in human resources. He is the author of the best-selling book *Human Resource Champions* and the co-author of *Results-Based Leadership* (both from Harvard Business School Press). Dave is also co-author of *Organizational Capability: Competing from the Inside Out* and *The Boundaryless Organization: Breaking the Chains of Organization Structure.*

Dave is a member of the PROVANT advisory board. He has served on the editorial boards of four publications and was editor of *Human Resource Management Journal* 1990–1999. His current research involves transformational leadership and organization theory.

CHAPTER SEVENTEEN

THE COACH-LEADERSHIP MOMENT

James A. Belasco

Everyone talks about being a coach rather than a director. Business cards sprout, like crocuses in the spring, with the job title "Head Coach" emblazoned on them. But what does a coach-leader do? Read on for some insight.

Welcome to the Tennis Match

They'd been hard at it for several hours, so involved that the scheduled break time came and went with hardly a movement of the chairs. The walls were plastered with butcher paper on which were scrawled "Opportunities," "Threats," and "Possibilities," the product of all those hours of brainstorming and heated discussion. Now stillness filled the room. Seven pairs of eyes turned toward the slight Chinese man who sat at one corner of the note-and-cup-strewn walnut table. The question hung like putrid cigarette smoke in a bar, "All right, George, what do we do?"

Well, there it is; the fuzzy little ball so deftly tapped into George's court. He sees it bounce toward him in slow motion. Now what? Welcome to *the coach-leader moment.*

I was midwife for the unfolding drama. George's electronic components business rang up $7 million in sales last year, up from $2 million three years ago. He saw lots of opportunity to grow to $12 million in the coming year and to $50 million within five years. George saw what he had to do. He hired several new managers, expanded his facilities, and set a vision for aggressive growth.

By lunchtime the table groaned under the weight of all the opportunities they'd uncovered. The "To Do" agenda couldn't have been accomplished in a billion-dollar organization. There was clearly too much on this small company's plate. Having surfaced the opportunities and threats, the seven members of the management team turned to George to decide which opportunities they would pursue. George knew the match would be a series of classic *coach-leader moments,* each proceeded by the question, "Now what do we do, boss?"

The Bobby Riggs Response

Engaging the Racquet and the Heart

We anticipated this moment. It happens many times a day in the life of most leaders. The ball ends up in your court. Everyone watches carefully to see whether you make the decision or engage others in making the decision. It's the classic play that reveals your view of your role in this very serious team sport. It's a test. It's the *coach-leader moment.*

I've learned to use the Bobby Riggs lob approach in these coach-leader moments. Bobby Riggs built a very successful tennis career by mastering the art of the lob. Rather than trying to overpower his opponent with the speed of his serve or the power of his backhand (both of which were very ordinary), Riggs lobbed the ball back to his opponent and let him make the unforced error. He won lots of games with this strategy.

George knew about the Bobby Riggs approach. He was ready for the question. He paused, allowing the silence to clear the air and set the stage. Turning to his controller, the most junior member of the staff, he asked, "Melly, what do you think are the most important items for us to pursue?"

The awkward stillness was broken only by the shuffling of feet and the shifting of chairs. After what seemed like an eternity—but likely was only 45 seconds—Melinora artfully passed the ball back to George, "I don't know, George. You know this business better than any of us. What do you think we ought to do?"

Bap! The racket made contact. George was steadfast. "Anybody want to help Melly decide? How about you, Jack?" George asked, turning to his executive vice president. Not being the shy and retiring type, Jack rushed the net. Bap! The room sprang alive with conversation. Lunchtime came and went unnoticed. The "To Do" list shrank to a more manageable size.

Using Questions to Engage People in the Business of the Business

The lesson: *coach-leaders engage people in weighing alternatives and making tough decisions.* Opportunities always outnumber resources. There's always more to do than there is time to do it. Coaching leaders engage others in making tough choices. Coach-leadership—engaging people—can come from anywhere in the organization. You don't have to be the CEO. Sure, the CEO engages from the top, but every individual from the shop floor to the back office can engage people in the business of the business. Being a coach-leader is a matter of spirit, not spotlight; a function of purpose, not position.

More than Just Questions

Make no mistake, coach-leaders don't *just* ask questions. Coach leadership is not a passive activity. George knew his marketplace. He saw what he thought were the best opportunities, but he wanted more knowledge on the table to make the best decision. George knew that a team decision would be more enthusiastically executed than a solo decision. He'd read the book. He knew the drill. Engage the people or suffer the consequences of poor implementation.

What else do coach-leaders do, besides ask engaging questions? There are several other critical activities:

Avoiding the Moses Mind-Set

It's About Us—As a People

Coach-leaders are not like Moses going up the mountain, hearing God talk, and getting a vision to tell everyone else. No, coach leadership is *about us, as a people*. Fall in the Moses trap, believing that it's all up to you, and you guarantee failure, coach leadership is about "of, by, and for the people."

Saying Farewell to Superstar, Hello to Dream Team

If you believe you're going to play the superstar and run the whole show, doling out pieces to others, then don't even start. You'll fail. It doesn't matter how bright you are or how energetic you are. It doesn't even matter how much money you're making. You'll fail, because no one can do it alone. Even Moses came to realize that he couldn't do it all himself. The Israeli camp would have shut down had his sagacious father-in-law, Jethro, not helped Moses see the reality of his own limitations.

Moses saw Jethro's wisdom and divided up the work of leadership among key people. In reality and in the future, dream teams will produce the wins. That's the way to the Promised Land.

Getting Out of Your Own Way

A high-profile CEO asked me to stop by for a "chat." The daily business press had chronicled his difficulties and disappointments in gory detail. "It's a much tougher slog than I thought. This group of folks just doesn't move fast. They discuss and discuss and discuss some more. Our market position continues to deteriorate faster than I can react. We've got lots of cash for the short term, but. . ." and his voice trailed off as he stood looking out at the foggy morning.

"Any stars on whom you can depend?" I asked.

"Stars?" he exploded. "Never seen anything like these people—they're like store manikins. I've got to do everything. If I don't do it, it doesn't get done. Strategy is a foreign word around here. Responsibility is unknown.

People talk, but don't execute—and no one cares. I'm no introvert, as you know, but even my temper tantrums don't move them. I'm at my wits' end for what to do. Any suggestions?"

"Polish up your résumé?" I said, smiling.

"Right," he grimaced, "and who'd take me after I've presided over the demise of one of the premier names in our business? Nope, I've got to make this one go. Let me try again. Any suggestions?"

I spent the next two hours scoping out several ways he might engage the several thousand people still in the business. My parting words to him summarized our theme, "At the end of the day, all of these activities will only work if you stop trying to do everything yourself. You need to *get out of your own way.* As long as everyone looks to you—and you believe that you've got to do it by yourself—you're creating the best short-selling opportunity in the market today, and you can't even capitalize on it." Can the leopard change his spots? As they used to say at the Saturday afternoon serials I watched as a kid, "Come back next week and find out."

Unlearn, to Learn Anew

Mort Meyerson thought he knew all there was to know about leadership. After all, he'd had one of the best teachers, Ross Perot, and a very successful track record building EDS into the power it is today. He had his priorities straight. Work came first, second, and third; family, community, and other obligations came after that, if there was time and energy. His leadership system worked. EDS grew at a phenomenal rate and created thousands of employee millionaires. He'd found the mother lodestone. What could be better?

There were a few bumps along the way. Employees often dropped like flies from working seventy to eighty hours a week. Customers often were shortchanged. The hyper-focus on short-term results often hurt the organization in the long term. But the dollars kept rolling in and the stock price kept going up, so it was easy to ignore these minor issues.

When Meyerson became CEO at Perot Systems, he saw the corrosive impact of the emphasis on profit-and-loss to the exclusion of other values. In the April/May, 1996, issue of *Fast Company,* he wrote that everything he thought he knew about leadership was wrong, so he embarked on a new coach-leader strategy. He engaged the people in an extensive information gathering process as a coach, not an executive. Rather than telling them what to do, he'd encourage them to look in the mirror at themselves and each other, rather than at him as the leader. Only by not stepping in all the time, as he had done previously, could he create a collaborative environment in which people could succeed through teamwork.

He also learned that he needed to be accessible. Meyerson replied to thousands of e-mail messages a month. He found that the single most important tool he had to break through the old organization and the old mind-set was e-mail. Through e-mail he could be an instant participant in any part of the organization.

Meyerson learned a new coaching approach to leadership: engaging people by giving up the flowing robes and long white beard of a Moses.

The Agile, Amphibious Coach-Leader Works Above and Below the Water Line

Don't let me mislead you. Coaching leadership does not require a vow of silence. Far from it. Be engaged. But the key word is "engage," not "control." In a crisis, a team of paramedics is more valuable than the solo virtuosity of the world's greatest surgeon.

But when do you control, and when do you contribute? When do you decide, and when do you question? The "high visibility" water line is the dividing line between these two approaches. Participate in topics and issues that are above the water line. Mistakes here cause embarrassment, but are not fatal to the organization. Decisions below the water line, however, are cats of a different color. You still want others to make the below-the-water-line decisions, but you can't afford to allow a bad decision. People might drown.

On decisions above the water line, learn to question, question, question; get out the spotlights and spades and work to make the decision as fact-based as possible. But at the end of the day, like George, move aside on any above-the-water-line decisions. Use the same questioning and searching activities as you did for decisions below the water line. Only redouble your surfacing efforts, because if the group comes up with what you believe to be a wrong decision, you will have to intervene.

It's not an easy call. When do you play the trump card? It'll take the trick, but it often doesn't win the game. I've learned that I lose every time I have to trump someone else's decision. Yet, I can also lose when I take over on a decision below the water line. It takes lots of patience and education to bring out the leadership talents of others, and during the learning process, the casualties can be high.

For instance, in one business I worked hard to narrow the product focus from twenty industries to something smaller. I believed that three was the magic number. Try as I might, I could not get the group to agree to any fewer than six. I bought off on six, hoping that I could come back the next year and narrow it again. Only this time, there was no next year. Heavy losses forced them to abandon major portions of the company's activities. The new leaders of the next corporate reinvention narrowed their focus to three products. My "right" answer came too late for me. There are risks in this engagement game.

In another situation, I moved too quickly. In my specialty chemical venture, the management group wanted to invest heavily in a new product venture. I wasn't convinced that there was a market for the new products, so I vetoed the proposal after long and heated discussions. A competitor launched exactly the same product and swept the market, costing us multiple points of market share. The unspoken "We told you so's" hung around like bad pennies for a long time. It's a judgment call. You win most and lose some.

"Mea Culpas" Clear the Air and Reinforce the Heart Connection

When you do lose—and we all do—call the folks together and declare your fallibility. Apologize for the error, figure out how you can do better next time, and move on. I did that with the specialty chemical management team. They accepted my apology, and we figured out how to counter the competitor's new product with some innovative ideas of our own. Everyone knows that no one, not even the leader, is perfect. It helps to reinforce the heart connection when you remind people of your own fallibility.

Coach-leaders at all levels can stand up and admit a mistake. In their Sept. 7, 1992, issue, *Sports Illustrated* reported the turning point for the Washington Redskins in the early 1990s. It occurred when pass receiver Art Monk, a usually quiet member of the team, stood up and called a mandatory team meeting. The team was in a slump and struggling. Addressing them in dead earnest, Monk told them that everyone, including himself, could play a lot better, and that he was rededicating himself to doing better right now. That simple but powerful admission coming from a star receiver made all the difference. The Redskins beat the Dolphins 42 to 20 the next day, and won all but one game on the way to the play-offs.

It's not only undesirable, but suicidal, to pretend you are infallible in any role you play. You can't romanticize your record—you've made mistakes and witnesses were present. You may as well admit it, or hear about it at an awkward moment from an unexpected source!

Words Are Prophetic: Paint the "Us" Picture

Words paint a picture. Coach-leaders carefully choose their words to paint a Rembrandt that celebrates and honors "us" rather that "I."

For instance, there's a big, big difference between the words "girl" and "woman." One describes an immature, dependent female. The other describes an independent, mature female. Which word picture would you prefer if you were a thirty-seven-year-old CFO of a Fortune 20 company? A woman we know told us of the following personal experience.

She's earned an M.D. and a Ph.D. and is the president of a start-up company looking for venture capital funding. The venture capitalists are due at 2 P.M. She's pacing the entry hall anxiously awaiting their arrival. At 2:05 the three male venture capitalists hurry through the door, led by the senior partner. He takes off his coat, gives it to her and says, "Here, girl, please tell Dr. Smyth that we're here. And I'd like some coffee, black with one sugar."

She hangs up the coat, gets him the coffee, and offers it to him with the words, "Here you are, boy. Dr. Smyth at your service."

"Maybe it was his guilt, but it was the easiest $7 million we ever raised," Dr. Smyth told us.

Words paint a picture. Be certain they paint the picture you want.

So, there you have it: ask engaging "What do you think?" questions; drop the Moses mind-set; radar out the water line in your activity and adjust your activities accordingly; prepare for the inevitable mea culpas; and watch your language. It's easy to write about, and hopefully easy to read. It's just very hard to do. But it must be done, so let's get on with it.

About the Contributor

James A. Belasco is a professor of management at San Diego State University and the founder and CEO of a global software and service firm. An experienced consultant, he has worked with such companies as AT&T, Royal Dutch Shell, McDonnell Douglas, Frito-Lay, BMW, and Heineken Beer.

Jim is a dynamic speaker on topics of strategy, leadership, change, empowerment, and customer service, and a successful entrepreneur and coach-leader in specialty chemicals and computer software companies. He is the author of nine books, including the bestseller *Teaching the Elephant to Dance: Empowering Change in Your Organization.* His newest book is entitled *Soaring with the Phoenix: Renewing the Vision, Reviving the Spirit, Recreating the Success of Your Organization.*

CHAPTER EIGHTEEN

LEARNING STRATEGIES FOR NEWLY APPOINTED LEADERS

Julie M. Johnson

Congratulations! You've just been promoted. While you envision exciting challenges and expanded responsibilities, your new boss delights in your enthusiasm. Hopes are high. Unfortunately, no one is talking about defining goals or setting benchmarks, because everyone is basking in a kind of glow. In an environment in which executives can afford only the briefest of honeymoon periods, however, you'll need a well-planned strategy for taking charge of your new position.

The Pressure to Measure Up

Whether you are a newly appointed chief executive officer or sales manager, you are expected to get up to speed fast. As an executive coach, I am frequently called in to help leaders manage their job transitions. Quality initiatives and the current "lean-and-mean" climate have produced a demand for strong, measurable results in short time frames. The pressure is greatest at the top. Shareholders and boards are subjecting the performance of CEOs to closer quantitative scrutiny than ever before. No wonder many newly appointed leaders fall short and fail fast.

The High Rate and Cost of Failure

When someone assumes a new or different leadership role today, he or she has about a forty percent chance of demonstrating disappointing performance, voluntarily leaving the position, or being terminated within twelve to eighteen months (Betof and Harrison, 1996). In addition, an American Management Association study revealed that nearly twenty-two percent of employers surveyed had, in the past two years, fired a professional or manager after he or she was in the position for less than three months (Betof and Harrison, 1996). Failure is costly both to the executive and to the organization. The more senior the executive, the higher the cost. A recent survey of why newly appointed leaders fail (Manchester Consulting, 1997) shows that executives often derail because they don't manage relationships well:

- eighty-two percent fail to build partnerships and teamwork with subordinates and peers;
- fifty-eight percent are confused or unclear about what is expected of them; and
- fifty percent lack the required internal political savvy.

Mastering the Soft Skills

What gets you into a new position won't necessarily keep you there. As shown in Figure 18.1, although technical skills may have accounted in large part for your past achievements, they may not be the key to your success going forward from a professional to an executive position. The higher your position in an organization, the more important the personal skills, such as listening and empathy.

As part of his inquiry into the qualities that make a strong leader, Daniel Goleman (1998) analyzed competency models from 188 companies. He found that emotional intelligence played an "increasingly important role at the highest levels in a company, where differences in technical skills are of negligible importance." When he compared "star performers with average ones in senior leadership positions, nearly ninety percent of the difference in

FIGURE 18.1.   CHANGING REQUIREMENTS FOR SUCCESS

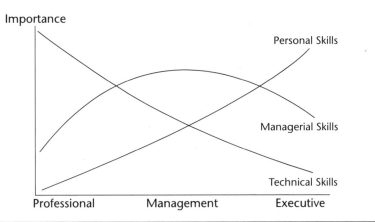

Reprinted from *Preventing Derailment: What to Do Before It's Too Late* by Michael M. Lombardo and Robert W. Eichinger. Copyright © 1989 Center for Creative Leadership.

their profiles was attributable to emotional intelligence factors." The five components of emotional intelligence, as defined by Goleman, are *self-aware-ness, self-regulation, motivation, empathy,* and *social skill* (Goleman, 1998, p. 95).

Take the case of the young derivatives trader who has experienced a meteoric rise through the ranks of a blue-chip Wall Street firm. This "Master of the Universe" had successfully managed a small, close-knit group of traders. Thanks to his stellar financial results and keen understanding of financial markets, he has just been promoted. In his new role, he has cross-functional responsibility for three hundred traders and salespeople. To succeed in the weeks and months ahead, he must shift away from his analytical and technical skill base. Winning the full support of his direct reports and other key stakeholders will demand softer skills (for example, the ability to build relationships and leverage influence across the organization).

A Proactive Approach to Effective Relationships

Because you cannot count on your organization to guide you in your new role, you must proactively manage your own transition. That means creating strategies for managing your expectations, as well as those of your boss and your team. By initiating open dialogues about the issues of greatest importance to key stakeholders in your success (for example, peers, internal clients, and boards of directors), you will strengthen the relationships that are vital to achieving your objectives.

Imagine a newly appointed CEO, selected because of his outstanding financial advisory skills. Having enjoyed a long, successful career consulting with clients and making sound recommendations, he assumes that his financial abilities will carry him through this new position. Unfortunately, this person fails to recognize the importance of building relationships with his staff, as well as with the board of directors. Uncomfortable at board meetings, he falls back on technical strengths—speaking in numbers. The staff feels micro-managed, and the board members have trouble following him. This person is on the fast track to derailment. In order to better understand the expectations of the board and staff, he should have invested time up front in building relationships, managing expectations, and learning how to delegate at the executive level.

In the remainder of this chapter, you'll find learning tools to get anyone who is newly promoted off to a running start in the right direction. They are designed for the following purposes:

- To help you move more effectively into your new leadership role;
- To provide a systematic framework for taking charge, getting information, and setting expectations;
- To illuminate the type of situation you are entering (startup, turnaround, and so forth); and
- To force you, your boss, and your team to be more thoughtful about business and transitional issues.

Managing Up

You may think your new boss is going to spell out for you the goals and business issues critical to your success, but that isn't necessarily the case. There can be many reasons for this lack of clarity. Often the most important information is not surfaced soon enough, so don't be afraid to push for definition and to establish your own benchmarks for your performance and progress.

Consider the operations executive who has been promoted into a much larger position. A highly capable project manager with strong technical skills, she really "knows her stuff." Yet, she is about to face some unanticipated challenges. Her boss, for example, does not understand or appreciate her technical competency and talent for detail. In a culture that values style over substance, he is primarily concerned that she demonstrate visible enthusiasm. To satisfy her boss and succeed in the culture, she will have to delegate more and shift her skill set. It's a big stretch, but possible with the tools below.

Learning Tools: Your Boss's Expectations

- Identify your key clients, customers, and stakeholders.
- Define what you are held accountable for in your new role in terms of:
  —People
  —Financial Resources
  —Results
- Understand what your boss really wants from you. For example, he or she may say: "I want you to implement change," but the underlying meaning is: "I want you to cut the dead weight in the organization."
- Know the expectations of the board (if you are a CEO).
- Determine a timetable and methodology for getting feedback from your boss. For example, schedule meetings with your boss to evaluate your progress in three months and six months.

Building Your Team

To streamline the assimilation of newly appointed leaders, major corporations such as Ford Motor Company, Exxon, Citibank, GE, and J. P. Morgan are using a highly interactive approach originally developed by the U.S. Army. One company calls this process "Jump Start." According to Bill Hunt, program manager, Organization and Staffing, GE Power Systems, this intensive getting-to-know-you program "reduces by three to six months the time it normally takes to build an effective team. It's the best

way to iron out rumors, to confront the issues that arise with a new manager, and to create a climate of openness" (*Fast Company,* 1998).

As a result, valuable time is not wasted speculating about who you
are and how to work with you most effectively. Everyone quickly gets information that might otherwise take six months or a year to come to light
or that might not surface at all. You'll learn what people are wondering
about, in terms of everything from revenue targets to organizational rumors about you. The process of getting acquainted is systematically condensed into six to eight hours of meetings.

Imagine an investment banker with an impressive track record. He
has a strong reputation as a fix-it, turnaround expert in various parts of
the organization. As a result of the CEO's trust in him and confidence in his
ability to manage people, he is appointed head of the private banking division. In this new position, he is faced with learning a new business and managing a team that doesn't know him. To make matters even more difficult,
many of his reports feel they should have been considered for his position.
The perception is that he is an outsider and one of the CEO's favorites. In
order to tackle this new role, he must first clear the air and dispel false perceptions. Armed with the right tools, listed below, he can do just that.

Learning Tools: Your Team's Expectations

- Work with an outside facilitator to create a framework for you to develop
  relationships with your entire team.
- Ask your team to get together as a group with a facilitator to generate
  questions for you, to provide information about the themselves, and to
  outline the key business challenges you'll face together. The questions
  might include:
  —What do we already know about the manager?
  —What do we not know about the manager, but would like to know?
  —What do we want most from the manager?
  —What does the manager need to know about us as a team?
  —What are the major business issues the manager will face in the next
   six to twelve months?
  —What are your specific suggestions for addressing these issues?

- Have the facilitator brief you on the collective input from your team.
- Meet with your team and the facilitator to respond to the questions and information they provided. For example, your reports may have heard rumors that you fire people indiscriminately. This format gives you the opportunity to address their concerns in a group setting, so no one is confronting you alone.
- Right after that meeting, review with the facilitator the commitments made and actions to be taken.
- Six months later, ask your team to provide the facilitator with an assessment of its functioning as a group, how you're fitting in, what you're doing best, what the team would like you to do more of (and less of), and what you're not doing that you should be doing. Then meet with your team and the facilitator to respond to that feedback.

Knowing Thyself

Self-awareness and self-regulation can be invaluable assets to the newly promoted leader. According to Goleman (1998), people who are self-aware "have a firm grasp of their capabilities and are less likely to set themselves up to fail. They know, too, when to ask for help."

People capable of self-regulation have "a propensity for reflection and thoughtfulness; comfort with ambiguity and change; and integrity—an ability to say no to impulsive urges" (Goleman, 1998, p. 99).

Take the case of the newly appointed general counsel, promoted from the ranks of the legal department. She quickly recognizes that managing an entire group requires skills that were not necessary when she managed a small team of legal specialists. In addition, her peer group has changed. It now consists of other business unit heads and the staff officers of the corporation. How can she gain a clearer understanding of her own strengths and weaknesses, foster trusting relationships with new peers, and develop a realistic picture of her radically different role and context? Here are some tools that can help.

Learning Tools: Your Own Expectations

- Meet with the departing manager to explore key learnings and lessons of experience, to gain insight into the power structure and informal networks, and to identify sources of information/data that can be most useful to you. Spend your first few weeks developing trusting relationships.
- Exchange information with peers and colleagues. Information is power. Be generous with information that isn't necessarily going to benefit you, so that when you need information from someone else, he or she won't assume it's self-serving. Share not only technical information, but the organizational information that helps build trust with other people.
- Watch out for your natural human tendency to fall back on the technical skill that may have won you the promotion.
- Recognize the significance and importance of the fact that people who were once your peers are now direct reports.
- Realize that you are in a new role. Reflect on your strengths and developmental needs in terms of your past and current roles. Consider what might derail your career moving forward.
- *Seek feedback!*

The simple tools and approaches I've outlined here can assist you in avoiding the pitfalls that derail many newly appointed leaders. Invest some time and effort up front in managing your new boss, building your new team, and taking an honest look at yourself in your new context. Understand that the softer skills become more important as you move up; use them to build the inner qualities and organization-wide relationships crucial to your success.

About the Contributor

Julie M. Johnson is a senior executive coach who helps companies improve business results by maximizing the performance of key individuals. Focusing on leadership, management style, and organizational change, she consults on management succession, high-potential and leadership needs assessments, management of executive transitions into new leadership positions, and resolution of interpersonal business-related conflicts.

Julie brings twenty years of human resource management expertise to each assignment. Her experience encompasses industries as diverse as investment banking, brokerage, cable television, consumer products, construction, retailing, and chemicals, as well as major law firms. A partial client list includes Aetna, Ann Taylor, BASF, Bayer, Bristol-Myers-Squibb, Chase Manhattan Bank, CitiGroup, Ernst and Young, Fleet Bank, Ford Motor Company, Hearst Corporation, International *Herald Tribune*, Lucent Technologies, J.P. Morgan, the *New York Times*, Pitney-Bowes, Rockefeller & Company, The Rockefeller Foundation, Shearman & Sterling, State Street Bank, Union Camp, and Union Carbide.

Julie is a founder of the Reid Group in Fairfield, CT; prior to that she spent four years as practice head of executive coaching at The Strickland Group, she was vice president of executive development at Merrill Lynch, vice president of executive education at the Merrill Lynch Executive Institute, manager of human resource planning at General Foods, and manager, management development, at Warner Amex.

Julie began her career as placement director at Stanford Law School. She then spent three years at the Vinson & Elkins law firm, where she created a system for recruiting, staffing, and organizing attorney offices that became a standard for law firms across the country.

Recently, Julie published a case commentary in the *Harvard Business Review*, "When a New Manager Stumbles, Who Is at Fault?" She holds a B.A. in liberal arts from Carnegie Mellon University, an M.A. in social psychology and counseling from Southern Methodist University, and an M.B.A. from the Harvard Business School.

CHAPTER NINETEEN

CONTINUOUS IMPROVEMENT IN PLACE OF TRAINING

Liz Thach and Tom Heinselman

For the last fifty years, our society has been steeped in the classical methods of learning through formal classroom environments and experiences. We have experienced it at the elementary, secondary, and university levels, and it has continued into the workforce as formal classroom training and weekend seminars. Only in the last few years have organizations acknowledged other constructs as better than the classroom for learning. One of these newer constructs is *coaching*.

The purpose of this chapter is to explore the cultural shift from formal learning constructs to a new era, in which traditional classroom training is combined with ongoing coaching to create an atmosphere of continuous learning and improvement. We will begin with a brief review of our current state of leadership development and then move into descriptions of how the new shift is being applied in the areas of medicine, sports, and management. Finally, we will provide a robust coaching model for leadership development.

The Current State of Leadership Development

In general, our approach to leadership development has been similar to our haphazard approach to the development of parents. In our society, some parents pursue development and some do not; some parents do not want to be bothered with mastering good parenting skills, but still want to be parents (that is, leaders of children). For those of us who have been parents, there is unanimous agreement that good parenting involves the mastery of a particular set of skills needed in few, if any, other endeavors.

In many organizations, leadership development follows a similar course, one that relegates leadership to a low priority position on the skill ladder. We approach leadership as if anyone can do it, as if the skills are acquired by osmosis. Why is it that while there is enough time to strategize and make decisions, and there is certainly enough time to set business goals, review plans, and inspect the numbers, there is seldom enough time to make leadership development a priority? It seems that we believe leadership effectiveness has nothing to do with making a profit. Picture yourself walking by your manager's office and observing your boss reading a book on leadership. Would your response be, "Why doesn't he (or she) get to work? What a waste of time. Doesn't he (or she) already know what he's doing?"

In businesses in which there are formal leadership development programs, many are still based on traditional models. Each leader attends the required two weeks of training each year, then checks off the development box on performance appraisals and succession planning forms. Often, rounds of golf and evening cocktail parties accompany the training, and leaders completing the sessions comment on how valuable the networking was. But what about the learning?

Some progressive organizations, however, have begun to put their time and resources into developing excellent leaders. These companies value training and development so much that they have put their developmental funding into a corporate account to preclude any division from using it to cut costs. Like these companies, all organizations must see leadership development as an area critical for success. Leadership development must be made a priority, or it will never follow the robust model that is necessary for mastery.

Today, an increasing number of organizations are assessing the impact of developmental activities on leader effectiveness, and a few organizations are changing the cultural meaning of leadership development and how it occurs (that is, continuous learning versus a once-a-year experience). Let's examine how these organizations are doing this, and how they combine training with ongoing coaching.

New Approaches to Learning Via Coaching

In the Medical Field.   One of the most fascinating approaches to this new trend in learning can be found in the field of medicine. For many years, medical schools offered the traditional four years of medical school and two years of residency to train doctors. Now, many schools have only two years of formal classroom training to teach the basic medical concepts and to build a frame of reference for the discipline. In the third year of medical school, students are placed in a hospital, where they continue their learning under the guidance of specialized coaches, "residents". Under the direction of these residents, medical students learn by doing. The residents not only accelerate learning for the students, but also keep their failures small and inconsequential. After graduation, the student then goes on to complete the traditional two years of residency (coaching).

In the Sports Field.   Another example of the new approach to learning comes from the field of sports, but in actuality it is not so new. Think about the drafted quarterback in professional football. This is the classic coaching-mentoring relationship. Seldom does the rookie quarterback play in a real game. The quarterback takes some classroom training, and there is some textbook work. The rookie must begin by knowing the offensive plays on paper, and most of his learning comes in practice. Typically, the rookie runs the opponent's offense as the team prepares for next week's game. On occasion, the rookie will run the home team offense in practice to fine-tune the execution of the game plan.

A coach is responsible for helping the rookie learn, grow, and become a more effective quarterback, but there is an element of preparation that even the coach cannot supply. That element comes from the starting quarterback, who acts as a mentor to the rookie. This happens for several reasons: (1) it is expected of the starter, that is, it's in the job description; (2) someone did it for the starter and the legacy is passed on; (3) if the starter is injured the rookie may be in the game, and the outcome of the game and the season may ultimately depend on the rookie.

In the Management Field.   Finally, we have encountered several corporations in the last few years that have adopted this new trend of continuous leadership development through coaching. They have done this for several reasons: (1) traditional classroom methods were not providing the desired results as quickly as needed; (2) the accelerated work pace and hectic schedules made it difficult to spend time in classroom training; and (3) much of the new research in leadership development suggests that eighty percent of leadership development occurs on the job (Morgan, 1992), often through interactions with others, such as a coach or mentor. These corporations did not throw away traditional learning methods—instead, they supplemented them with one-on-one executive coaching over a period of six months to a year, depending on the specific developmental needs of the leader. With this combination, many were able to demonstrate measurable results in terms of lasting skill-knowledge development and progress in leadership interactions.

The leadership development model that follows describes the key components required for implementing a robust system that utilizes coaching as a core process. It allows organizations to move from "learning-as-an-event" to *learning as a continuous improvement process* and part of the fabric of organization life.

A Robust Coaching Model for Leadership Development

The critical success factor of any leadership development model is a commitment to learning on the part of the leader. However, there are many obstacles to achieving this commitment. So before we examine the model, let's review why personal commitment to learning sometimes fails:

- The person believes there is no room for a new priority and might say, "My plate is full and I just don't have the time for one more task."
- The person is working on the wrong issue, sometimes even on symptoms of a larger issue, so efforts to improve seem futile and are soon abandoned.
- The person is working on something because he or she thinks it *should* be done, rather than because he or she desires to make the change and believes it will return positive benefits.
- The person chooses a developmental goal that is too ambitious; progress is difficult and efforts to change are abandoned.

- The person does not have a good structure or process for making the change.
- The person does not accept personal accountability for making the change.
- The person takes a "hit-and-miss" approach rather than consistent action.
- The person is unable to measure progress and, therefore, is unable to celebrate small victories, becomes frustrated, and abandons the developmental effort.

The more robust leadership development model we recommend can positively impact several of the above lapses and failures. Organizational interventions or different personal approaches can impact others. We will suggest some possibilities for each of these areas in the rest of this chapter.

Coaching Model for Leadership Development

Our coaching model for leadership development, shown in Figure 19.1, is modeled on the cycle of continuous improvement. The coach is available to assist the leader through the process steps, but once the leader has grasped and ingrained it as a natural ability for continuous learning, the coach will gently exit and the leader will take full responsibility for his or her development. There may be times when the coach re-enters for specific learning situations or to provide encouragement, but the goal is to have the leader operate independently of the coach.

The coach can be an external source or someone internal to the organization who has the proper experience and training to be a coach. In either case, the coach must be someone whom the leader can trust to work with him or her over the long term.

Examining the Model Phases

As illustrated in Figure 19.1, our coaching model for leadership development has four major phases.

Assessment. It begins with an *assessment* of leadership skills. This can be accomplished through a variety a means: traditional assessment center;

FIGURE 19.1. THE COACHING MODEL
FOR LEADERSHIP DEVELOPMENT

360° feedback; the coach conducting interviews and providing feedback; or any other method that results in quantitative and qualitative data that the leader can use to select developmental areas on which to focus. The idea here is to set a base, or benchmark, of current leadership competency that can be measured to determine progress. Regardless of the method used, the coach is involved in debriefing the assessment data with the leader and assisting him or her in identifying developmental areas.

Developmental Plan.   The next phase is the creation of a *developmental plan* or contract. Here two things are critical. First, the leader selects only *one or two high-impact areas* on which to focus. This enables him or her to have a better chance of achieving the developmental goals given the hectic work schedules of many leaders. Second, the leader is free to choose the goal. We call this *volition.* If one does not desire or choose to deal with a goal, the probability is lower that there will be any sustained effort over time. A mindset of "I don't want to do this, but I suppose I must since everyone is saying that I must" is generally a killer to goal attainment. One will unconsciously sabotage the effort or, at a minimum, will engage in avoidance behavior.

Here's the tough side of goal choice. Some leaders receive feedback regarding an area of leadership that, while not desirable, must be dealt with. For example, suppose a leader receives feedback that he or she "shot the messenger" when being given bad news or critical feedback. This is an area that many leaders would avoid, because it's not fun or easy to deal with. At the same time, reasonable people know it's important that others feel safe, not threatened, in being the bearer of bad news. Even though this "bad" news could prevent failure, embarrassment, and needless wasted effort, it's still not fun or desirable to deal with it.

In such a case, the leader must identify the personal benefits dealing with the issue. In the above example, a leader might increase commitment by focusing on the importance of early warning. In the execution of a business plan, the ability to adjust quickly certainly enhances the chances of success. The coach assists the leader through this process, applying a mixture of support, validation, and "tough love," to help the leader identify development areas that will make an impact and around which the leader has some passion and energy.

Public Announcement.   The third phase is the *public announcement.* The literature describes this as "publicness" or the degree to which others are aware of the leader's goal. Most people have a need to be viewed by others as consistent in their words and actions. If one does not tell anyone else about a planned goal, then it is relatively easy to release the goal. However, if others know of the goal it is more difficult to back away from, because one would risk appearing inconsistent and irrational to others.

There may be some developmental goals that should be kept personal (for example, issues around integrity, ethics, honesty, or respect for others), but most developmental goals should be made public to those who observe and interact with the leader frequently. Making the goals public offers two benefits to the leader. First, it raises his or her commitment to the announced course of action. Second, it lays a foundation for periodic follow-up conversations with the observers to assess progress on the goal. The coach will assist the leader in planning how to make the "public announcement," but in most cases it will be through informal one-on-one conversations tacked onto the end of other business agendas. An example might be: "Do you have a minute to talk? I wanted to thank you for providing me with feedback on my leadership skills and let you know that I have identified two areas to work on. . . . This is what I'm thinking of doing. . . . Do you have other suggestions for me?"

Implementation. Next comes the *implementation* step, which is comprised of *developmental activities* and *informal follow-up* with feedback participants. Implementation is customized to match the identified developmental areas. It may include attending classroom training, but the majority of it will be improvements in on-the-job interactions with other employees. The coach is available to meet with the leader face-to-face as needed—often in regularly scheduled monthly conversations. In addition to support, encouragement, and occasional prodding, the coach may take on the role of tutor and provide tools and tips to help the leader progress on developmental goals. The coach will also follow up with e-mail messages, phone calls, and other supporting mechanisms to help keep the leader focused on integrating development into his or her everyday thinking. In this way, it slowly becomes second nature, and a culture of continuous leadership development begins to permeate the organization.

Follow-up with feedback participants is also part of the implementation phase. We recommend that this be done every sixty days or so, and that it be an informal conversation—much like the public announcement. A sample conversation might be: "Do you have a minute to talk? I wanted to follow up with you on my leadership development. As you know, I'm working on the two areas of. . . . Have you noticed any progress in these areas? Do you have any other suggestions for me to improve in this area? Thanks for your feedback. I know I'm not perfect, but I really do want to continue to work on these two areas to improve my leadership skills." By having these quick follow-up conversations, the leader is keeping the issue alive and communicating to people that he or she is trying to improve. This helps create the impression in peoples' minds that this leader is serious about leadership development.

Then finally, the leader begins the cycle again with another *assessment*. Here the leader can either repeat the same assessment process he or she used at the beginning or do a mini-assessment focusing only on the developmental areas on which they have been working. The coach will assist them in determining the best approach and the best time in which to complete the assessment. In general, people need to see a leader working on developmental areas for at least six months before they are willing to say the leader has improved, but in some cases this period of time can be shorter or longer. Regardless of the length or timing of the assessment, the results should be reviewed carefully. There should be a time of *celebration* for areas in which the leader has achieved some successes. There should also be a reintegration of some of the areas into the leader's *updated development plan*. Development does not stop just because the leader improved in a few areas. The coach must encourage the leader to identify new areas to work on and also must encourage him or her to proceed on the journey of continuous leadership learning.

The Benefits of Coaching

The coaching aspect of the above model has many benefits. These are as follows:

- *Coaching allows learning to be tailored to the leader.* The classic training model holds time constant and has varied learning. That is, every person goes through the same structured experiences that last for the same amounts of time and happen at the same intervals. A learning model (such as the coaching process), on the other hand, holds learning constant and varies the time. A leader acquires some particular competence, even though more time may be required for some leaders than for others. Additionally, the competence that is appropriate for one leader may not be appropriate for another leader.
- *Coaching allows the methods to be varied according to the needs of the leader.* The classic training model provides the same experiences for everyone. A learning model can vary the methods and experiences depending on the leader and his or her needs.
- *Coaching allows the teacher/mentor to be tailored to the learner.* In the classic training model, one instructor/facilitator handles the needs of all student leaders. Typically, the instructor handles the instruction process based on what he or she does best, not what is the best learning method for the student. In a learning model, one can tune the coach/mentor/ consultant to the needs of the student, much like a patient would use medical consultants depending on the nature of an illness.

Organizational Interventions to Support Leadership Development

It is not only the relationship between the individual leader and coach that makes leadership development successful. Several organizational interventions support the ongoing process and really make the coaching model pay off in terms of business results. The organization must see to the following:

- *Leadership Development Definitions.* The organization must formally define what constitutes leadership development, paint clear expectations, prescribe any stand-alone experiences, workshops, or seminars only as an element of a long-range development plan, and ensure that such experiences have purpose well beyond checking a "completed" box.
- *A Systems Approach.* The organization must integrate leadership development into performance and human resources systems so they make sense and paint a seamless picture. Examples include staffing and recruiting, succession planning, performance appraisal, and retention programs.
- *Accountability.* The organization must establish accountability for the continuing pursuit of developmental plans in the same sense as they do for job performance. Developmental discussions should be integrated into performance reviews and evaluations, along with job performance.
- *Continuous Learning Philosophy.* The organization must hold leaders accountable for following a pre-determined process. It is important to think about "following" the process versus "completing" the process. As in Deming's PDCA (Plan—Do—Check—Act) process (Deming, 1982) of continuous quality improvement, one never completes it. It is a way of life; it's how one goes about work. The organization must build a picture for leaders that leadership development is not to be viewed as another task to accomplish, but rather a different way to go about work. Learning must be seen as a life process, not a task.
- *Balance.* The organization must help leaders see that neither personal nor professional life is broken into three boxes labeled "learning," "working," and "playing." Life is always all three at the same time.

- *Measurement.* The organization will require periodic mini-surveys so that leaders can assess their progress toward becoming more effective leaders. The assessment results can also be tallied confidentially to provide measurable return on investment (ROI) data for the organization to determine the payback on the leadership development system.

Concluding Thoughts

As our society delves further into the age of information technology and the speed of work and time accelerates beyond anything imagined fifty years ago, it is interesting to see how our learning needs have shifted from the collective classroom format to a cry for one-on-one coaching. Many would say that the craziness of our work schedules precludes us from attending traditional training; others theorize that with all of our technological speed—where whole days can be spent productively in the isolated parallel work universe of e-mail, voice mail, computer programs, and teleconferences—we now feel more sharply the elemental human need for face-to-face interaction. At any rate, leaders crave the personal relationships that coaches provide, because the coaching context is not only a place for competency development, but also a touchstone to be human again.

About the Contributors

Liz Thach is director of leadership and organization development for MediaOne Group, a $7.4 billion broadband and international wireless business based in Denver, Colorado. She currently has over sixteen years' experience in the field of human resource development, specializing in international leadership development and the application of communication technology to workplace performance. Her experience encompasses organization development, executive/leadership development, training delivery, change management, instructional systems design, total quality management, distance learning, educational technology/multimedia, adult education, team building, and technical writing.

Prior to joining MediaOne Group, Liz worked for Amoco Corporation, Compaq Computer, and Texas Instruments in managerial positions in learning and organization development. She has worked on projects in over fifteen countries, including Kazakstan, Azerbaijan, England, Norway, Switzerland, the Netherlands, United Arab Emirates, Trinidad, Colombia, Venezuela, Argentina, and Mexico. Liz is an avid writer, who has published twenty-two articles in the field of HRD. She holds a doctorate in HRD from Texas A&M University; an M.A. in organizational communication from Texas Tech University; and a B.A. in English (summa cum laude) from the College of Notre Dame in Belmont, California, as well as a semester abroad at Warnborough College in Oxford, England.

Tom Heinselman is a principal in Keilty, Goldsmith & Company (KGC), one of America's key providers of customized leadership development. He specializes in providing consultation and training services in the areas of leadership development, organizational values, team building, and executive coaching.

Prior to joining KGC, Tom gained first-hand leadership experience as vice president of human resources for a national personnel consulting firm and in various management positions at IBM. His background at IBM includes ten years in direct sales and sales management and six years in human resources, including personnel operations management.

Tom earned his B.S. degree in mathematics from Harding University and his master's degree in mathematics and educational psychology from Ohio University.

CHAPTER TWENTY

RE-GROOVING CRITICAL BEHAVIOR

David Allen

Knowing what to do and doing it automatically are two very different things. We can watch a video, read a book, or attend a seminar that imparts useful information and perspectives; however, much that is required of the new leadership style is not about what we know, but about how we operate when the heat is on. And we often need professional help in real time to instill new behaviors and to attain the enhanced levels at which we want to function.

It's not about what we can spout at the next staff meeting. It's about consistently applied, high-leverage responses and activities that happen when we're on cruise control. It's about what we can be trusted to be *doing* under pressure from the real world. To rapidly make those kinds of permanent changes and enhancements to our lives and work styles, we need models, mentors, and—most importantly—personal coaches with whom we spend real time learning to do what we need to be doing.

As leaders we *want* to work differently, and when we understand *how* we can work differently, we want it to happen *yesterday*. But, self-propelling strategic conduct will seldom occur by itself and certainly does not become second nature quickly.

We can shift our behaviors through will power, but only for a limited time. If you are especially strong-willed, it may take a few days. If you're on a retreat in the mountains, with no phone, fax, or computer, it may take a week. But soon, the intense onslaught of your temporal engagements is back at your door. There are too many things to focus your conscious attention on, and you don't have the personal bandwidth to keep going in the new direction. In other words, you *know* better, but you don't *do* better.

We all have our weak points, and some of those may be in mission-critical or values-critical areas. For example, let's say that not long ago your results-oriented personality was required to help get your company off the ground. Now that same personality is limiting the initiative of your senior team. Or let's say that not long ago your tolerance of incomplete projects was required so that you could stay sane and focused on the company's goals. Now, you're paying the price for agreements others have not kept.

There are many things we all need and want to learn—to give us the edge we want or to unlock the potential we strive to fulfill. One of the two greatest values of a coach in the consultant's role is to give us new and useful points of view. *Perspective* is the slipperiest and most valuable commodity on this planet. We must learn to see "outside the box," and we need to hear non-vested opinions about what we're doing and how we're doing it. This is, and always will be, the value of consultants.

If we want change to happen *now,* and we want it to *stick,* we must put ourselves in the hands of a trainer who coaxes and coaches us through the new behaviors we desire in real time, in the real world. We need and want someone to be the stake in the ground that we can hang on to, someone who will help us get past the deep grooves of our unconscious habits. We need a tether that will hold us steady against past conditioning and the present demands on our lives that distract us from learning new behavior.

The most effective way to change our patterns is to commit to a coach whose job it is to hold us to a focus and a format that helps us retread. It could be a new way to think, a new way to feel, or a new way to act and respond, but if it's a "new way" at all, it's unfamiliar territory for us, and it must be made much more friendly to our basic nervous systems. We want to become "unconsciously competent." We don't want to be burdened or beholden to another person to keep us in line forever. We know that ultimately we need to *do it ourselves,* but we must acknowledge that the path to that freedom is not free.

I have found it useful to review with my clients an old behavioral model that identifies four stages of moving to permanently changed conduct:

1. *Unconscious Incompetence:* "I don't even know that I don't know what I don't know." Many people wander around in the miasma of not realizing that what they don't realize is a problem. They're just in it and basically numb. Pain-aspiration (and therefore change) factor = zero.
2. *Conscious Incompetence:* "I now know where I ought to be and what I ought to be doing, but I don't know how to get myself there or how to get myself to do it." They now know things could and should be different from the way they are, but are not sure how to make them different. "I know that we should be at the cutting edge, facilitating innovation, but what do I do to reach that end this afternoon?" Pain-aspiration factor = variable, depending on the commitment to the new standard. This is the stage people often find themselves in after a great book, seminar, or other educational and eye-opening experience.
3. *Conscious Competence:* "I know now how to make it happen and I know I can do it, but I have to keep reminding myself to stay on track." Pain-aspiration factor = variable, depending on commitment to the new standard and the delta between current reality and that standard. This is tricky ground. We've been to the seminar; we've tried and tested some things ourselves; we've *really* gotten enthused because we know that we can do it and how to get there; but we aren't able to maintain it.
4. *Unconscious Competence:* "I just do it. I only think about it when I *don't* do it, and I then *have* to go do it." This is real motivation, and it happens when you would feel awkward if you *didn't* do it. Of *course* you empty your voice mail and your in-basket every day. Of course your staff is happy and eager to come to work. If they weren't, it would feel too weird—you just don't let that happen.

The challenge in reaching the level of unconscious competence is to frame the subtle behaviors that limit or expand our effectiveness in the world. The first step in meeting this challenge is to find the person or people who have models and formats designed to help re-groove our patterns of thinking and acting. Those leaders who have the confidence to enter this new territory of coaching, who are willing to leverage the best tools in order to restructure their automatic response systems, will be able to create ever greater opportunities for their organizations and for themselves.

About the Contributor

David Allen has more than twenty years' experience as a management consultant, productivity coach, and educator. He has conducted performance enhancement workshops for more than 250,000 professionals, with current ongoing programs in government, aerospace, financial services, retail, and information technology.

As well as being president of the management consulting and training company David Allen & Co., David is also a founding partner of Actioneer, Inc., a San Francisco-based software company.

David has developed and implemented management and productivity programs for such diverse organizations as Microsoft, LL Bean, Lockheed, QVC, Fidelity Investments, Massachusetts General Hospital, and the United States Navy. Having logged thousands of hours individually coaching managers and executives, he has developed a revolutionary, unique system for implementing personal and corporate goals within customized personal systems and organizational structures.

David has published articles in professional journals, and has been featured in both audio and video training programs. He is a regularly featured keynote speaker on the topic of individual and team productivity for many national and governmental organizations, including the National Office Products Association, the Young Presidents' Organization, and the United States Department of Justice.

CHAPTER TWENTY-ONE

CAREER DEVELOPMENT—ANYTIME, ANYPLACE

Beverly Kaye

What does a manager set aside when another project or problem is piled on, and there just isn't time to do everything?

- The calculations for the annual budget process? No way, managers reason. Those have a deadline.
- The weekly meeting with the boss and other unit directors? Not on your life. The boss wouldn't stand for it.
- The negotiations with outside contractors? Not possible. Nobody else really knows how to handle them.
- The activities related to developing employees, such as performance reviews or counseling sessions? Well, maybe. After all, those can wait until things settle down.

Even though most managers readily agree that people are their most important resource, they find it easy to postpone human resource development in favor of other pressing concerns. The career counseling they have been meaning to do slips to the bottom of the mental in-box, right next to performance appraisals and requests for training. Too often, employees find their managers inaccessible. They see their managers infrequently and speak to them even less. When employees do initiate interaction, managers have a way of "tossing it off"—responding to employees' questions and concerns with palliatives like, "Hang in there!" or "Let me think about that."

This isn't because managers don't care about the developmental needs of employees. They know that companies pay a price for dissatisfied workers who find few challenges or career opportunities in their jobs. They understand the costs of having to recruit and train new employees. They understand that high staff turnover cuts productivity. They recognize that career development and counseling create a better "fit" between employees and their jobs, which increases efficiency and elevates morale. But they still don't make employee development a priority. Why? Listen to these typical comments:

- "I know I should sit each employee down for a chat about his or her future here and career in general. That would be ideal. But I have twelve people who report to me directly; then there are dozens under them. We're talking about an enormous task."
- "I guess I'm really wary about raising expectations that we just can't meet, like pay raises and promotions. If we start talking about career goals, we could be opening a Pandora's Box."
- "Those sessions on, 'Let's spend an hour talking about you,' seem so forced. To really counsel my employees, I'd have to be much more skilled in that area. I'm a planner and an organizer, not a counselor."
- "If we're going to get into career development, it has to include everyone. And that would take a lot more time than we have right now. So, at least for the foreseeable future, employees are going to have to deal with career issues on their own."

Just Do It

Contemporary organizational practices rely heavily on managers' abilities to get the most from their employees. But with the ranks of middle managers shrinking, those who remain have more responsibilities and less time to devote to employees' critical developmental needs.

Employees can't put their career needs on hold until managers accumulate the time and talent to offer them comprehensive career guidance. HRD specialists can help managers substantially meet employees' needs by teaching managers to incorporate career development into their day-to-day routines.

Some managers do this naturally—they recognize employees' interests through casual conversation or by observing how employees work. They give feedback that can help workers develop professionally. These managers take advantage of "coachable moments"—opportunities that occur in the context of ongoing work and open the door for valuable, if brief, career counseling. "Coachable moments" help managers address career development within the small amount of time available.

Coachable moments represent an informal, spontaneous opportunity for career development. Coachable moments do not substitute for formal programs and in-depth counseling, but they can produce important results.

To take advantage of coachable moments, managers first need to understand and commit to the need for career development as a way to use human resources productively. To act on that commitment, managers must take three steps: recognize, verbalize, and mobilize.

Managers need to *recognize* opportunities for coachable moments when they occur, picking up on cues from employees whose words and actions indicate an openness to immediate developmental feedback.

Managers need to *verbalize*. They have to take time to talk to employees in a way that helps both parties understand and "check out" developmental options.

Last, managers need to *mobilize*. They should suggest, on the spot, next steps that can help employees develop their careers.

With those three steps, in just a few minutes, a manager can serve as a catalyst for an employee to undertake his or her own enrichment and developmental activities.

Recognize Opportunities

Five common cues from employees can tip off managers to opportunities for "coachable moments."

238 | Coaching for Leadership

An Employee Demonstrates a New Skill or Interest. Lynne, a secretary in the word processing pool, hands her manager a flyer she produced on her computer. It looks almost as good as one that might have come from the company's graphics department. Lynne mentions, "I've been doing some fiddling with that new graphics program and the laser printer."

This type of cue indicates that an employee is taking a crucial step in career development: self-assessment. Most who take this step will not end up in an entirely new career or different job. But with help, by broadening their skills, they can expand their contribution to the organization and gain more satisfaction from their work.

An Employee Seeks Feedback. Marc, a new supervisor, has drafted a detailed proposal for reorganizing tasks in his purchasing unit, including a budget that demonstrates annual cost reductions. Several days after submitting it to his boss, he asks her: "Did you get a chance to check out those figures in the budget I gave you for the new organization?"

An employee who asks for feedback or evaluation might be examining strengths and weaknesses, not just fishing for a pat on the back. This type of cue indicates that an employee is conducting a reality check, the second critical step in career development. When managers recognize these coachable moments, they should relate feedback on the activity to the employee's potential; this helps the employee discover areas to enhance and develop.

An Employee Is Thinking About Change in the Organization. Lindsey, a computer programmer, mentions to her manager, "I heard that the advertising office might develop a slot for its own network-management person. Is advertising growing that fast, or do a lot of departments already have their own network managers?"

When employees show interest in better understanding the organization's structure and development, they might need an opportunity for organization study. Managers can help employees see how their aspirations fit with organizational realities and directions. Employees might use this information to develop a career path that eventually could take them outside their current units; in the meantime, they will add value to their present positions.

An Employee Is Experiencing a Poor Job Fit. Barry, a payroll supervisor, recently has become the subject of complaints about sloppy work in his unit. When his manager points out an error, Barry responds, "I guess that one just slipped by. The only way to make sure nothing slips is for me to monitor my people more closely, and I really don't want to do that. That's not my job."

When an employee sends cues about poor job fit, it might mean the employee is considering his or her options and goals, a vital aspect of the career development process. An employee might have outgrown the job, or the job might not match his or her interests or abilities. If managers recognize these signals as opportunities for coachable moments, they might be able to help unhappy employees find a better match.

An Employee Is Searching for Development Opportunities. Julie, who deals with new-client prospecting for a large construction-management firm, tells her manager, "You can probably count on me being here in this job forever. I thought I might be good at project planning, but those people are all hired from outside with previous experience."

Most employees who have clear goals in mind but don't know how to achieve them need only minimal encouragement and suggestions to help them map out career plans. But typically, they don't ask for help outright. Instead, they vent frustration.

Managers must recognize that these employees are not just asking for empathy; they want help in planning the actions they should take to attain their goals.

Verbalize Support

This step opens a dialogue and establishes a rapport that says, "I noticed; I care." By verbalizing, managers confirm that they have read employees' cues correctly, and they demonstrate their interest.

For some employees, a coachable moment requires only a brief verbal response—assured of support from above, they are motivated to pursue their own career development. Other employees need more help in sorting out how they want to direct their energies and develop their careers. In either case, the verbalization step is not meant to provide solutions, but to help employees define their goals and needs. Let's look at some examples of verbalizing that might follow the cues offered in the previous cases.

New Skill or Interest.   When Lynne showed her boss the flyer and mentioned that she had produced it with new software, her manager could have taken advantage of the coachable moment by saying, "This is really good. Is it something you'd like to do more of?" Or, "Nice job. I had no idea you were interested in graphics." This type of brief response shows approval and opens the door for the employee to discuss a new area of skill or interest. It goes beyond the disinterest of, "Thanks. We can use that."

Evaluation or Feedback.   When Marc asked his boss if she had checked the budget figures in his reorganization proposal, his manager could have responded, "I like your use of a program budget rather than an expenditure budget. How did you decide that would prove your point best?" Or, "Budgeting really seems to be a strong point for you."

This opens a dialogue that might prompt Marc to talk about specific job interests—the skills he might want to enhance and develop in his work. Dialogue would be cut off if the manager had simply responded, "I've only skimmed the report, but it looks fine."

Change Within the Organization.   When Lindsey asked if many departments have their own network managers, her manager could have said, "Sales and research have their own network managers, and I think we'll be seeing more departments going that route." Or, "We're growing in that direction. Is it something you'd be interested in?" This kind of response provides the desired information and the opportunity for the employee to confirm his or her interest in a different area of the organization. If Lindsey's manager had simply said, "I'm not sure; you might check with personnel," the coachable moment would have been lost.

Poor Job Fit.   When Barry said it was not his responsibility to prevent errors by supervising his staff more closely, his manager could have asked, "What do you see as the critical functions of your job?" Or, "Why don't you want to monitor your people more closely?"

The key is to open a dialogue that can help identify the source of the problem. Is the employee bored or disinterested? Does the employee lack training or knowledge? Managers need to confront these situations, not just shrug them off with a vague directive. ("You're going to have to try to eliminate those continuing errors.")

Searching for Development Opportunities.   When Julie told her manager that she believed her lack of experience would prevent her from ever trying project planning, her manager could have suggested, "Some of your experience in our area could be applicable, with just some additional training." Or, "If you're serious about it, there might be some ways you can get similar experience here." Such a response lets Julie know her manager supports her development desires and has ideas that can help.

Verbalizing requires a commitment on managers' parts to keep the conversation going, but it does not require a lengthy interaction that seeks to explore and solve all issues. Even if a manager decides to stop at this step, verbalizing can make a valuable contribution to an employee's pursuit of career development.

Mobilize the Employee

Once a manager has recognized a cue and opened a conversation with an employee, the manager can "mobilize" the employee by suggesting steps the employee can take to develop his or her career. At this stage, the key for managers is to be candid and specific. Mobilizing still leaves the responsibility for career development with the employee, but it helps the employee focus on realistic, doable steps. Here are ways in which managers in the previous examples could mobilize their employees.

- After recognizing Lynne's new skill at computer graphics and confirming her interest, Lynne's manager could say: "You might want to take a shot at the invitations for Steve's retirement party." Or, "Why don't you ask Michele down in graphics what other new programs are available that you might want to learn?"
- After Marc has requested and received feedback on development of a budget proposal, his manager could suggest: "Let's put this on the agenda of the next administrative meeting so you can show the other supervisors how performance budgeting might help them." Or, "This year, why don't you draft your unit's budget for my review, instead of me doing it?"
- After Lindsey has expressed an interest in computer-network management positions within the organization, her manager might mobilize her by saying, "If it's something you're thinking about for yourself, you might want to talk to Jane Hunter, who does computer personnel work, about the kinds of training those positions require." Or, "A computer-network manager is something our division might eventually need, too. Why don't you talk to some of the network managers in other divisions and work up a proposal for me about when and how our unit might phase into that?"
- After confirming Barry's poor job fit, Barry's manager might say, "You have some valuable skills, but we might not be using you in a way that fits your interests. If you make a list of your skills and interests, I'll look at it with you to see what we can do to improve the situation."
- After Julie has indicated that she can't identify strategies to develop the opportunities she seeks, her manager could suggest: "You got to know Alan pretty well when he was planning the university project. Why don't you talk to him about courses and projects that might help you learn the ropes; then bring a list of them to me so that we can see what we can do." Or, "If I were you, I'd review some of the job descriptions for planning positions to check out qualifications. Then you'll have an idea

of exactly what gaps you might need to fill and what you already have to offer."

Mobilizing employees takes more creativity and awareness than time on a manager's part. This step leaves an employee with concrete suggestions he or she can act on and demonstrates that managers are interested in employee developmental needs and willing to be involved.

Seize the Moment

With practice, acting on coachable moments can become routine and almost instinctive for managers. Seizing the opportunity for "coachable moments" creates a caring environment that can alleviate many employee frustrations about development on and beyond the current job.

Coachable moments can go a long way toward meeting employees' needs for job satisfaction and the organization's need for effective use of employee talent. These brief encounters enable managers to seize the moment for employee development when lengthier discussions and planning sessions aren't possible.

Acting on a coachable moment might add up to only a five-minute discussion, but that discussion can initiate important partnerships between caring (but extremely busy) managers and employees who need help and encouragement to focus on career goals.

About the Contributor

Beverly Kaye is president of Career Systems International, Inc. Her cutting-edge management and career-development programs are used by such leading corporations as American Express, Dow Corning, Chevron, Chrysler, Nations Bank, Nortel, Marriott International, and Sears. Bev is a prolific writer, popular lecturer, and management consultant.

In the early 1980s, Bev published her now classic book, *Up Is NOT the Only Way*, which forecast how individual careers would be affected by the move to leaner and flatter organizations. Her latest research is about management strategies for retaining knowledge workers, and she has recently co-authored *Love 'Em or Lose 'Em: Getting Good People to Stay*.

Bev has received many honors and awards, including the National Career Development Award of the American Society for Training and Development. Most recently she received the Best Practice Award from ASTD for her work with global client Dow Corning. She earned a doctorate at UCLA and did graduate work in organization development at the Sloan School of Management at MIT. Her career development materials are produced by Career Systems International, Scranton, Pennsylvania.

PART FOUR

PRACTICE AND TECHNIQUES OF COACHING

In this part, our authors present a compendium of good practices and also highlight potential pitfalls.

Paul Hersey and Roger Chevalier remind us that coaching is situational and present their models that match appropriate leadership behaviors with specific coaching situations. Victoria Guthrie and John Alexander present the "process advisor" as a personal development approach using a key learning partner, and contrast this approach against other definitions of coaching. Alan Fine looks at some pitfalls that relate to decision making in the organization and gives the reader a well-rounded view as to why people need coaching. Bert Decker offers another valuable model for coaching, providing a practical 3 × 3 Feedback tool that works in coaching key leadership qualities. Judith Bardwick approaches the subject from a counseling stance and shows relevant techniques that may be brought into coaching, as well as providing a comprehensive overview of eight critical communications skills. Joe Folkman discusses what is required in coaching others to accept feedback, a critical topic because accepting and giving feedback is so integral to successful coaching and leadership. Bill Hawkins and Tom Pettey include an actual coaching process that is directed toward creating organizational change. David Noer suggests some things to look for in the coaching relationship and offers some warnings to avoid major derailment factors.

CHAPTER TWENTY-TWO

SITUATIONAL LEADERSHIP AND PERFORMANCE COACHING

Paul Hersey and Roger Chevalier

In many organizations, the performance management process has become a periodic intervention rather than a continuous process or ongoing cycle. It has been reduced to a once-a-year appraisal session that can best be described as an "end-of-period autopsy." Another challenge to the process is that very often during these sessions supervisors take on judgmental roles that limit their ability to truly improve the performance of their people.

As a result, performance management has been limited to meeting organizational needs for information with which administrative decisions for such things as promotions, terminations, pay raises, bonuses, and training are made. But what about the needs of the individual for clearly communicated expectations and timely feedback on performance?

The roles of executives, managers, and supervisors should include three distinct phases of performance coaching of their direct reports: *preparation, execution,* and *review,* as shown in Figure 22.1.

At the beginning of the performance coaching cycle, people are *prepared* by clearly defining expectations for each management period. At this point, both means (activities) and ends (results) should be identified and discussed, and performance standards should be set.

FIGURE 22.1.   THE PERFORMANCE COACHING CYCLE

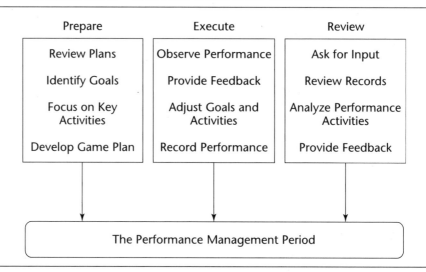

For a new or poorly performing person, clearly communicate expectations in terms of the activities needed to succeed (such as learning specific skills, working as a team player, or treating customers with respect) as well as results to be gained (such as projects to be completed, reports to be submitted, or specific goals to be met).

For experienced and successful people, focus primarily on the results, allowing the experienced person to participate in defining the activities needed to accomplish the goals and, if possible, in setting the actual goals.

During each performance management period, directly observe performance, obtain feedback from others who have contact with the individual, and review productivity against goals. Provide timely feedback on performance to each person, adjusting their activities and goals if necessary. Focus feedback on the individual's performance, and reinforce what is being done right as well as identify what needs to be improved.

Throughout the performance management period, adjust goals as necessary. Activities must also be *reviewed* to ensure that they are contributing to goal accomplishment. Because most managers and supervisors typically have many people reporting directly to them, and because the performance coaching cycle can be as long as a year, it is important to keep written files that document performance for each follower.

This final stage of the performance management period calls for feedback in a counseling session that closes out the current period and begins the next. It is helpful to have each person submit a written self-appraisal that identifies accomplishments and shortcomings. This forces them to assess their own performance, while providing the leader with insight into how they see the period.

Review all performance results, comparing the person's accomplishments to the goals. Records of direct observations and feedback from other sources should similarly be reviewed. Counsel the person before the formal annual performance appraisal is filled out. This will allow the leader to gain greater insight, as well as "the other side of the story" prior to making the final assessment. (Feedback from participants of our performance training programs has reinforced our belief that the final counseling session should take place before the appraisal is written.)

Situational Leadership®

Situational Leadership can be used as a framework to give leaders the guidance they need to coach their people throughout the performance coaching cycle. During the initial meeting, Situational Leadership guides the leader in setting the degree of participation for the planning and goal-setting process. During the rest of the period, it guides the leader in each interaction with the follower.

The underlying principle in Situational Leadership is that leaders should adjust their leadership styles to their followers' readiness level (ability and willingness) to perform a given task. Leadership is the amount of task behavior (direction) and relationship behavior (support) given by a leader. (See Figure 22.2.)

The same principles apply to the leadership roles in the performance coaching process. To be effective, leaders must adjust the ways in which they counsel their people based on their level of readiness for each task that they are expected to perform. Performance coaching is a unique application of the principles of Situational Leadership that guides leaders in the day-to-day transactions with their followers.

FIGURE 22.2. SITUATIONAL LEADERSHIP MODEL©

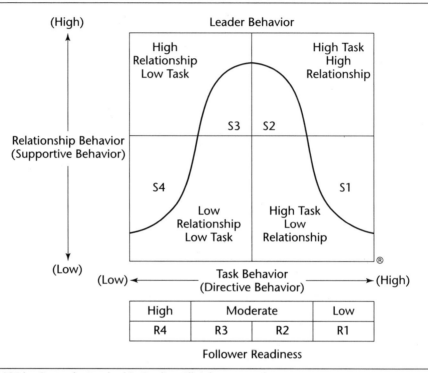

© 1985 by Center for Leadership Studies. All rights reserved.

The lowest readiness level (R1) for a group or individual is described as *not willing and not able* to do a given task. As seen in Figure 22.2, the appropriate leadership style (S1) is that of providing high amounts of task behavior (direction) and low amounts of relationship behavior (support). The next readiness level (R2) is described as *willing but not able*. The appropriate leadership style (S2) is that of high amounts of both task and relationship behavior.

The next readiness level (R3) is described as *able but unwilling* in that the individual lacks confidence or commitment. The appropriate leadership style (S3) is that of high amounts of relationship behavior and low amounts of task behavior. The highest readiness level for a group or individual to do a given task is *willing and able* (R4). The appropriate leadership style is low amounts of both relationship and task behavior.

The Situational Leadership Model provides a framework from which to diagnose different situations and prescribes which leadership style will have the highest probability of success in a particular situation. Use of the model can make supervisors more effective in that it illustrates the connection between their choice of leadership styles and the readiness of their people. As such, Situational Leadership is a powerful tool for supervisors to use in the coaching process.

The Performance Coaching Guide©

The Performance Coaching Guide© performance aid that follows describes a process that is highly effective when used in formal interviewing, counseling, and coaching situations. The guide is divided into two phases that focus on assessing follower readiness and then choosing an appropriate leadership style. The first phase uses leadership Styles 4, 3, and 2 to prepare, open the lines of communication, and diagnose the follower's readiness level for the tasks necessary to be successful.

During the performance period, the follower perceives a Style 4, as the leader observes, monitors, and tracks performance. The follower continues to perceive low amounts of direction and support as the leader prepares for counseling sessions by reviewing relevant materials, such as performance records for the period and, in the case of an end-of-period session, follower input.

At the beginning of the meeting, the leader moves to a Style 3, increasing support by building rapport, by opening up the lines of communication, and by reinforcing positive performance or potential. In this step the leader works to assess how the follower sees his or her performance by asking open-ended questions.

The leader then moves to Style 2 to focus the discussion with direct questions to gain further insight into the follower's perception of performance and identify how the person perceives any shortcomings. For each task that is critical for the follower's success, the leader must assess the person's readiness (ability and willingness) level so that the leader can choose the best style with which to intervene. The assessment phase is described in Figure 22.3.

FIGURE 22.3. ASSESSMENT OF FOLLOWER READINESS

Assessment of Follower Readiness		
S4: Prepare →	*S3: Assess* →	*S2: Diagnose*
Low Relationship Low Task	High Relationship Low Task	High Task High Relationship
1. Observe, monitor, and track performance.	1. Build rapport, trust, and personal power.	1. Focus discussion with direct questions.
2. Review your records and employee input.	2. Begin session with open-ended questions.	2. Identify readiness level for each issue.
3. Set counseling goals; develop a strategy.	3. Identify issues and problem ownership.	3. Select an appropriate leadership style.

After assessing the follower's readiness for each critical task, the leader selects the appropriate leadership style based on the follower's readiness level from the diagram. As is the case with the Situational Leadership Model, the critical tasks must be clearly defined before a readiness level can be determined.

Followers can be at several different task-relevant readiness levels for the different tasks that make up their jobs. Once the readiness level is decided, the corresponding high probability leadership style is chosen to begin the intervention. After the initial intervention, if the follower responds appropriately, the leader then moves to the next style to further develop the follower. The selection of the high probability intervention style is shown in Figure 22.4.

If the follower is unable and unwilling or insecure (R1), initially, the leader uses a Style 1 (Prescribe) to inform, describe, instruct, and direct. If the follower is unable but willing or confident (R2), the leader initially uses a Style 2 (Develop) to explain, persuade, guide, and train. If the follower is able but unwilling or insecure, the leader initially uses a Style 3 (Reinforce) to encourage support, motivate, and empower. After making the initial intervention, the leader moves through the remaining styles to Style 4 to follow up on the meeting by observing, monitoring, and tracking performance.

The Performance Coaching Guide shown in Figure 22.5 is a performance aid derived from the Situational Leadership Model, and it describes the process used to develop people. The performance coaching process

FIGURE 22.4. SELECTION OF LEADER'S STYLE MATCHED TO FOLLOWER READINESS

S4: Follow-up ← Low Relationship Low Task	S3: Reinforce ← High Relationship Low Task	S2: Develop ← High Task High Relationship	S1: Prescribe High Task Low Relationship
1. Document session in performance record.	1. Reinforce self-worth and self-esteem.	1. Discuss goals to improve performance.	1. Clearly communicate expectations and goals.
2. Follow through on all commitments.	2. Assess understanding and commitment.	2. Reach agreement on best course of action.	2. Define role as both means and ends.
3. Observe, monitor, and track performance.	3. Encourage, support, motivate, and empower.	3. Guide, persuade, explain, and train.	3. Inform, describe, instruct, and direct.
Selection of Leader's Style Matched to Follower Readiness			
Able and Willing or Confident	Able but Unwilling or Insecure	Unable but Willing or Confident	Unable and Unwilling or Insecure
R1	R2	R3	R4

follows a pattern that typically includes varying the amount of direction and support given followers as the leader prepares, assesses, diagnoses, prescribes, develops, reinforces, and follows up.

The assessment phase is critical to the coaching process in that the leader must prepare, assess, and diagnose prior to making the actual intervention. In effect, the leader must "earn the right" to intervene. All too often leaders intervene without taking the time to truly assess the follower's readiness. At this point, the follower will become defensive—and there will be little hope for improving performance.

While the initial intervention style is chosen based on the follower's readiness for a given task, the goal is to develop the follower by using successive leadership styles as the leader moves on the continuum from prescribe to develop, to reinforce, and then to follow up.

By describing the process and by giving examples of what is done at each step, the Performance Coaching Guide can assist you in structuring the formal counseling process. The Performance Coaching Guide is one member of a family of performance aids and training programs that apply the principles of Situational Leadership in such areas as coaching, customer service, advocacy and consultative selling, and facilitation.

FIGURE 22.5.   PERFORMANCE COACHING GUIDE®

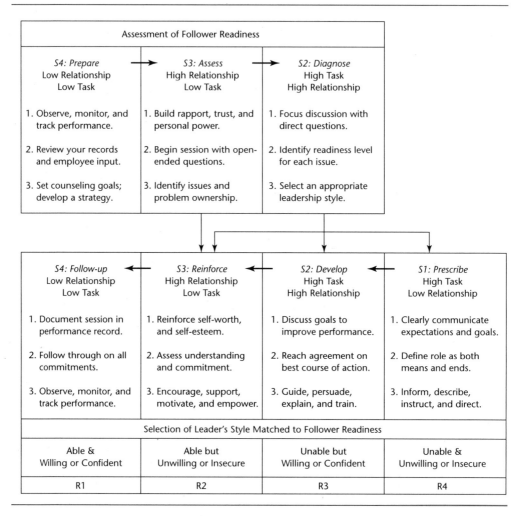

About the Contributors

Paul Hersey has helped train over 10,000,000 managers and salespeople from more than one thousand businesses and other organizations. He is an internationally known behavioral scientist and highly successful entrepreneur.

Paul is recognized as one of the world's outstanding authorities on training and development in leadership, management, and selling. In addition to his teaching, he is a consultant, on a continuing basis, to industrial, government, and military organizations. He is a former faculty member of Northern Illinois University, California State College at Chico, University of Arkansas, and Ohio University. Paul served in the roles of chairman of the Department of Management and dean of the School of Business, and has also served as project director for the Industrial Relations Center of the University of Chicago, training director at Kaiser Aluminum & Chemical Company, and department head at Sandia Corporation.

Paul has authored or co-authored numerous books, papers, and articles, including *Management of Organizational Behavior: Utilizing Human Resources; Organizational Change through Effective Leadership;* and *Selling: A Behavioral Science Approach.* He also authored the books *The Situational Leader* and *Situational Selling: An Approach to Increasing Sales Effectiveness.* His latest release is *Situational Parenting.*

Roger Chevalier is an independent consultant specializing in the design of systematic and systemic performance improvement interventions. As a trainer, he has personally developed and delivered leadership, coaching, customer service and sales training programs to over 25,000 individuals since 1977.

Major corporate and government clients have included Century 21 Real Estate, Johnson & Johnson, Hewlett-Packard, Agilent Technologies, Medtronic AVE, E. & J. Gallo Winery, Parker Hannifin, Siemens Energy and Automation, Phoenix Contact, Storage Dimensions, TRW, Vistakon, Realty World, Champion Chemicals, Borg Warner, the U. S. Coast Guard, and the Department of Veterans Affairs.

A consultant to Century 21® Real Estate Corporation for eighteen years, Roger served as vice president of their Performance Division, guiding the design, development, implementation, and evaluation of training and other performance improvement initiatives for 4,600 offices and 60,000 sales associates. He also co-developed the Managers as Leaders Program, personally presented it to over four thousand brokers and managers, and facilitated the executive management team in the development of their strategic plan.

Roger has authored numerous articles on leadership, human performance technology, management of change, customer service, and sales techniques published in a wide variety of professional and trade journals. He is the human performance technology forum field editor for the American Society for Training and Development's *Performance in Practice*. Roger has a Ph.D. in applied behavioral science and master's degrees in personnel management and organizational behavior.

CHAPTER TWENTY-THREE

PROCESS ADVISING: AN APPROACH TO COACHING FOR DEVELOPMENT

Victoria Guthrie and John Alexander

As the demand for executive coaching increases, there has been an accompanying proliferation of different philosophies and styles of coaching. The challenge for professionals is to carefully match the appropriate philosophy or style to the specific needs of the individual being coached. Over the past decade, one approach we've found to be consistently effective is the *process advisor* (PA) role. This technique has allowed us to offer a sustained, focused coaching experience to a relatively large, diverse pool of managers and executives as part of an extended leadership-development process.

Process advising is a specialized form of coaching that emphasizes learning, personal development, and effective action in a specific leadership situation. We conceived of the PA role more than ten years ago as a way to enhance and reinforce leadership development for executives and managers. The idea was to move beyond a one-time training event and create a process that would enhance an individual's ability to take effective actions in his or her real-life leadership situation, learning on the job as he or she interacted with employees and worked through challenges.

Role of Process Advising

Jim had just accepted a new assignment within his company. He felt well prepared for his new post because, as a supervisor for the last seven years, he had been "steeped in the authoritarian style of the organization." The entire group he worked with had spent their careers in this environment, so it felt easy for Jim to pick up the ball and run with it.

However, things changed as he moved into his new job, and he quickly got the message, "We do things differently here now." He spent the next three years working an average of seventy to ninety hours per week; he gave up nine of the twelve weeks of vacation he had earned. The workforce was very young; he saw them as inexperienced, but willing to try anything and work hard.

For Jim, the definition of success on the job had changed. His previously effective leadership style and processes were failing him, but he didn't know what to change or how to change. Jim turned to our organization for insight into how he might become more effective in his new environment.

We knew from our research and experience with executives like Jim that leadership development takes place over time and requires ongoing assessment, challenge, and support. Our clients, from corporate executives to entrepreneurs, told us they needed more real-time, real-world leadership development to enable them to manage the complexity and turbulence of today's work environments.

One client articulated the needs of many: "We want development experiences that go beyond awareness and move to action, that go beyond teaching heads to moving feet."

To meet this need, we and our organization designed multi-session programs, typically taking place over a six-month period, that addressed specific, individual leadership challenges. Within that framework, the PA model was created.

The term *process advisor* was carefully chosen as we began to define the role itself. *Process,* defined as a natural phenomenon marked by gradual changes that lead toward a particular result, was at the core of our development processes that emphasize future action.

Just as important, we wanted the role to be a blend of advocate, partisan, and adherent. We found that the best word to combine the support, assistance, fidelity, loyalty, and help in keeping something going was *advisor*. Thus, the PA would be a key learning partner, who would help individuals determine the best course of action in their current work situations.

Seven Key Competencies of the Process Advising Relationship

The role of a PA can be complex; however, we've identified seven key competencies that guide the process advising relationship. Process advisors and their advisees must:

1. Deal effectively with interpersonal relationships;
2. Think and behave in terms of systems;
3. Approach decision making from the standpoint of tradeoffs;
4. Think and act with flexibility;
5. Maintain emotional balance by coping with disequilibrium;
6. Clarify and maintain the sense of purpose; and
7. Be able to learn how to learn.

Effective and successful PAs come from a variety of backgrounds, such as clinical psychology, organizational change, career development and counseling, and management or leadership development, but all have a thorough understanding of human development and adult learning processes, and all have the ability to surface and work through challenges and issues.

Typically, the advisees are experiencing some form of personal or professional turbulence, such as downsizing, new management, culture or job change, or health, family, or psychological problems; and they are seeking ways to adapt or cope. In this context, PAs are process experts who are able to aid advisees in taking the action or making the personal change necessary to be more effective leaders. As one advisee explained, "The PA helped me visualize needed changes and showed me how to focus on the *where* and *how* of accomplishing my goal."

Although personal styles may vary, PAs are carefully trained to work within the focused objectives of the program and the advisee's specific challenges. Yet, like any coach, they must remain flexible to deal with the dynamics that evolve as new information is introduced. A PA provides the advisee the discipline and support for the implementation of change, but recognizes the impact of specific work and personal situations on the development process.

Effective PAs also possess a motivation to teach others, keen observation skills, the ability to understand the advisee, a way to sense personal issues underlying the situation, and a strong desire and belief in helping others grow and change.

As with any form of coaching, the most effective PAs view process advising as an integral part of their work, not as a sideline role. They work with two to three advisees from several programs for a six-month period, through a set number of phone conversations and face-to-face meetings.

During this defined period of time, the PA provides the opportunity for the advisees to develop their leadership skills and move from "management-by-objective" thinking to process-management thinking.

In the advising sessions, the PA's major job is to focus the advisee on effective action by asking two key questions:

- "What does the situation call for from me as an individual, as a team or group leader, and as a contributing member of an organization?"
- "What is the ideal or purpose I am striving for?"

By clarifying the situation, current needs, and larger goals, the advisee is able to focus on finding new solutions. The PA helps the individual clarify strengths and potential blocks, provides perspective, gives feedback, and inquires and offers support. The advisee determines his or her action plans and developmental needs and evaluates his or her progress and learning.

For example, one advisee had just made a change from a secure job at a local college to a risk-taking entrepreneurial position. Her PA helped her learn that her creativity and global perspective often kept her from examining the small details that were critical to the success of her new business. As a result, she developed a process for addressing the specific needs of the business, as she worked to expand her leadership and decision-making skills.

"My process advisor constantly pushed me to the edge of my comfort zone," she reported. "I was cognizant of a gain in confidence, listening skills, and open and honest feedback. I am learning to listen to suggestions for changes in my new entrepreneurial work with increased confidence and receptiveness."

Over time, we have found that, regardless of the specific work environment or challenges, the individual outcomes often include:

- *Greater Self-Empowerment.* Following the takeover of the company by new management, one executive reported that he "fell from grace and no longer felt like an exemplary leader." The program and PA "helped me figure out a way to adapt my leadership style to changing situations. . . . It helped me get through the anger, the disappointment, and the doubts and empowered me once again to be myself."
- *An Expanded View of Leadership.* "Getting the job done is no longer enough," explained one manager. "I learned how and why to change my personal habits to become a more sensitive leader. Leadership has a new meaning to me now; I certainly see things through a different lens."
- *Greater Focus on Systems-Level Interventions.* Advisees often gain a greater appreciation of forces affecting organizations and their own relevance to the organizations. Kay's organization was in a period of radical change, and she was perceived as being unable to implement the new strategy. With her PA, she developed a plan to develop new skills and behaviors that helped her initiate the changes needed in her department.
- *Improved Understanding of Diverse People and Viewpoints.* Advisees typically gain greater awareness of how differences add strength to teams and organizations. "I learned to reflect with others from diverse backgrounds, new ways of looking at things, and new ways of working with others," noted one advisee.
- *Greater Flexibility.* Advisees learn to visualize individual and organizational possibilities and how to engage others in developing a shared vision. One executive, who attributed his success to "brute force," learned that much of leadership is about developing a personal leadership plan that

includes letting others lead, building consensus, connecting with others, and sharing ideals and vision.

- *Commitment to Continuous Learning.* Many advisees see the PA process as just the beginning. In the words of one manager, "My learnings have just begun. I am continuing to learn and grow both as a person and as a professional."

Jim, our overworked, ineffective manager, worked with a process advisor through one of our organization's multi-session programs. Jim's process advisor helped him see his strengths as well as his weaknesses. He recognized his tendency to become reactionary and learned how it was affecting the team he managed. With his PA, he has developed a process to recognize and control this behavior. Jim's colleagues and subordinates further encouraged this change, commenting that he was becoming more effective. Jim committed to further growth and learning. He found a mentor in the organization and discovered a role in which he can be an agent for positive change.

Process Advising Versus Coaching

During the ten years that we have been working with the process advising model, we have seen the roles PAs play reflect many, but not all, of the roles typical in a coaching situation.

Process advisors provide process expertise, reflective thinking, feedback, dialogue, accounting, positive reinforcement, counseling, historical reference, and continuity. Process advisors do not offer content expertise or focus on specific management skills, nor do they serve as consultants to the business. Process advising is not executive coaching, which is usually one-on-one interaction at senior levels and seems to carry a greater sense of urgency for the organization's strategic success.

Process advising, because of its focus and its combination of face-to-face dialogue and telephone work, is a development method that is available to a larger number of people concurrently. As a consequence, we've found it to be an efficient and effective way to extend the benefits of a training and development program.

Also, PAs report that process advising is less intense than executive coaching. This may be because it operates within a specified time frame and given structural framework that includes a clearly articulated intent with specific goals of the developmental relationship, a set of competencies to use as reference points, and a focus on the demands of the individual's situation. This creates an interaction in which the individual selects the situations or issues he or she wishes to work on, and, with the guidance of the PA, develops an ongoing action plan.

Process advisors themselves stress the assessment, challenge, and support responsibility of process advising, which expands a typical coaching role. They emphasize the following:

- Process advisors do not need to know all the answers. The foundation of the relationship lies in the PA's ability to understand fully what the situation calls for from the individual, not by competing with the individual for the right answers.
- Process advisors need to remain nonjudgmental. They must establish trust and a strong sense of confidentiality.
- Process advisors need to blend candor with belief in the individual. Less successful PAs tend to be those who flinch or hedge when giving feedback.
- Process advisors must respect and work with the changes the individual decides to make.
- The ongoing relationship and counseling aspect can result in both personal and professional or work-related impact.
- The PA brings reality (feedback); hope (what's possible); and a learning process (structure, steps, stress management, and a safety or holding pattern) to the relationship.

Interestingly, although we see the PA role as a special form of coaching, the term *process advisor* is more palatable than *coach* to many of our clients. This became evident at one organization when the president immediately dismissed the idea of coaching. He said that when he heard the word coach, he thought of teaching someone something, such as a sport or a sales technique. However, when the concept of the PA was explained, he felt it was exactly what the individuals in the organization needed.

The Future of Process Advising

Our experience has taught us much of what works and what doesn't work in a process advising model. We know that to be effective, any process advising model must:

- Establish a clear development goal;
- Establish key competencies and guiding questions;
- Train, coach, and develop skilled process advisors;
- Set specific parameters on time, frequency of contact, and modes of interaction between advisor and advisee;
- Set specific objectives and expectations for both parties;
- Establish regular contact between process advisor and organizational sponsor;
- Establish a learning community to expand the advisors' knowledge; and
- Design evaluation and quality checks to ensure a successful process.

At our organization, we continue to explore and evaluate new ways that the process advising model may be used in our programs, as well as through new technologies. For example, we are increasingly adding process advising to our customized programs and working with companies to incorporate process advising into their internal development systems. Our hope is to make this technique even more widely available to today's leaders, who are increasingly expected to perform well on the job, in the moment, and to learn and grow while doing so.

About the Contributors

Victoria Guthrie is a senior fellow and director of innovative program initiatives at the Center for Creative Leadership (CCL). Her responsibilities include bringing fresh initiatives to established programs, as well as generative ideas for future program development. Prior to this position, Victoria headed up the Organizational Leadership Group, which included programs that enabled participants to act on and apply their individual developmental learning in the context of their organizational situations.

Victoria is co-designer of three of CCL's programs: LeaderLab, Leading Transitions, and Leading Creatively. In addition to her leadership role at CCL, she holds teaching roles in all three programs and also designs and conducts client-specific programs for international organizations worldwide.

She is author of *Coaching for Action: A Report on Long-Term Advising in a Program Context* (CCL, 1999) and co-author of a number of other publications, including *Training for Action: A New Approach to Executive Development* (CCL, 1992); "The Lessons of Life at Work: Continuous Personal Development" (*Career Planning and Adult Development Journal*), and two chapters in *The Center for Creative Leadership Handbook of Leadership Development* (Jossey-Bass and CCL, 1998): "Feedback Intensive Programs" and "Enhancing the Ability to Learn from Experience."

John Alexander is president of the Center for Creative Leadership (CCL), an international, nonprofit educational institution devoted to behavioral science research and leadership education. Founded in Greensboro, North Carolina, in 1970 by the Smith Richardson Foundation, today CCL is one of the largest institutions in the world focusing on leadership.

John came to CCL in 1990 after more than twenty years as an award-winning career as a journalist and newspaper editor. He has received numerous state and national awards for his writing, including the Scripps-Howard Walker Stone Award for editorial writing and first place in editorial writing from the North Carolina Press Association. In 1979, John was a finalist for the Pulitzer Prize in editorial writing. He most recently co-authored "Leading Across Cultures: Five Vital Capabilities," a chapter in the Peter Drucker Foundation's *The Organization of the Future* (Jossey-Bass, 1996).

CHAPTER TWENTY-FOUR

DECISION VELOCITY: A TARGET FOR COACHING

Alan Fine

The pace of social and technological change is probably faster now than it has been at any time in history, and it shows no sign of slowing down. As economies become more global, people in organizations have more to do in less time. They have to live with the prospect of reorganization, right-sizing, and the changes in the social contract that often go with these initiatives. The consequence is that both individuals and organizations have to be more responsive and flexible than ever before. They have to take action more and more rapidly in order to stay in touch with a market that changes at an ever-faster rate.

The Changing World: A New Game

This new "game" compounds the impact of organizational inertia. In the dictionary, *inertia* is defined as the "indisposition to change." Organizational inertia is made up of the combined interference (the mental and organizational noise that colors our perceptions, creating different points of view) of the people in the organization. At best these different views promote diversity and creativity; at worst they lead to resistance and more inertia.

One indicator of interference is a gap between how people *think* they perform or behave and how they *actually* perform or behave. The more interference that is present, the more inertia the organization experiences. Inertia generates interference, interference generates inertia. It's a vicious cycle.

Closing the Performance Gap

Keeping an organization performing is a constant battle. Every organization is trying to overcome its inertia, to gain momentum, and to become more productive. This battle with inertia means there is constant change—change that people often resist, deny, and frequently become angry about.

Ultimately, everyone in the organization wants higher performance. This occurs at its highest levels in spite of resistance to change when people are clear what their team or personal goals are; understand the business outcome that their team or personal goals contribute to; and ensure that each task they do supports these goals.

One way to raise the performance of an organization is to help all individuals become more efficient and effective in their daily tasks. Historically, leaders have tried to develop this effectiveness and efficiency in their people by using two approaches:

1. *A command-and-control approach:* Controllers lead their people as if they are herding sheep. Their mind-set is to train their people well enough to be able to control them. It works, but it costs a lot of time and energy.

2. *A knowledge-based approach:* It is often assumed that if people have more information, they will be able to do things better based on that information. This is the organizational equivalent of reading a book on golf and expecting to be able to play at the level of a professional. More often than not, it is not a lack of knowledge that blocks performance, but a lack of consistent, accurate implementation of the knowledge that people already have that blocks individuals, teams, and organizations from performing at their best. People in organizations are rarely stupid, but they often suffer interference that blocks their performance.

Performance

In sports the measurement of performance is easy and obvious. The media show us the dollar earnings and world rankings. The coaches gather huge amounts of data to help identify less obvious measures—critical variables for the athletes to improve. In sports such as golf, athletes spend a lot of time improving what we could call swing velocity. (We are borrowing from physics for this concept.) In physics, velocity is speed in a direction. If the golfer can increase his or her swing velocity, the speed and accuracy of the swing, he or she will hit the ball farther and more accurately—a big advantage in golf.

Decision Velocity©*

As in sports, effective coaches in the workplace are clear what performance they are trying to improve. To this end, the concept of decision velocity can be of value. (See Figure 24.1.) *Decision velocity* is the speed and direction (or accuracy) of decisions. *Performance* is the outcome of specific actions that people take to implement the strategy of the organization.

FIGURE 24.1.   DECISION VELOCITY

Decisions ➡	Actions ➡	Performance
At the heart of everything we do	Taken because of decisions we make	The outcome of specific actions

Increasing the *speed* of decision making alone is not necessarily helpful to the bottom line, because if the decision is not accurate you will get poor performance. Increasing the *accuracy* of decision making on its own is also not necessarily helpful, because if it is not fast enough then your competitors get ahead of you. However, increasing *both* the speed and the accuracy of decision making can be a source of competitive advantage because these activities underpin everything people do at work.

Unlike under the command-and-control approach, when an action is chosen by an individual, then that person's commitment, energy, and focus for action are far greater. In other words, when the sheep want to get into the pen, the shepherd and his dog have less work to do. Similarly, when people make and own their decisions, they devote their discretionary effort to these activities. Discretionary effort (as distinct from mandated effort) is what people put into their private lives when they get up at 3:30 on a Saturday morning to go fishing, or work on a rape crisis hotline, or coach Little League teams. This kind of effort cannot be mandated or written into a job description, but it is the "stuff" of peak performance. It is given by performers, not mandated by leaders.

Coaching

Decisions lie behind all the actions that people take. Workplace coaches accelerate decision velocity, and are therefore a high leverage point for creating change at any level in an organization. Leverage comes from leaders being coached, coaching others throughout the organization, and focusing that coaching on decision velocity.

The word *coaching* came into common usage in the fifteenth century, when it described something that "conveyed valued people from where they are to where they want to go." This definition, of course, referred to a stage-coach. Although simple, the words are revealing when we think of excellence in coaching:

- "Conveying valued people"—Great coaches ensure that coachees are able to leave a coaching interaction with their self-esteem enhanced. The coach does this by preserving the self-respect and dignity of performers—even when they have to be tough with them and/or they do not like them.
- "From where they are"—This sounds obvious, but many coaches/ leaders give their followers more information than they can digest at one time (for example, a new hire's orientation program in which a huge amount of new information is thrown at people, most of which doesn't stick). The rationale is that "we don't have time to do this in 'digestible'

amounts." It is convenient if people can start from where the coach is (that is, able to deal with all the new information). However, people will always start from where they are, not where the coach wants them to be.

- "To where they want to go"—Of course everyone in the organization cannot go in whatever direction he or she wants. What people do has to add value to the strategy, and the strategy defines the direction the organization needs to go in. However, unless the employees choose to make a decision that is consistent with the organizational strategy, they will wait for and comply with directives from above, merely delivering minimum standards of performance. To meet the high levels of performance demanded by today's competitive environment, we need people to *choose* to give their discretionary efforts. We have to help them *want* to go where they need to go, and coaching their decision velocity is a way to do this.

Increased Decision Velocity

Watch master coaches execute their special skills and one thing becomes apparent: they seem to be effortless in their execution. They know the few high-leverage things that have to be attended in order to deliver high performance—the critical variables of the task. Observers always comment on how simple skilled coaches make it look. One could say they bring simplicity to complexity.

Among the many models for describing how human beings make progress, one very simple process is in four stages: *goals, reality, options,* and the *way forward*—G.R.O.W.®* We might call these stages *critical variables* in making progress—critical because if you leave any stage out it can be problematic, and variable because the content of these stages is different in different situations.

The significance of these four stages as critical variables comes from looking at how human beings and organizations make decisions. People and businesses have current situations or problems that they want to change in some way—their *reality.* They define in what way they would like this situation to be different—their *goal.* They then develop ways in which they

---

* ® Registered trademark 2000. InsideOut Development L.L.C. All rights reserved.

can close the gap between their reality and their goal—their *options*. Finally they commit to some action, based on the options that they have energy about and believe will create results—their *way forward*. So we could call these stages the critical variables in decision making.

For progress to be made, people must go through these stages. If they miss or are unclear on any of them the downsides at each stage are as follows:

- The goal—we don't go anywhere or we solve the wrong problem;
- The reality—we don't know what we are dealing with;
- The options—we have fewer ways to bridge the gap between the reality and the goals; and
- The way forward—we don't have a clear sense of, or commitment to, next actions.

One or more of these downsides tend to show up when people are "stuck" in their decision-making process. It is common for people to follow a specific path when they are thinking or conversing about a situation. They start in reality and wander around (often complaining) before trying to set a goal. Then they return to reality and wander around some more, develop one option, and immediately return to reality and decide it will not work.

They try once more to develop an option and half-heartedly choose a way of implementing it that they are not really committed to executing. It is like trying to score in baseball by running in a few circles and over to the stands between stepping on each of the bases. It is much more difficult to score a run this way. They may get there eventually, but there is a lot of wasted time and energy along the way. By systematically focusing on each of these stages in the decision-making process, we can go through the stages faster—one of the elements in increasing decision velocity.

Reduced Interference

Inherent in the systematic targeting of these stages is a reduction in interference. How this works can be seen from the work of Professor Mihaly Cziksentmihalyi (1975) on "the psychology of optimal experience." He has found that if people perceive the challenge of the task they are working on as being greater than their skill set, they become threatened. This results in their becoming worried and anxious. If they perceive their skills to be greater than the challenge, they become bored (and if bored for too long, anxious). In both cases, if they perceive either one as being greater than the other, they experience interference. People do their best "stuff" when they perceive their skills as being enough to meet the challenge of the task they are currently doing, but only just enough. The task needs to challenge them enough to demand most of their attention, but not be so challenging that it threatens them. This puts them in what Cziksentmihalyi calls their "flow state"—the optimal state for learning a new skill or performing a skill they already have.

A key "task" in decision making is thinking. It is by thinking that we make decisions. When people try to think about a problem that they hold as difficult to solve, it represents a challenge that they perceive to be greater than their skill to think about it. This therefore moves them out of their flow state by creating interference. Focusing on the four stages of the G.R.O.W. model focuses the decision-making process by breaking it into smaller discrete steps. These smaller steps represent less of a challenge (in relation to skill) and therefore create less interference, helping people get into their flow state to do their decision making. Clarifying each of the stages in the model is much easier in the flow state, and so the decision making happens more rapidly—an increase in decision velocity.

Discipline and Coaching

What coaching does in a corporate context is something that athletes have long recognized as having value. Coaches systematically help performers overcome their interference. They clearly understand that "winning" comes from small increases in effectiveness and efficiency. The coach brings discipline, which helps them stay focused on the critical variables of their tasks. The corporate coach can bring this to bear for individuals, teams, and organizations. And, given that the decisions people make are the precursor to their actions, the coach can help them focus on the critical variables that drive all their decisions.

Teams and Teams of Teams: Organizations

At the individual level then, decision velocity is increased by focusing on these four critical variables in the decision-making process—goals, reality, options, and way forward. The same is true for teams. With a group of people, developing clarity at each of these stages is more complex and takes more time, but they still have to get through these four stages in order to make a decision.

Although clarity of perception is needed at all four stages, consensus is only essential in the *goals* and the *way forward*. Diverse views of reality help in the development of a wider range of options. One of the coach's tasks with a team is to bring discipline to the discussion, so that the stages are undertaken systematically.

Summary

Everyone suffers with interference in decision making at some time or another. A large part of this interference is because of the gap between how people think they behave and how they actually behave, and the effects of that gap on others. Interference creates organizational inertia, which slows down decision velocity—the speed and accuracy of decision making. However, coaching can be used to increase decision velocity by reducing interference—closing the gap between how people think they behave and how they actually behave.

About the Contributor

Alan Fine, founder of InsideOut Development, has over twenty years of experience coaching world-class athletes and Fortune 500 companies. Alan began his career as a professional tennis player, and later was certified as a professional tennis coach by the British Lawn Tennis Association. As a coach he has trained many nationally ranked players, such as Britain's former number one tennis player, Buster Mottram, and he has advised several British Ryder Cup golfers, including David Feherty.

Alan's work now extends to some of the most demanding Fortune 500 companies. His interest in how people learn and perform under pressure led him to develop a coaching method of performance improvement that he applies not only to athletes, but also to individuals, teams, and organizations.

Alan is the author of *Mind Over Golf,* a book and video published by the BBC and is a columnist for *Golf World* magazine. His work has caught national interest, and he has been featured in the *Sunday Times Business Supplement,* Edward de Bono's book *Tactics,* and on the BBC television program *Business Matters.*

InsideOut's clients include some of the best athletes and companies in the world. Thousands of people from companies as diverse as BellSouth, KPMG Peat Marwick, Chevrolet, Pharmacia & Upjohn, DuPont, Procter & Gamble, AT&T, and NASA to the British Institute of Management are using InsideOut coaching methods to help their individuals and teams achieve breakthrough levels of performance.

CHAPTER TWENTY-FIVE

COACHING LEADERS WITH 3X3 FEEDBACK

Bert Decker

Bob was like many of the men and women who came into my executive speaking seminars. As soon as we videotaped his talk and got into the private coaching session, he said, "Okay, just tell me what I'm doing wrong so I can fix it." Direct and to the point, like most overachievers who just want to find the problem and fix it. It's as if they were machines—all performance and no feelings. But leaders have the same feelings as anyone else and, as we'll see, feelings are an important area of coaching that is often neglected.

I've used a simple system for giving communications feedback that I've found also works for any behavior or characteristics in which you may want to give, and receive, coaching. It's called the 3×3 Coaching Model, and I will describe how it works, then apply it to what I've found to be key leadership characteristics that make the most difference in long-term effectiveness.

This methodology works very effectively for leaders. It ensures there will be the balanced feedback that the overachiever professes to eschew. It is quick and continuous, and it can easily be adapted to a variety of situations in which a leader might want to solicit feedback.

The 3×3 Coaching Model

The coaching model uses the 3×3 rule, a process of giving feedback that I developed to use when I had no audio or video feedback available. It is short, sweet, balanced, and particularly appropriate for leaders who want to get right to the point.

The model is to give *three strengths* (keepers) and *three weaknesses* (improvements) when analyzing performance and behavior. It forces you to give balanced feedback, because you are giving three positives along with three areas to work on. In any situation there are literally dozens of pros and cons about someone's behavior, if you really think about it. With the 3×3 model, you emphasize only the first ones that come to mind. They don't have to be the most important, nor the most profound—just the first ones that occur to you. If they stand out for you, they are probably the same ones that stand out for most people, and thus become the most important in practical terms.

Many people are comfortable giving the positives and uncomfortable giving the negatives. Some people can be overly critical, leaving few strokes of encouragement for the person coached. Neither method is productive for the person receiving the feedback. A forced choice is created by 3×3 feedback. You are forced to give a balanced 3×3 assessment, so the person feels supported while taking away valuable lessons to work on. This is as important for the leader as for anyone else.

Three is a good number. Don't ask for a dozen keepers and a dozen improvements. That's too many for people to give and too much for the receiver to remember. For the best learning and skill development for yourself and others, just remember the 3×3 rule.

Three by three feedback can be given in almost any setting. It can be solicited by the leader during or after a speech or meeting. It can be given by an executive coach to a leader on a systematic basis. It can be focused on certain characteristics or be given in general and broad terms. It is flexible and adaptable. It is most useful when you solicit it for yourself and give it to others often.

Receiving three bits of feedback at a time allows people to make course corrections, like a guided missile, as they keep moving onward and upward. They continuously receive feedback, continuously update the awareness of their skills and habits, and continuously make course corrections. This is the best way to hit the target.

Leadership Characteristics

So what do we coach leaders on? There are thousands of books out on leadership, and perhaps as many opinions on the "essential" qualities of leadership. In my experience of teaching and training, three stand out and these are also easily coachable: *communication, competence,* and *care.*

Leaders Communicate

Of all the potential skills of leadership, knowing how to communicate effectively is the most important. Leaders listen to their people and their world, synthesize, and then speak in order to influence others to action. Leaders communicate with energy. They speak with a confidence and certainty shown through voice, eye communication, movement, and gestures. They smile at people, and they listen.

Here is a sample of a brief written 3×3 *communication* of a leader who has just finished giving a quarterly update in an open forum to 150 employees:

Keepers

- Good and focused content; you considered their interests;
- Started on time and ended on time; and
- Humorous

Improvements

- Reading the speech cut down on your energy and eye contact;
- Your voice was hard to hear at times; and
- The room was too crowded and hot.

Leaders Are Competent

Measurements of performance and accountability set the standards in the business world. The specifics of the numbers are important feedback tools for leaders, but they are not the subject here.

What is important is to have feedback and coaching on the skills that lead to superior performance in an organization. The shadow of a leader falls long, and the behavior of the leader has impact far beyond the immediate results, because the leader is always showing by example. What the leader does speaks so loudly that it often communicates more than what is said, particularly if it seems to be inconsistent with what is said. So coaching in the following three leadership competencies has the greatest payoff in creating action in others and results:

Focus.   The truly great leaders have a singleness of purpose. They have a mission. They are passionate about it. They set targets and goals. Those goals are *specific, physical, time-oriented,* and *measurable.* They repeat the vision, mission, and goals often. Repeating good ideas is worth repeating. Repeating good ideas is worth repeating.

I'm Responsible.   Leaders don't wait for things to happen; they *make* things happen. They do not wait for direction from others, but they *give* direction to others. Leaders like accountability and thrive on achievement and creation. The best leaders do their achieving and creating with and through others. They are not Lone Rangers. Good leaders can be entrepreneurs or managers, but if they are going to reach their optimum, they will leverage any talents they have through the collaborative efforts of others. Leaders take responsibility, but they delegate and keep others accountable. Most leaders I know are harder on themselves than they are on others.

Forward Lean.   Years ago I made a documentary film on Robert Kennedy, and the writer of the script wrote a memorable line to describe Kennedy's arrival as a new Senator in Washington, D.C.: "Senator Kennedy hit the ground leaning forward." That captures a quality that has struck me as most important to success in anyone—going about life with a "forward lean." For instance, leaning forward is to volunteer to take on a job, agree to give a speech, look for the opportunity in adversity, or look to oneself as a leader, model, and mentor for others.

Leaders need coaching in three important qualities in this area (notice that the "Rule of 3" is continuously at work!):

1. *Staying in the Disciplines.* The pressures and stress of leadership require a certain amount of organization and routine in life. Leaders are usually disciplined people, who regularly exercise, or read, or pray, or have dates with their children, or eat certain foods, or a combination of these things—and many others.
2. *Leaders Are Not Sarcastic.* In relating to others, leaders have a forward lean of encouragement. They are cheerleaders. Sarcasm, caustic banter, and double-edged kidding can be fun; the problem is that when you might be "kidding," people don't know whether you're kidding or not. That lack of complete trust can be a real detriment to a leader's credibility and effectiveness. It's best to be a cheerleader.
3. *Leaders Are Savvy.* The leaders of the future (not excluding the present) are tech savvy. They know and use the computer and the Internet. Today is a new age of communicating and commerce—by voice, phone, cell, e-mail, PDAs, Internet, and wireless. Leaders know what means of communication to use when they want information or when they want action, and they are able to use all the tools. It is effective to be an "early adopter."

The competence of leaders can be a laundry list of desired characteristics, but coaches would go a long way by just giving 3×3 coaching on focus, accountability, and "forward lean." A sample of a 3×3 on *competence* is shown below. This was given to a leader of a national service organization after he requested some accountability and feedback. He has several hundred people reporting to him with a budget of over $10 million.

Keepers

- Great focus; you continuously organize people into single purpose teams;
- Strong example of discipline by running and praying every morning; and
- Always straightforward; people can trust what you say.

Improvements

- E-mail and computer skills are poor;
- Late adopter; better to model competence by learning new tools that are available and using them; and
- You do too much; others can do some of the things you do. Let some things go; delegate to individuals as you do to teams.

Leaders Care

This is probably one of the most neglected characteristics of strong and effective leaders. Good leaders *care* about the people they lead. What is the purpose in leading if it isn't for the betterment of a body of people? Where it is just for the glory of the leader himself or herself, then that leader will ultimately fall short.

Listening is critical to both the communications and caring nature of the leader. Good leaders are good listeners. They not only pause often in their communications, but they also stop talking and just look, nod, assent with "uh, huh's" and other vocal acknowledgments, particularly when there is conflict, misunderstanding, or hostility in the air. Listening is not lip service, but ear service with the eyes.

Caring means knowing the names of people, responding promptly, smiling, acknowledging with a nod or touch (careful on the appropriateness of touch), and ultimately hanging out. Tom Peters well-worn cliché of "managing by walking around" is worth remembering. By being out with your people, you show you care and are accessible, while also gaining valuable information.

Coaching Caring

Of the 3 C's, *caring characteristics are probably the most difficult to coach,* because it is subjective and sensitive. Coaching should only be done by trusted individuals, and the leader must be open to it and fully committed to the principle that caring is important. Then the 3×3 Coaching process becomes the most effective. A sample of what a written 3×3 on *caring* might look like on a leader who has asked for feedback follows:

Keepers

- You send handwritten notes on birthdays/events;
- Very candid in employee open forum sessions; and
- Your natural smile connects with people in casual contact.

Improvements

- Could spend some time out in people's work areas;
- Often interrupt meetings to answer phone calls; and
- Listen well (eye contact and nodding), but often finish people's sentences and sometimes interrupt before they finish.

Pros Are Always in Training

Professional athletes are in training year-round. They want continuous improvement. Should we do any less as leaders than be in continuous training? Coaching leaders should be just like coaching athletes. Using the 3×3 Coaching Model gives a simple system of practical feedback that you can use on a regular basis for any leadership characteristics you choose to emphasize, measure, and improve.

About the Contributor

Bert Decker is a major figure in the communications field. He has been on NBC's *Today* show many times as a communications expert, often commenting on the presidential debates. He is the author of the best-selling book, *You've Got To Be Believed To Be Heard,* as well as video and audio programs such as "High Impact Communication" and "Creating a Powerful Presence" for Nightingale Conant. Bert has been featured in the *Wall Street Journal* and on ABC's *20/20,* as well as in *Business Week,* the *New York Times,* and *Success Magazine.* His book, *Speaking with Bold Assurance,* is scheduled for publication in 2000.

Bert is founder and chairman of Decker Communications, Inc., specializing in training executives and managers in the spoken word. His company is now a wholly owned subsidiary of PROVANT, Inc., a publicly held international training and development company with over two thousand people. Bert also personally coaches CEOs, such as Charles Schwab, and major sports figures, such as Olympic champion speed skater Bonnie Blair.

Bert now spends much of his time writing books and speaking on the impact of communication in the Marketplace, where he was a main platform speaker at the Million Dollar Round Table. He graduated from Yale University with a degree in psychology, has served on the cabinet of United Way, and served on the board of directors of the National Speakers Association. He is currently on the board of directors of PROVANT, Inc., and CBMC, and also serves on the Westmont College board of advisors.

CHAPTER TWENTY-SIX

INTERPERSONAL TECHNIQUES FOR LEADERS

Judith M. Bardwick

Providing both positive and negative feedback to subordinates is an extremely important managerial responsibility, because it guides individuals, teams, and organizations toward success. Yet, most managers, if they provide feedback at all, provide it badly.

Where Counseling Fits

The best feedback is straightforward, honest, and specific, and it is rooted in behavior. In contrast, poor feedback is vague, evasive, or hostile (involving a criticism of a person rather than of the person's behavior). Honest, specific feedback creates an opportunity for positive development. Hostile feedback causes resentment, which precludes the creation of a climate in which a developmental conversation of development can take place. A manager's feedback should inform or teach a subordinate. Critical

Note: This chapter shows how some techniques used in life counseling may be usefully brought into a coaching context. Those managers who are not also qualified psychologists should never attempt to apply these techniques outside the agenda of work-related coaching.

evaluations should be structured in a constructive way, giving the person the information he or she needs to make changes.

Coaching involves telling people specifically what they are doing well and what they are doing badly in areas limited to their work. Once a manager has communicated the problem and what improved performance would look like, both parties form an expectation of the future. *Counseling,* on the other hand, engages people with issues that are deeply important to them and about which they hold strong feelings. These issues may go beyond the work situation and are often large and difficult to define.

The advantages to counseling include: (1) the client presents the problem to the counselor—in contrast to the work situation, in which the employee may feel there is no problem or the manager and employee may disagree about the issues; and (2) a qualified counselor is present with diagnostic and communication skills—whereas workplace situations may become very "touchy," because one or both parties are uncomfortable talking about the issues or don't want to listen.

It is naturally more comfortable and less intimidating for managers and subordinates to discuss work issues rather than personal issues, but profound emotions also frequently affect work performance. When this is true, the emotions and any personal issues behind them should also be addressed and resolved. Managers may find any of the following situations among subordinates:

- Emotional impact of divorce on their work;
- Impact of drug or alcohol abuse on work;
- Work implications from a child in trouble;
- A mid-life crisis;
- Unrealistic expectations;
- Fear of retirement;
- Poor interpersonal skills; or
- A work plateau.

Any of these situations is likely to have both a life component and a work-related component.

Effective Counseling

Counseling is effective when it results in people changing their perceptions, attitudes, and behavior to solve their problems and improve their lives. Good employee counseling requires a manager to have an open attitude, good communication skills, and an understanding that the issue under discussion may only be the tip of an underlying problem.

People's thoughts and feelings often seem contradictory and inconsistent when important and sensitive issues are involved, so counselors have to listen well and concentrate on what is being said in order to ask the questions that will lead to insight on the part of the person being counseled. The manager-counselor's goal is to enable the employee to see alternatives and choices and to make good decisions.

To be an effective counselor you must understand yourself, your own values, and any obstacles that may hinder your progress. An effective counselor does not react emotionally or defensively, nor is he or she afraid of others' emotions. Expressed emotions are clues; they provide data and insight into another's outlook. As an effective counselor, you must not become emotionally involved. Of course, you may feel compassion, pity, sadness, irritation, or even anger, but it is imperative not to be vulnerable to the content of the problem or feel responsibility for the problem. As counselor, your goal is to be appropriately objective. Do not be so involved as to respond emotionally, but be empathic enough to feel sensitively.

Emotion and Miscommunication

The most difficult conversations are those in which there is a great deal of emotion, because emotion increases the chance that messages will be obscured or distorted. When there is a lot of emotion—either because of the nature of the relationship or because of the content of the message—there is a good chance that the message will be distorted by one or both parties. People tend to highlight and remember the positive and forget or exaggerate the negative.

Misperceptions and miscommunications often occur because people prefer to avoid uncomfortable emotional situations. People may not want intimate information about how someone else feels and they may also be reluctant to expose how they feel. The paradoxical result of these tendencies is that when the need to communicate well is high, the probability of not communicating well escalates.

Counseling requires more awareness, sensitivity, and skill than does coaching, because it addresses significant, underlying issues that are deeply personal and grounded in emotion. It is crucial that communication be accurate, relevant, and comprehensive. Because the very significance of the situation makes communication difficult, managers must be taught the following eight skills, appropriate components of counseling, to use in real-world situations.

Eight Skills of Counseling

One: Establish Rapport and Stay Calm

Establishing rapport means creating a mood for the dialogue that is about to take place—to create a sense of comfort so the other person is willing to listen and talk. Begin by taking the time to make sure both of you are at ease.

You will feel more comfortable if you are physically relaxed. You will want to master a breathing or relaxation technique to use when you must remain calm with an emotional or upset employee. You can start to create rapport in the usual verbal ways by which we make people feel welcome. Create contact non-verbally: smile and look at the person, keep your posture open, and lean gently toward the other person. Demonstrate your interest by facing the other person and maintaining eye contact.

The goal of rapport is to create a mood in which trust leads to real communication. Rapport is the result of your being ready to listen and to respond. You may have called the meeting because you are upset or displeased, but you must refrain from making the other person feel defensive. Don't prejudge. Your objective is for both of you to learn. With rapport, the mutuality of your relationship is emphasized. Only after rapport has been established will you be ready to move to the content of the dialogue.

Two: Listen and Ask Responsive Questions

The key to counseling, *active listening*, involves more listening than talking. Active listening also requires concentration and energy, because you must actively think about what you hear. First, focus completely on the other person. You do not have to agree with him or her, but you must concentrate on what the person says and does, without thinking about what you want to say in reply. (It is *not* appropriate when counseling to tell someone what *you* think.)

When counseling, you may offer opinions and provide information, but withhold your advice and do not give orders. Instead, *ask questions*. Find out what is going on in the other person's head. The other person may come up with answers that hadn't occurred to him or her before. This makes the issue clearer for you and for the other person. An advantage of asking questions is that you do not have the responsibility of coming up with the "right" answer for someone else's major decisions.

Another advantage of active listening is that it can enable you to transform an emotional encounter into a cognitive task. Answering a question, especially those that involve facts such as "What was said?" and "What happened next?" diffuses the emotional intensity. Questions can change the focus from "How do you feel?" to "What did you do?"

Three levels of questions are essential for active listening. The levels vary in the amount of interpretation required.

Level One.   Repeat what someone said, but use different words. Summarize or paraphrase what the other person said. For example, in response to a statement such as, "I can't accept the promotion. The move would be too difficult right now." You might say, "The timing is no good right now, is that it?" You have not introduced anything new to the discussion, but the nature of your response invites the other person to continue talking and thinking.

Level Two.   Talk about what you think the other person implied by what was said. Such a response to the same statement would be, "Would your family be upset if you moved?" While the person hasn't said that his or her reluctance stems from family attitudes, it is such a common source of resistance to moving that it's a plausible inference. A Level Two question indicates your involvement by the fact that you went further in your

observations than the person explicitly stated, but your questioning observation is not a challenge. The use of a question indicates your tenta-
tiveness and willingness to listen.

Level Three.   A Level Three question interprets a statement even further;
you articulate feelings that may run deep and of which the person may not
be aware. For instance, "Are you reluctant to move because you don't want
to put your wishes ahead of those of the family?" This can be the most useful response, because you are inviting the person to discuss the crucial issues. Level Three responses should be used only when you believe that the
underlying issue must be addressed in order for the most important aspects
to surface, and only if the result will be that no substantive progress will
occur otherwise. Level Three responses should be used only if you are a
skillful counselor and you have a trusting relationship with the person,
because they are intrusive and can open issues that the person may not be
aware of or want to disclose.

Level Three questions are often based on a feeling you have when the
person speaks. It's normal for emotions to rise. Asking a Level Three question says you trust your intuition and you're willing to experience an emotional response. Although a Level Three response is the riskiest, it is also
potentially the most productive.

Three: Hear with Your Eyes and Ears and Emotions

Be Aware of What Is There and What Is Missing.   Most of us have had
a lot of training in how to think, but we receive much less training in how
to feel or be intuitive. Ours is a culture that prefers cognitive information
to feeling data. But not paying attention to feelings means that you ignore
and lose vital data about how someone else feels and why they make the
choices they do.

Intuition—or how something makes you feel—is especially valuable in
making you aware of what is being said without words. Your intuition is
most receptive to the messages that are being sent by tone of voice, pattern
of speech, intonations, facial expressions, and posture and body movement.
Intuition helps you hear what is not there—what is avoided, evaded, or

missing—but which you sense ought to be present. Often, what is missing is at least as important as that which is present.

Beware though, as managers are not qualified psychologists or psychiatrists; therefore, they can question in order to gain clarity, but must not probe beyond what is comfortable and appropriate. You may only ask about an issue either to open it up or to help you decide whether you should suggest a professional counselor.

Read the Non-Verbal Clues. Although it has become fashionable to interpret facial expressions and body language in great detail, it is unnecessary and probably invalid to do so. It is sufficient to become sensitive to the general message that is being conveyed non-verbally. Check the following, for example:

- Is the body posture closed so that the spine is curved, the head lowered, the arms held close to the body? Does that convey timidity? Depression?
- Is the body slunk down, the voice a whisper, giving a sense of low energy? Does that imply depression? Powerlessness? Futility?
- Is the energy level high, the torso and head thrust forward, the eyes directed at you? Does this intensity convey a sense of importance? Anger?
- Are the eyes focused anywhere but on you? Is the person embarrassed? Fearful?
- Is speech interrupted by sounds such as, "aaah, errr, or mmmmm?" Is the person uncertain of what to say or uncomfortable saying it?
- Is the person's voice uncharacteristically high? Does it sound tentative?
- Is it uncharacteristically low and deliberate?
- Is there an unusual level of formality? Is the person uncomfortable?
- Is there a sense of spontaneity and honesty—or of control and evasion?
- Did the person's mood change suddenly? What were you talking about when the tone altered?
- Is there a basic incongruity between the words being said and the body's message?

Being sensitive to messages that are sent without words is intuition. Pay attention to what is there and what is missing. Pay attention to how you feel and what it makes you think of. Because your goal is to learn about people, practice being aware of these cues. Respond to signs of tension by asking responsive questions, especially those at Level Two. Be aware that body language can be a sign that something of emotional importance is occurring. Ask about it, but don't over-interpret it, and don't take it literally.

Four: Stick to What Is Happening in the Situation

It is always tempting to dwell on the past. The past is interesting, and by understanding it we gain understanding of someone's present perceptions and choices. Often, the past feels psychologically safer to someone; after all, the past has already happened.

However, the past cannot be changed; therefore it should not be the focus of discussion. Moreover, in the past there were unsatisfactory behaviors that may cause you to judge and blame. So, although you may talk about the past, make it a minor theme. Focus on what the person is doing *now* and where he or she is going.

Generalities are often evasions of what is important; they lend themselves to emotional exaggeration. Try to keep the conversation specific and steer it to the present, especially to what is going on during your conversation, because that is what is most vividly real.

People usually talk about their *experiences,* their *behaviors,* and their *feelings.* Of the three, it is easiest to talk about an experience, because it is something that has already happened. Describing an experience means that we can be charming, funny, poignant, or dramatic without disclosing ourselves. But the point of counseling is tapping into the motivation behind our actions and to prepare for change; disclosures on the part of others should lead to self-awareness. Therefore, use the questioning techniques of Levels One and Two to help the person to describe exact behaviors and feelings in specific situations; help people to emphasize the near past in the current conversation.

You will know the person is comfortable talking with you when his or her non-verbal communications and your intuition agree. Only then are you in a position to ask: "What will you do now?"

Five: Don't Solve the Problem; Emphasize Choices

An objective of counseling is to empower the other person. The goal is for people to be active in their own lives. When you tell people what to do, you reduce their power; when you help people make their own choices, you give them power. Personal power allows people to initiate, evaluate, decide, and ultimately to create their own futures.

The most basic help you can give someone is to help the person make his or her own decisions. In short, try not to give advice, even if you are directly asked for it. Instead, present suggestions, options, and alternatives. People who are currently experiencing a problem are usually able to perceive only a narrow band of what is possible. They are simply too close to what is going on to gain a larger perspective. It is appropriate and constructive for you to point out alternatives and the feasibility and possible consequences of different decisions. You can offer opinions about different options, but that should be the limit of your input.

Six: Be Open to Emotions

Many people are uncomfortable with emotional responses from those with whom they interact at work. We may not want the burden of an intimate friendship because we do not want to be an emotional support for a co-worker or we may experience their emotion as a threat to us. Don't be afraid of other people confronting you and being angry. Emotions are a major key to their understanding and clarifying significant issues. An expressed emotion is vastly more constructive than the alternatives: passivity, silence, evasion, and denial.

The way to handle an emotional situation is to observe the emotions. Try to understand why they occur and what has provoked them, but do not become emotionally involved yourself. It is easier not to become involved if you do two things: (1) think of emotions as data, and (2) remember that you, as a symbol of the organization or as someone with power over the other person, often become the target of the emotion. Simply ask the right questions and provoke awareness.

In counseling you want to become aware of others' responses. Equally important, but more difficult, you have to become sensitive to how you feel and the circumstances that give rise to your own emotions. This is the first step to controlling your responses so that you are free to concentrate on the other person.

Sensitivity to emotions means not only being aware when they are present and powerful; it also means being sensitive when emotions ought to be present and they are not. When there is too little emotion around the topics under consideration, that is usually a signal that something important is going on and more is involved than is obvious. You can probe this possibility using the questioning techniques of Levels One and Two, or you may disclose your own discomfort. Say something like, "I have a feeling that something is going on, but I don't know what it is."

If the emotional responses of the other person trigger significant emotion in you, and the intensity is so great that you are uncomfortable, you should stop the conversation and say, "I'm having difficulty handling this." A more effective use of a strong emotion is to transform it into a cognitive disclosure rather than an emotional one. You can do this by saying, "I can see that you feel very strongly about this. Can you tell me why?" This is a Level One question: it asks for information, but offers no interpretation.

You can ask, "How are you feeling right now?" This question really implies, "How do you feel about talking about serious matters with me? Do you feel okay with me?" While you may sense that the person is comfortable and trusts you, when you ask someone how he or she feels, you are empowering the person to choose to end the conversation.

Seven: Don't Judge the Other Person

Not judging and the skill that follows, "Be honest," are the most difficult. Effective counseling requires us to be forthright in our opinions, but our opinions must not become judgments.

Of course we all have opinions. In fact, a major responsibility in our lives is to evaluate and decide whether a procedure or a behavior, an idea or an outcome is good or bad. An important part of a manager's role is to judge ideas and performance—to decide whether something is good or bad. The acuity of your judgment is an essential criterion in distinguishing whether you are merely an adequate or a truly outstanding manager. In coaching, which involves directing someone in daily work, it is appropriate to judge. In counseling, you must not judge.

Judging increases your power over the other person, and naturally it increases the person's feeling of powerlessness or dependence. Judging, in itself, increases the probability that the other person will ultimately resent you, be angered by what you say, and not hear you. In a subtle but pervasive way, the premise that you have the "right" to judge sets up an antagonistic exchange. Because you, as manager, are in a more powerful role, your subordinate may not display those feelings, but the feelings will be there—and they are counterproductive.

Your task as a counselor is to comprehend other people's perceptions, choices, expectations, and attitudes. What are their values? What do they think they need to do? When you understand, you can evaluate—but not in terms of good or bad. Rather, you may ask to what extent they believe their perceptions are accurate or inaccurate. In what ways are their behaviors effective or ineffective? Are their goals achievable or unachievable? Is the person's sense of self appropriate or inappropriate? Remember, the goal of counseling is to help another person see himself or herself more clearly and accurately and to help uncover the range of choices from which to make decisions and set goals. You want to increase the person's ability to take appropriate action and sense of empowerment.

Eight: Be Honest

The ultimate mark of respect for people is when you regard them as capable of managing their own lives. By being honest, you convey your belief in them. Actually, we are rarely dishonest. Instead, we are *not* honest. Usually, when we are not honest with people it is because we think they cannot handle the truth. Dishonesty, in this sense, is not the act of lying. Rather, it is evading, and evasion can be as potent as lying in bringing out feelings of mistrust.

Trust between people requires *communication,* but that does not necessarily mean *agreement.* You may agree or disagree, but if you can see the other person's point of view and state your own, you will build a relationship built on trust.

Honesty involves disclosure and feedback. You want to convey information, and you want the other person to know that he or she can do the same. Honesty is the essential firmament of trust—and it must be mutual. Honesty involves responses that are both supportive and challenging. Honesty requires that you give both positive and negative feedback. You must also be willing to hear about yourself.

When you disclose what you think and feel, and make it clear that you want the same kind of response in return, you create an atmosphere of honesty. It is one in which neither of you has to be defensive. This is because disagreeing becomes only a starting point from which you move on to create more and more agreement. Disagreeing, then, is not confrontation. It is merely the exchange of information. In order to gain helpful responses, you must treat others with respect. Thus, in a progressive climate, you both completely ignore any power difference between your roles at work.

Dishonesty is destructive because evasion allows individuals to remain in the purgatory between hope and tense despair. You do not do yourself a favor—and you do not do your employees a favor—when your lack of honesty keeps them in a state of uncertainty and anxiety. Honesty makes issues clear. It is only when issues are on the table, specific and definable, that they can be addressed and solved.

While counseling is never easy, you may come to find it is among the most significant and satisfying things you do as a manager.

About the Contributor

Judith M. Bardwick is founder and president of Bardwick and Associates, an influential management consulting firm. In addition to her many academic achievements, Judy has been an active business consultant for more than two decades. Since 1978, she has concentrated on issues relating to improving human and organizational effectiveness. She is a leading expert on these subjects and has combined respected cutting-edge research with its practical application throughout her career.

Well-known for her exciting and challenging speaking style, Judy has been a leader in the field of the psychology of women for thirty years. Her roster of clients includes dozens of Fortune 500 companies, such as AT&T, Hewlett-Packard, Nissan Motor Corporation, IBM, CONRAIL, 3M, Bell Atlantic, Lyondeti Petrochemical Company, Schering-Plough, NORWEST Bank, and the U. S. Treasury Institute. Bardwick and Associates has a high proportion of repeat engagements, reflecting the productive relationships formed between the firm and its clients.

Judy earned a B.S. degree from Purdue University and an M.S. from Cornell. She received her Ph.D. from the University of Michigan, and subsequently became a full professor and associate dean of the College of Literature, Science, and the Arts. She left the University of Michigan in 1982 and served as a visiting professor of management at the School of Business Administration at San Diego State University for a year. Since then, she has devoted herself to consulting and business-related research and writing. She is currently a clinical professor of psychiatry at the University of California at San Diego.

Judy's most recent book, *In Praise of Good Business,* was published in 1998. She is the author of four other books, *Danger in the Comfort Zone, The Plateauing Trap, In Transition,* and the *Psychology of Women,* and the editor of *Readings in the Psychology of Women* and co-author of *Feminine Personality and Conflict.* In addition, Judy has published more than one hundred articles and book chapters on a wide range of topics.

CHAPTER TWENTY-SEVEN

COACHING OTHERS TO ACCEPT FEEDBACK

Joe Folkman

Possibly the most valuable gift we can receive from another person is honest feedback. Receiving feedback about how to improve our performance and effectiveness can lead to life-enhancing improvements. And, although negative feedback is frequently unappreciated, those who receive it must occasionally be reminded that receiving no feedback at all would be much worse.

Feedback establishes a connection between what we think and what we do, between our intentions and how others perceive our actions. Without good feedback we can never be sure how our behavior affects others. We are left on our own to figure out what others think and feel.

Most coaching relationships begin with helping those being coached to accept feedback. This article will present four steps that will help you coach others to accept feedback and turn it into positive change.

Step One: Hearing the Feedback

For many people it is difficult to tell the difference between feedback and noise. One of the most intriguing characteristics of the human body is its ability to filter what we hear. We teach ourselves to pay attention to some noises and to ignore others. As you read this, stop a few times and notice the noises occurring around you.

Today's organizations are full of noise: voice mail, e-mail, announcements, memos, interruptions, meetings, discussions, and other messages abound in most offices. With such a high volume of noise from incoming information, it becomes impossible to pay attention to every message. To cope, we develop fairly sophisticated mental filters that help us pay attention to some and ignore others.

Coaching others to hear feedback begins with helping people pay attention to feedback that has been ignored in the past. Many who need this coaching were originally hired and placed in important positions because of their clear points of view and strong opinions. As they progressed in their positions, they became confident and tough-minded; they made difficult decisions and moved their organizations forward on issues for which there might not have been 100 percent agreement. These managers needed to develop thick skins, and so they ignored some feedback to accomplish more effectively the jobs they were hired to do.

Often, the peers and direct reports of this group observe that these managers "just don't get it." Given the above scenario, such observations are correct. Many people teach themselves to ignore the feedback they are given. In a similar example, one of my children is often easily distracted by the events going on around him. Occasionally I must place my hands gently on both sides of his face, point his eyes directly at mine, and then talk to him before I am sure he is paying attention and listening effectively. Sometimes coaches must do the same thing, figuratively, for others to genuinely hear their feedback.

Step Two: Accepting the Feedback

We are unwilling to change what we do not believe needs to be changed. Beyond simply coaching people to hear or to become aware of feedback, coaches must help others to accept the feedback provided. If the feedback is not accepted, no change will occur.

For example, it is frequently said of alcoholics that although they are given plenty of feedback, and often demonstrate awareness of the feedback, many initially deny it: "I'm not an alcoholic! I can stop whenever I choose!" When people are in a state of denial, no change or improvement can be made until they can "own" the problem. Part of the acceptance process involves admitting that the feedback received is accurate. In Alcoholics Anonymous meetings, this step is placed at the very beginning of the process, when people introduce themselves by saying, "I am John [or Jane] Doe, and I'm an alcoholic."

Acceptance means more than a passive acknowledgment of the feedback. It means receiving or embracing it and believing that the perceptions of others are valid. It is possible to hear, and even believe, feedback from others while continuing to think, "Who cares?" "What do they know?" or "This doesn't really matter." For example, someone may admit, "I understand that those I work with think I'm indecisive," while saying to himself, "If those morons only understood the complexity I have to deal with, they might understand that I just take the time to analyze a problem thoroughly before making my decisions." Acceptance means believing that we do, in fact, "have a problem."

Acceptance also means that we understand the feedback and are clear about what the behavior looks like, when the behavior occurs and does not occur, and how the behavior impacts others. For example, someone who has not fully accepted feedback might say, "I understand that my direct reports would like to be better informed." But someone who is accepting the same feedback would understand, "When I don't keep my direct reports well-informed, they do not spend their time productively and they feel dis-empowered." Similarly, acceptance means understanding how the behavior impacts our personal effectiveness: "My job would be a lot easier and this project would run more smoothly if people were kept well-informed."

Step Three: Prioritizing

A key to coaching people to make a successful change is to focus their efforts on only a few critical behaviors. Trying to change too much inevitably results in changing nothing at all. The 80/20 rule of individual performance helps capture the philosophy of prioritization: eighty percent of our performance comes directly from only twenty percent of our behaviors.

This concept can be used to demonstrate that a few critical behaviors account for the bulk of our performance. The central idea is to focus our efforts on the critical behaviors that leverage performance.

One difficulty with feedback is that frequently the behaviors we receive feedback about most often are *not* key drivers of our performance. Those who provide feedback do not typically prioritize their feedback. They provide feedback about what is bothering them and what they observe, and they tend to do it in the order in which these things come to mind. As a result, when we receive highly negative feedback, we sometimes feel overwhelmed because the feedback seems to indicate problems in every aspect of our behavior. But the reality is that poor performance in a few critical areas can drag down the perceptions of others about our other behaviors. I call this a "negative halo effect." When others are extremely frustrated with us about some aspect of our performance, it is difficult for them to acknowledge that this one behavior is bad while all the other behaviors are good. Instead, they tend to form general impressions and adjust their perceptions about other behaviors to fit those impressions. Thus, poor performance in one critical behavior tends to produce a negative halo when providing feedback.

For a successful change effort to occur, we must review the feedback we receive and determine the key drivers of our performance. Coaches can help to identify these critical behaviors and help to create dramatic change. Expending great effort to change a behavior that will have little impact on the perceptions of others will not lead to the required level of performance. But if we can change a few critical behaviors that leverage our performance, then our focused efforts will help to create a "positive halo effect." Just a few noticeable changes can cause others to change their general impressions.

The following paragraphs show how to determine the key drivers of performance:

Clarify the Key Objectives or Expectations of the Job. It is impossible to improve performance without establishing clear and specific performance objectives. For many, this process alone will help to leverage performance.

Often, poor performance is the result of unclear expectations ("I didn't know I was expected to do that!") or competing expectations ("I can't manage all the details of this project if I have to take on three projects at the same time!").

Determine Whether Making a Change in a Particular Behavior Would Significantly Improve Overall Performance. For many behaviors it is not clear how a change would improve performance. In one instance, a manager had received strong feedback about his cynicism. Although the cynicism bothered some people, it was unclear whether changing this behavior would have a substantial impact on the bottom-line performance of the group. So, rather than trying to change the behavior, he decided to keep his cynicism private. He determined that involving others in decisions and keeping them informed would have a greater impact on the group's performance.

Find Out Which Behavior the Person Desires to Change the Most. Behaviors or characteristics for which people have passion, commitment, and a desire to change have a significantly higher probability of changing. Too often, people try to change behaviors for which their desire to change, their "felt need," is low. The inevitable result is that nothing changes. Review the feedback and determine whether one of the issues would be easy to change. Finding a "quick win" can provide both momentum for the person making the change and optimism for those who provide feedback and can demonstrate that the person is serious about change. Some behaviors are more difficult to change than others. For example, *things are easier to change than people,* and *personality traits are more difficult to change than basic skills or knowledge.*

Step Four: Making Change Happen

Many of us approach personal change with great enthusiasm but little planning. Although enthusiasm is important, perhaps even critical, enthusiasm alone is rarely enough. When quizzed about how we plan to carry out a change, we generally answer, "I'll just do it."

I like to think of the many different approaches to change as "levers." As when moving a large rock, the more effectively positioned the levers are, the higher the probability that the rock will be moved. Some approaches to making changes work better for some people than for others, and some approaches make more sense with some change issues than with others. The key to increasing the probability that change will happen is to increase the number of levers used and the effort applied to each.

Three of the most important change levers include: (1) making the change goal specific; (2) creating a clear vision; and (3) obtaining support from others. (For a more complete list of these levers, refer to Folkman, 1996.)

Making the Change Goal Specific.   Usually, when we begin a change effort we start with a general goal. We say we are going to "become a better communicator," "be more sensitive to others," "exert more leadership," "better motivate our direct reports," or (my personal favorite), "become a better person." Although these are all desirable goals, they lack specificity. The problem with general goals is that it is difficult to tell whether we are succeeding or failing, or to know what actions we should take next. To make effective changes, our goals must be specific and must indicate explicit, measurable behaviors. When our goals are specific, it is easier for us and for others to measure our success and to determine whether we are succeeding or failing.

Creating a Clear Vision.   I recently took my five-year-old son skiing for the first time. As we began our ski day, I helped him put on his skis and explained to him the basics of skiing. The first thing you must learn is the "snowplow," for which you make an upside-down "V" with the skis, which helps you to slow down and to turn.

As I explained the concept to my son, I could see a blank look on his face. On the way to the ski resort that morning we had seen a snowplow, but it had been pushing a single blade, pointed sideways, along the road. My explanation was not working.

As we got to the top of the hill to begin our first run, I heard a ski instructor ask his student to "make a piece of pizza." The student quickly positioned her skis in exactly the same manner I had tried to explain to my son.

I thought to myself, "Now, if there is one thing that my five-year-old is clear about, it is the shape of a piece of pizza." Then I asked my son if he could make a piece of pizza with his skis. The light visibly went on in his eyes.

He replied, "Sure, Dad. Do you want me to make a big piece or a small piece?" Once my son had a clear vision in his mind, it was much easier to learn this new behavior.

Often, we begin our change efforts with only a very vague vision of our ultimate goal. A clear vision is:

- *A Destination.* A vision should describe a place we want to go, not a place we want to avoid. We should be clear not only about what the vision *is,* but also about what it is *not.* It is just as important to describe where we are *not* going as where we want to go.
- *Visual.* We must be able to picture a vision in our minds. The picture often starts out as a distant object that is not totally clear. Later, as we get closer, the vision becomes more clear.
- *Simple.* Complex visions are difficult to clarify and often lead people in multiple directions. Simple visions are the most focused and the most compelling.
- *Challenging, But Realistic.* The vision needs to be attainable.
- *Consistent with Our Personality.* Visions that do not connect with us, that require us to be something other than ourselves, do not have the energy to carry us forward.

Obtaining Support from Others.   Persuading other people to support your change effort is potentially one of the most powerful change levers (although many powerful people tend to want to "go it alone"). Enlisting help from others keeps us honest, because others are watching. Others can often help us avoid the traps that lead to problems. For example, for people who have a difficult time controlling their anger, several easily observable behaviors often precede the explosion of anger. These behaviors are often discernible to others, but not to the person with the problem. Having another person help us recognize such patterns of behavior is a wonderful monitoring device. Eventually, we learn to monitor ourselves.

But enlisting others to help us make changes is often difficult. Some people believe that asking for help diminishes their position or reputation. One person commented to me, "It's like admitting you have a problem." We sometimes deceive ourselves into believing that other people don't know we have a problem. Although a few people might be surprised, most people already know the problem exists. Asking for help allows others to see us as authentic or teachable. As you begin your change or coaching effort, take the time to identify people who will support that change effort.

Conclusion

Both hearing and accepting feedback are critical skills that help us to improve our effectiveness. A coach's role in helping others to "get it" is absolutely critical in bringing about such change. Once people can understand and accept the feedback they receive, they should prioritize the issues they plan to change. Although it is difficult to change many things at one time, those who are motivated can create dramatic impact by changing one or two critical behaviors that leverage their performance.

Remember that a change in one critical behavior can generate significantly greater performance than can trying to change five things at once. Coaching people to use different approaches or "levers," such as setting specific goals, clarifying vision, or enlisting the support of others, helps improve the probability of a change occurring.

About the Contributor

Joe Folkman is a managing director at Novations Group, Inc.—a PROVANT company. He leads the firm's survey feedback practice. His book, *Turning Feedback into Change®: 31 Principles for Managing Personal Development Through Feedback,* suggests how to use feedback in intelligent ways to bring about genuine and positive change in personal behavior. Joe is also the author of two books on employee surveys: *Making Feedback Work: Turning Feedback from Employee Surveys into Change* and *Employee Surveys That Make a Difference.*

CHAPTER TWENTY-EIGHT

COACHING FOR ORGANIZATIONAL CHANGE

Bill Hawkins and Tom Pettey

In today's marketplace, companies must continually re-create themselves or perish. Scott McNealy, the chairman, CEO, and president of Sun Microsystems, estimates that ninety percent of Sun's current business is in products developed within the past twelve to eighteen months. In this dynamic world, business leaders are looking at the way they do business with a critical eye, because an organization's ability to adapt to market conditions, address new technology, and develop and quickly market products can make the difference between prosperity and sinking stock prices.

In response, executives in the most successful companies are examining every aspect of their business to provide capacity for adapting to the changes unique to their marketplace. These executives are clarifying strategy, amending business objectives, and establishing new systems. As a result, organizations are removing layers of management, setting up cross-functional teams, establishing self-directed teams, reducing bureaucracy, and driving decision making to lower levels.

The Challenge

The challenge is to get people in the organization to embrace the changes and focus on attaining the goals set forth by the executives, and this requires a change in behavior. Real cultural change can only be achieved if people at all levels in the organization behave in ways that support the strategic direction and goals. Obviously, people need to know what is required of them in the "new" future. Not so obviously, however, people need to understand the differences between their current behavior and future expectations. That is the responsibility of the leaders in the organization, right?

Single-source assessment, in which the leader provides feedback to direct reports on performance, typically occurs once a year for the purpose of providing management with information for pay and promotions. Supervisors typically dislike these appraisals, so they put them off or avoid them completely. Recently, while working with a senior executive team in a large organization, we found that only two people out of fifteen at the vice-presidential level had received a performance review in the past year. Another negative aspect of single-source assessment is that even under the best conditions these assessments represent only one point of view. Add to this the fact that the boss, who has responsibility for dozens of people, may be new to the position or may work in a different city, country, or time zone, and the assessments become even less accurate. One middle-level manager told me in an interview, "I now have sixty-five people reporting to me. Giving each one a meaningful performance review is unrealistic. I'm pleased when I can remember everyone's name."

A Tool for Alignment

The most popular tool used to align organizational expectations to individual goals and performance expectations is to create a profile of specific leadership behaviors expected in the future and to provide leaders in the organization an opportunity to receive feedback on their performance against this profile. Although there are a number of good "generic" leadership models available, many clients choose to develop a custom leadership profile. This profile is typically composed of two parts. The first part centers on values or principles that are held dear to the company. It involves issues such as integrity or respect for people. Johnson & Johnson calls these the "Credo"; American Express identifies them as their "Blue Box Values." The second part identifies a set of core competencies and leadership behaviors critical to future success. These might include such issues as: "communicates information across organizational boundaries early and often" or "effectively manages individuals whose behavior undermines teamwork."

If created thoughtfully, this profile will align organizational goals to individual performance expectations. It is an ideal tool to reinforce the corporate values and communicate the new set of competencies needed for future success to all employees and leaders. It can also be a strong motivating factor for encouraging change in leadership behavior in managers who receive feedback from co-workers.

Making It Happen

Create a Profile of Desired Leadership for the Future

A useful way to begin this process is to interview the president and the executive team to validate the vision, mission, values, and broad organizational goals of the company. Once these have been clarified, focus groups (including people at all levels and in all areas of the organization) can go to work identifying the core competencies and behaviors needed for future success. The purpose of these focus groups is two-fold: first, the involvement of people at various levels from all parts of the company ensures that the profile accurately captures the success factors for the entire company, not just headquarters. Second, and just as important, their involvement ensures ownership of the final product. This leadership profile isn't a theory from some college professor or something that senior management has imposed. It is a unique set of competencies and leadership behaviors that they helped create. The list is then returned to the president for final approval.

Determine Who Can Provide Meaningful Feedback

For best results the feedback providers should render the feedback anonymously and be valid, credible sources who know the leader's work best. This would almost certainly include the boss and any direct reports. Other valid sources might be team members, internal customers, peers, or external customers.

Conduct an orientation meeting (led by a senior executive) to introduce the process and provide training on how to provide feedback to others. This is a step frequently overlooked, because the process appears so straightforward that no explanation is necessary. However, both those giving and those receiving feedback approach the process with some anxiety, so a kickoff meeting can be used to explain how and why the leadership profile was put together. This meeting is also used to instruct respondents on how to complete the survey, to answer any questions, and to put people's minds at ease about the absolute confidentiality of the results for the person receiving feedback and the anonymity of those providing feedback.

Collect the Feedback

Technology exists today to collect everything on-line via Internet or intranet and still preserve confidentiality for the manager and anonymity for those providing feedback. The feedback is compiled by an outside party into a summary report. This is given directly to the manager being coached.

The Coach

Analyze the Results and Develop an Action Plan

At first, most managers are overwhelmed with the volume of information provided in the summary report. There are percentiles, written comments, company averages, and category summaries. The first responsibility of the coach is to help the manager analyze the information looking for themes. What leadership skills and core competencies do people see as strengths in this manager? Is this a pleasant surprise, or is it how the person sees himself or herself? What areas are seen as opportunities for improvement?

The next step is to ensure that the coachee accepts the feedback as valid. Once the manager has accepted the feedback as valid and identified areas for personal growth, he or she wants specific suggestions from the coach. The key to the action plan is that it must contain specific advice on what and how to approach change. The successful coach needs to provide alternatives. For example, if the person wants to improve public speaking skills, one could suggest a public speaking course at a local college; Toastmasters; short presentations at the boss's upcoming staff meetings; hiring a professional speech coach; volunteering to make a presentation at a local church, school, or club; and/or using an audiotape to practice in the car on the way to work or a videotape for instruction at home. If enough alternatives are suggested, some will appear attractive.

Respond to Stakeholders and Follow Up

The manager should meet with the key people he or she will be working with during the next six to twelve months. In a short meeting, the manager should share the action plan and collect additional suggestions on how to improve in key areas targeted for improvement. Last, he or she should follow up with these people on a regular basis.

Keilty, Goldsmith & Company (1996) has published the results of a study conducted regarding the impact of feedback and follow-up with over eight thousand leaders in Fortune 100 companies. The results were dramatic, but not surprising. "The degree of change in perceived leadership effectiveness was clearly related to the degree of follow-up. Of the managers who were seen as *not following up*, over half were rated as unchanged or less effective by their direct reports eighteen months later. Of those who were seen as doing *some follow-up*, eighty-nine percent were rated as more effective." Unfortunately, only fifty-eight percent of the leaders followed up. Follow-up works, but how do you make it happen?

Ongoing Coaching

Most leadership programs initiated as part of organizational change projects have traditionally been approached from the following point of view: give the people feedback, target areas for improvement, provide training (usually a one- or two-day course), and success will follow. The problem, of course, is that even the most well-meaning and motivated managers return to work and are swamped. As Steve Covey (1996) points out in his book *First Things First*, the urgent phone calls, meetings, customer requests, and so forth tend to take priority over important but non-urgent issues. Personal development is important, but it can be put off. Before you know it, a year has passed and those development issues never made it to the top of the "to do" list.

Jim Bolt, chairman of Executive Development Associates, which specializes in designing custom development programs to support strategic change, recognized this problem. In our work with Jim over the last two years, he has included ongoing coaching in the programs he has developed. Coaches follow the format outlined above, but instead of saying, "Goodbye, good luck, call me if you have any questions" at the end of the feedback coaching session, they maintain an ongoing coaching relationship with the coachee. They continue contact via e-mail and telephone on a monthly basis. The coach is there to answer questions that invariably arise, provide additional input, suggest alternative approaches, and help maintain focus on the action plan for development.

The cost of this additional coaching is "peanuts," typically only an additional one percent or two percent, as compared to the cost of programs without the ongoing coaching. The impact is enormous. Every organization that has included ongoing coaching as part of the feedback process has dramatically improved the proportion of leaders who follow up, and consequently the perception of leadership effectiveness has improved. Following is a case study of the California Public Employees' Retirement System (CalPERS) wherein ninety-two percent of the *entire* executive team showed improved leadership in a four-month, follow-up study.

Multi-Rater Feedback

EXHIBIT 28.1. THE CALPERS STORY

CalPERS manages pension and health benefits for more than 1.1 million California public employees, retirees, and their families. With $156 billion in assets, we are the largest public pension system in the nation with a record of success. During our strategic planning process in 1996, however, it became clear that we would face increasing competition and tremendous challenges in the next decade.

Training and development was identified as one of five key projects in the strategic plan. We recognized that an inordinate share of CalPERS' resources were devoted to efficiency and effectiveness, and few to creating greater organizational capacity through expanded learning. The commitment to learning as a top priority in the organization came from the CEO.

We began with a comprehensive training needs assessment. The input of every senior manager in the organization was compiled and used as a foundation for identifying business challenges and key training opportunities. Next, focus groups, including people at all levels and all locations, were employed to fine-tune the issues. A key finding from these focus groups was that the vision and strategies of the organization were not widely understood. Silos and parochial thinking were evident and could potentially impair success.

We then developed a profile that incorporated the changing role of the leader of the future at CalPERS. This profile drew on the established organizational values in which we have always prided ourselves, such as integrity and quality. To that we added competencies and leadership practices that would be critical to future leadership success, such as communication of information across organizational boundaries.

Leadership Challenge Workshops were created to promote increased awareness of the changing roles of leadership. Multi-rater/360° feedback was a cornerstone of these workshops. Importantly, senior executives led by example by participating in the first workshop, in which the focus was receiving feedback and developing actions for leadership improvement. A senior executive then kicked off each subsequent workshop by explaining the changing role of leadership in the organization and sharing his/her own action plan for improvement, resulting from his/her participation in the feedback process.

The objectives of the three-day Leadership Challenge Workshops were for participants to:

- Gain an understanding and internalize the vision, values, strategies, and leadership challenges;
- Understand our marketplace realities and trends;

(continued)

EXHIBIT 28.1.   (CONTINUED)

- Learn and practice the common demands of the changing role of leadership;
- Increase teaming;
- Learn how to lead change and improve communication skills; and
- Receive feedback on the leadership effectiveness and create individual development plans for improving effectiveness.

As part of the workshop, each person met one-on-one with an outside consultant. During the session, the consultant interpreted the feedback and helped each person identify two individual opportunity areas and two group opportunity areas for leadership improvement. Then, action plans were developed. At the conclusion of the session, the consultant kept a copy of the action plan and arranged for ongoing communication over the next few months. Depending on the communication style preferences of each manager, ongoing dialogue (telephone, e-mail, and sometimes additional face-to-face meetings).

Four months later, each manager again surveyed his/her "key stakeholders" to assess improvement, not on the entire list of leadership behaviors, but on those specifically targeted for individual improvement in the action plans. The result met, even surpassed, our initial expectations. Over 90 percent of our executive group showed improvement and 86 percent of senior management showed improvement.

In retrospect, we feel we did a number of things that led to our initial success. The involvement of senior executive staff in the first multi-rater/360° feedback session set an excellent foundation for the remainder of the leadership team to share the same experience. The Leadership Challenge Workshops, scheduled away from headquarters, also provided an excellent learning environment to receive the feedback and to formulate action plans. Focusing on one or two individual opportunity areas with the support of the assigned coach yielded excellent results, as did the commitment to re-surveys after four months to assess progress.

During our initial work with the 360° feedback process, we also learned the importance of ongoing communication. We could have increased our effectiveness if we had established a communication link, via the CalPERS intranet, early on with each participant. Such a link would have been a great way to share personal success stories and to provide helpful tips and reminders to our participants. In the final analysis, the personal commitment of the CEO and the example he established made a real difference in our level of success.

About the Contributors

Bill Hawkins is an independent consultant specializing in the design and delivery of training to support leadership development, organizational values, team building, performance management, and organizational change. Prior to being a consultant, Bill worked for a division of Johnson & Johnson in sales, marketing, sales management, and product management positions. He then joined Boston Scientific Corporation as director of sales and marketing for the Microvasive Division. In seven years, the division grew from four employees to over five hundred, and Boston Scientific went public on the New York Stock Exchange.

During the last ten years, Bill has worked with and conducted leadership training in leading organizations on five continents. Clients served include American Express, AT&T, Bell South, Bloomberg, Boston Scientific, Budget Rent-a-Car, CalPERS, DirecTV, Dreyer's Grand Ice Cream, Johnson & Johnson, Kodak, Lutheran Brotherhood, Motorola, Nortel, PNC Bank, Raytheon, Sun Microsystems, Titleist, Union Pacific Railroad, Valvoline, and Weyerhaeuser. With his blend of consulting and management experience, Bill brings a breadth of understanding and insight to real world situations.

Aside form his work with major corporations, Bill has donated his services to the International Red Cross/Red Crescent, the New York Association for New Americans, United Cerebral Palsy Association, and the Girl Scouts of America. He holds a B.S. degree from Drake University and an MBA from Indiana University. Bill is a member of the Learning Network, is listed in *Who's Who in International Business,* and is a contributing author in the Peter Drucker Foundation book *The Organization of the Future.*

Tom Pettey is the chief of the Human Resources Division for the California Public Employees' Retirement System (CalPERS). As key policy advisor on human resource issues, he has primary responsibility for the implementation of HR strategies to support the CalPERS strategic plan. In addition to directing the core HR functions, over the past two years he has devoted particular attention to the development of specialized and innovative programs to recruit and retain a top-quality workforce.

CHAPTER TWENTY-NINE

THE BIG THREE DERAILMENT FACTORS
IN A COACHING RELATIONSHIP

David Noer

At a recent professional gathering of experienced management consultants, the moderator asked participants to describe the "kind of work you are doing these days." The response was both surprising and distressing. The surprise for me was that almost everyone in the room claimed to be doing some kind of "executive coaching." The distress came with my knowledge that many of my colleagues, although good consultants in their areas of expertise, did not have the training, orientation, or aptitude for maintaining the special kind of helping relationship necessary for effective coaching.

With the delayering of organizations and expanded spans of control, the coaching and mentoring role previously performed by managers is increasingly being farmed out. It is the hottest consulting game in town and, unfortunately, many organizations are not getting the maximum bang for the buck, and in some cases "coaches" cause more harm than good. This chapter addresses the three most common reasons coaching efforts run into trouble. I call these the big three derailment factors. I will look at each of these factors in turn from the perspective of the coach, the client, and the philosophical underpinnings of the coaching relationship itself.

Factor One: Confusion, Collusion, and Lack of Clarity as to Who Is the Client

The following is a condensed version of a recent meeting with a CEO, a vice president of human resources (HR), and me:

> "We've heard a lot of good things about your coaching work, and we have a senior vice president we'd like you to change," said the vice president of HR.
>
> "Technically, he's great, but he doesn't have good people skills," added the CEO.
>
> "What do you want me to do?" I asked.
>
> "You know, fix him, help him change, because he's in trouble," responded the vice president.
>
> "We don't have a lot of time to waste. How long would it take to get some tangible results?" asked the CEO, first looking at his watch, then to his desktop calendar.
>
> When I didn't respond, the vice president jumped in: "We've got a corporate budget to cover these kind of things. The cost of this effort would be invisible to him, so your fee shouldn't be a reason for him to say no." He smiled and winked at the CEO.
>
> "How's that for a deal?" asked the CEO.

It was the kind of a deal that I was ready to walk away from. It wasn't congruent with my values, the way I think coaches should work, and the long-term success of any helping relationship. Here are some practical lessons to be gained from that scenario:

From the Consultant's Perspective.   Contract with the person receiving the coaching, not his or her boss, an HR professional, a management committee, or any other third party. Who is the client in the above example? It certainly was not the person who would be the focus of the coaching. In this example it was the boss, who, I discovered after further discussion, hadn't told the person he was in trouble. I also found that the vice president of HR had already determined that the person would eventually be terminated and was more interested in documenting the file and performing "due diligence" that the organization had done all it could do to save the employee.

From the Client's Perspective. Find out why the organization wants you to have a coach and, if you choose to be coached, insist that you, not your boss, be the client. I am continually amazed that otherwise smart and analytical executives simply comply with the suggestion that they *need* a coach and passively accept the coach offered up by the company. My advice is to do some digging. Why do they think you need coaching? What needs to change? Is there a message your boss cannot or will not deliver? If you do choose to work with a coach, be assertive around your client status. If possible choose your own coach; if this isn't possible at least get veto power. It makes it much more professional if you pay the tab for coaching out of your own budget. If there is a corporate cost center, at least find out what the company is paying. Above all, insist on the three C's: *clarity* that you, not the organization, are the client; *confidentiality* that all information is yours alone and the coach makes no reports about your progress to your boss or others that you don't know about and endorse; and *control,* that you are in charge of the process and the only one qualified to decide whether it is helpful.

From a Philosophical Perspective. Confusion, and at times collusion to keep it confusing, as to the identity of the client and the purpose of coaching is a primary reason for failed efforts. If the boss or the system is the client, consultants are not coaching, they are helping with performance appraisal, communications facilitation, role definition, or setting objectives. All are legitimate consulting efforts, but they are *not* coaching. Consultants who tell the coachee that she or he is the client, but who are really serving the needs and direction of the boss, are not only unethical, they are setting themselves up for failure as a coach.

Factor Two: Solutions Looking for Problems—Coaches Enamored of a Single Model or Approach

A friend of mine, a well-published and well-known behavioral scientist, asked me for some advice. He couldn't understand why he was unable to make it as an executive coach.

"You're a solution looking for a problem," I said. (Our relationship had long since passed the need to pull any punches with each other.) "Your model is great. It got you published and lots of national recognition," I continued. "The problem is that it doesn't fit a client-centered helping relationship. Stick to speaking, writing, and selling your tools. You'll be happier, make more money, and not screw up any more coaching clients!"

This conversation with my well-published friend illustrates the dynamics of the second coaching derailment factor. Here are further implications:

From the Consultant's Perspective.   Effective executive coaching involves a helping relationship. The currency of the realm in any helping relationship is empathy, a nonjudgmental approach, and mutual exploration and diagnosis. Dogmatic adherence to a single model or a consultant-centered process will doom an authentic coaching relationship. Currently, I have three active coaching clients. All three are going different directions and require unique approaches. In one, the client is involved in a serious exploration of her career options. She isn't sure she is in the right job or organization. My coaching efforts have involved using aptitude measurement instruments, life and career planning activities, and a process of skill and reality assessment. The second client is working on his presentation and assertiveness skills, and my coaching has involved focused feedback and behavioral rehearsal efforts. The third client has a good shot at becoming CEO of his organization, and we are currently working on ways for him to gain more visibility and credibility with his board. All three of these efforts are the culmination of a great deal of listening, mutual exploration, and trust building. If, like my friend, I had come in and presented a one-dimensional approach using *my* model or *my* approach, I may have felt good about myself, but the client's need would not have emerged, and I would have failed.

From the Client's Perspective.   Beware of coaches who want to sell you on a single process or *their* solution to your problem. An effective coach will be an outstanding listener, much more interested in your ideas; your definition of what would be helpful; and your hopes, dreams, and aspirations than in his or her model or process. Be wary of coaches who use athletic models and metaphors. Athletic coaching is a totally different genre from executive coaching in organizations. Athletic coaches are content experts: they know the game and the skills necessary to optimize player performance in the game. Organizational coaches are not content experts: they are process experts. They don't know your product or service. You hire them to help you grow and develop; however, *you* define growth and development. Athletic coaches are part of the system; their bottom line is winning; they are paid by the system and fired if they don't rack up the requisite number of wins. Organizational coaches are outside the system. They are hired by *you* to help *you* decide what winning means to *you*.

From a Philosophical Perspective.   Help is defined by the person receiving the help, not by the person giving it. True coaching is a helping relationship and, like all helping relationships, it requires mutuality, openness, and focus on the client as a unique individual. Gimmicks, dogmatic adherence to a technique, and interventions that support the consultant's hypothesis sabotage authentic coaching.

Factor Three: Creation of a Dependency Relationship

The goal of all effective executive coaches should be to empower their clients and withdraw from the relationship. The goal should not be, as articulated by one misguided but honest consultant, "a long-term relationship with the client and a steady stream of income for me!"

Here are some thoughts and lessons for consultants and clients in regard to this third derailment factor:

From the Consultant's Perspective.   The essence of effective coaching is to create a self-reliant client and then withdraw from the relationship. Unlike the athletic model, where there must always be a coach, executive coaches should be aware of and reject the temptation to create a dependent relationship with their clients. Dependency perverts the coaching role, diminishes both the coach and the client, and trivializes the coaching process. A coach should never stay in a helping relationship for the money.

From the Client's Perspective.   Make sure you and your coach are on the same wave length as to when and how the coaching process will end. Resist the temptation to prolong the relationship; it is important and ennobling for you to solo! Coaching is much more effective when it is bounded in time and by predetermined objectives. Set these goals and limits early in the coaching process and stick to them. It is not good for you or for your coach to create a long-term, dependent relationship. If your coach overstays his welcome, fire him!

From a Philosophical Perspective.   Coaching is a temporary and artificial process, and it is essential that a termination plan be part of the initial contract. Colleagues who tell me about staying with the same client for multiple-year coaching engagements raise some red flags in terms of my assessment of their effectiveness and credibility. They have either created, or are in imminent danger of creating, unhealthy, dependent relationships. It is fine to withdraw and come back occasionally to monitor progress, but the goal is always to empower the client and terminate the relationship. Coaches and visiting relatives have something in common with dead fish: they begin to smell if they stay too long!

External coaching can be a powerful developmental tool. It can also be a contrived, shallow, and manipulative process that is ultimately harmful to both the coach and the client. It is my hope that coaches who want to ensure their effectiveness and clients who want to be wise consumers of coaching expertise will benefit from this chapter and develop plans to avoid the big three derailment factors.

About the Contributor

David Noer is an author, researcher, and consultant. He has written six books and numerous academic and popular articles on the application of human spirit to leadership. David heads his own consulting firm in

Greensboro, North Carolina. His practice involves executive coaching; team development; dealing with the human aspects of mergers, acquisitions, and downsizing; mission, vision, and value development; and strategic planning. The common thread of his work involves helping organizations and people through transitions by harnessing the power of applied human spirit. David has been designated an Honorary Senior Fellow of the Center for Creative Leadership and was previously senior vice president for training and education with worldwide responsibility for the Center's operational, training licensing, and educational activities.

PART FIVE

EXPANDING SITUATIONS

In this part, the authors look beyond coaching and into the business world. Here we find some real-life situations, current issues, and difficult problem situations. The challenge we set for coaching is to ask how it can help and what it can add.

Jeremy Solomons, Maya Hu-Chan, Carlos Marin, and Alastair Robertson take a unique look at global leaders and present an inventory that can be used for developing individuals in this role within a coaching context. Robert Fulmer presents a real-life case study that posed difficult problems and is a very useful aid to discussing the dynamics of the coaching approach. Roosevelt Thomas, Jr., addresses the need for coaching all people by all people and discusses important factors to consider in diversity. Nancy Adler takes in international view on women leader and shows how issues in their career development may be addressed through coaching. Marshall Goldsmith, Iain Somerville, and Cathy Greenberg-Walt look at the new free-agent workers and show how an understanding of their values can inform the coaching style of the leader.

CHAPTER THIRTY

BECOMING AN EFFECTIVE GLOBAL LEADER

Jeremy Solomons, Maya Hu-Chan, Carlos E. Marin, and Alastair G. Robertson

Are global leaders born? Or are they made? Is global leadership an innate competency? Or is it an acquired skill, learned and honed throughout a lifetime? On the "nature" side of the argument, there are strong beliefs in such factors as genetic predisposition and karmic pre-destiny. Some people are natural leaders; others are most definitely not. On the "nurturing" side of the argument, there are equally strong beliefs in the need for a caring and supportive family structure, a safe and healthy living environment, and a rigorous but broad education. Here are what some famous leaders have said on the topic:

"I suppose leadership at one time meant muscles; but today it means getting along with people" (Indira Gandhi)

"To lead the people, walk behind them." (Lao-Tzu)

"In a beginner's mind, there are many possibilities. In an expert's there are none." (Zen Master Suzuki Roshi)

Nature Versus Nurture

Although there may never be a definitive answer to the nature versus nurture question, most people will agree that no amount of nurturing can make someone into a global leader if he or she does not have a fundamental desire, passion, and talent to be one. And no potential leader, however naturally gifted he or she may be, can become fully realized without a tremendous amount of nurturing. Throughout childhood and adolescence, even the divinely reincarnated Dalai Lama had to undergo intense and lengthy preparation for his weighty role as the spiritual leader of Tibet. But the preparation does not stop at the onset of adulthood; in some ways, it is only just starting.

Potential global leaders must continue their formal education by expanding their theoretical and technical knowledge in various arenas of higher learning, but they must also begin to live the reality of being a global leader through practical experience, particularly traveling, living, and working in cultures and countries that are not familiar to them.

Built on Practice

In many ways, preparing to be a global leader is like a native English speaker learning a "difficult" language, such as Arabic, Mandarin, or Finnish. The leader must build a solid foundation of grammar, vocabulary, and syntax in the classroom, but at some point there is no substitute for becoming totally immersed in the language in a country in which it is spoken.

The reason why Esperanto—the international language invented by Dr. Ludwig Zamenhoff in Poland over a century ago—never took off is because there were neither native speakers nor a natural environment in which to practice it. It ended up being a purely intellectual exercise, proving that language, environment, and theory are impotent without practice. Fluency will not flourish in a static environment. Just as language ability can rust without regular polishing, so can global leadership skills. This is a particular challenge for potential global leaders who are already on a chosen career path.

How many leaders find the time in their hectic work and travel schedules to reflect on and define such issues as: "What does it mean to be a global leader?" and, more specifically, "What exactly constitute 'competence,' 'effectiveness,' and 'success'?"

Here the foreign language analogy begins to break down. A couple of weeks of business travel or a vacation in a particular country can be enough to brush up on one's linguistic fluency—and the results are pretty easy to quantify: either you can make an effective sales pitch or hold your own in a three-hour dinner conversation or you cannot. By contrast, honing global leadership skills is trickier, because the skills required are qualitative and effectiveness is difficult to measure.

From extensive formal and informal discussions with business people from around the world, we have come up with five key behavioral characteristics of effective and influential corporate global leaders. These characteristics are as follows: *trustworthy, respectful and caring, balanced between "doing" and "being," emotionally literate*, and *culturally self aware*.

Trustworthy

Leaders are viewed as dependable, sincere, nondeceptive promise keepers. They show integrity and moral fiber. In many countries, paying government officials to get a project off the ground is part of doing business, but true global leaders are those who would rather walk away from "a deal" than compromise their own or their company's integrity. In this way, they earn high levels of respect.

Respectful and Caring

Global leaders demonstrate a high regard for the dignity, worth, well-being, and autonomy of all people, including themselves. They are genuinely interested in learning from other cultures, and they are able to demonstrate cultural empathy by consistently "seeing the picture" from various cultural points of view, including his or her own. These leaders also show their desire to learn and "communicate" in the local language.

Many negative examples of global leadership show up in managers who view their assignments as "temporary." If the assignment is temporary, why should they go to the trouble of communicating and becoming more acquainted with the locals and their culture? Unfortunately, these leaders do not see their learning as an investment in their global leadership skills.

Balanced Between "Doing" and "Being"

A global leader has the sensitivity and skills to manage attitudes, values, and expectations around issues of performance and results in the cultural context of those he or she leads. For example, in Latin American and Middle Eastern cultures, there is much more of a "being" than a "doing" orientation. In terms of hiring or buying, who a person is and what sort of character he or she has may be considered more important than technical competence.

The global leader works effectively to accomplish the goals of the organization, while aware of this balance. The trust the leader inspires in others gives him or her license to set the performance bar on both variables: "being" (quality of life) and "doing" (business success).

Emotionally Literate

Emotional awareness, resilience, and persistence are important to global leaders. Especially under difficult or stressful circumstances, these leaders are aware of the source of their feelings and emotions. They are capable of sensing, understanding, and responding effectively in situations that are emotionally charged, and they can "witness" or view themselves on the cultural stage and direct their responses from this vantage point.

Culturally Self-Aware

Global leaders demonstrate the ability to recognize, and then learn from, the different behavioral expectations required of different roles, both in their own culture and in the cultural context in which they are operating. They learn to recognize and deal effectively with the different attitudes, values, and expectations placed on cultural variables such as power, competitiveness, time, space (physical proximity), individualism, performance, formality, and structure. This information gives them knowledge required to establish meaningful and effective relationships and to work successfully with people who operate from different cultural orientations.

Looking to the future, a new research study of over two hundred "high-potential" leaders in international organizations came up with similar requirements for the incoming cohort of global leaders in business, government, and elsewhere.

Defining a Global Leader

A research project, "The Evolving Role of Executive Leadership" conducted by Andersen Consulting and assisted by Keilty, Goldsmith & Company, produced fourteen essential skill categories for global leaders, listed below. Based on the experiences of more than one hundred twenty leaders around the world, these broad headings profile eighty vital competencies that global leaders possess. (See Figure 30.1.)

FIGURE 30.1. GLOBAL LEADERSHIP: THE NEXT GENERATION

1. Thinks Globally
2. Anticipates Opportunity
3. Creates a Shared Vision
4. Develops and Empowers People
5. Appreciates Cultural Diversity
6. Builds Teamwork and Partnerships
7. Embraces Change
8. Shows Technological Savvy
9. Encourages Constructive Challenge
10. Ensures Customer Satisfaction
11. Achieves Competitive Advantage
12. Demonstrates Personal Mastery
13. Shares Leadership
14. Lives the Values

Source: The Global Leader of the Future research project. 1999 © Andersen Consulting and Keilty, Goldsmith & Company.

In order to envision how an international business manager of today might become a truly global leader of the future, it helps to broaden the perspective and take a quick glance at what a universal leader might look like.

For some people, a universal leader has to have a global mandate. In this case, such people as the secretary general of the United Nations or the Pope would qualify. For others, a universal leader has to have a global impact. The most obvious examples of this are business leaders, such as Bill Gates of technology giant Microsoft, Anita Roddick of the Body Shop, and Jürgen Schrempp of DaimlerChrysler.

The majority of people, however, believe that universal leaders have to embody certain key universal qualities or traits, such as clarity of vision, strength of purpose, courage of one's convictions, and moral integrity, even if their mandate and impact are not necessarily global in scope. Current and former national leaders, such as Vaclav Havel, Golda Meir, and Ronald Reagan, are often mentioned in this respect. Such maverick business leaders as Ted Turner and Richard Branson are also frequently named. On the humanitarian side, Mother Teresa and Aung San Suu Kyi (of Myanmar) are cited as well.

Given these disparate views of what makes a universal leader, it is hardly surprising that there was little consensus in the global leadership study or elsewhere on how to measure a global leader's effectiveness. On a narrow level, the pope could be judged by the increase or decrease in the number of his followers around the world; Jack Welch (of General Electric) by his company's employee retention, shareholder valuation, and board support; and Vaclav Havel by the length of his term in office.

But do these essentially quantitative gauges really touch on the issue of quality global leadership? In one sense they do, because they all have a human, democratic element to them. If the leaders do not perform, then they will definitely lose credibility and support; they will probably lose their jobs; and they may even lose their lives. On the other hand, this type of assessment runs the risk of reducing the question of effective global leadership to a mass popularity contest, played out through the increasingly sensationalist media.

The authors of this chapter firmly believe that there must be a more personal way of assessing the quality of a global leader's effectiveness, whether in the narrower business world or in the broader universal context. For example, one could find out what the people who are closest to a leader think about the job that he or she is doing. Lack of confidentiality often inhibits peers or subordinates from saying what they really think and feel, but there are reliable human resource instruments, such as 360° feedback processes, to use to collect and analyze co-workers' opinions anonymously.

But this is not enough, because a universal leader, who often does not have a clear job description or boss, may not have the same willingness or obligation to listen and respond to feedback in a constructive and consistent manner. Of course, having one or two trusted advisors, mentors, or coaches can help to reinforce the main messages.

But this is still not enough. Even though the Pope may answer to a "higher authority," in most cases the only person who can gauge whether a global leader is effective or not is the leader himself or herself. This requires considerable reflection on what has been done and said; on the measurable impact of these deeds and words; on the successes and the mistakes; and on any changes that are necessary.

This introspection will lead to constructive and surprising changes if the leader goes about it diligently and honestly and, more importantly, continuously and consistently.

Five Questions

Here are five questions for global leaders to ask themselves on a regular basis:

1. Why am I a leader, and what do I hope to achieve?
2. Whom do I represent, and where are they located?
3. Why do they trust me to lead them, and how can I help them?
4. What results and other indicators will show me that I am doing my job in helping them to get what they want and need?
5. When is it time for me to step down, and who will replace me?

What makes a global leader of whatever ilk—mandate, impact, or character—effective is recognizing and accepting this belief: one of the main purposes of being a leader is to develop new leaders to whom the leader may pass the baton.

We assume that some potentially great global leaders, such as John F. Kennedy, Indira Gandhi, or Alfred Herrhausen (of Deutsche Bank in Germany), never had the chance to be so because their lives and careers were cut short by assassins. Many other leaders have been ousted by election, back-room intrigue, boardroom revolt, illness, or death. Prime examples of this phenomenon are Winston Churchill and Margaret Thatcher of the United Kingdom. One notable exception in recent years is Nelson Mandela, who decided to resign as president of South Africa after only five years in power. But then, he had nearly thirty years in prison to reflect and prepare for his time as a truly global leader.

Conclusion

An effective global leader requires not only passion and talent, but commitment and practice. From our studies, we have found that corporate global leaders must be trustworthy, respectful, and caring, balanced between "doing" and "being," emotionally literate, and culturally self-aware. Global leaders must also take the time to reflect diligently and honestly on a continuous and consistent basis to be successful. And most importantly, global leaders must take responsibility for developing new leaders capable of taking on leadership roles in the future.

About the Contributors

Jeremy Solomons is an independent consultant, speaker, and writer. He provides customized coaching, facilitation, and training in career development, conflict resolution, cross-cultural communication, global leadership, international management, multicultural team building, and strategic planning to individuals and groups around the world. Jeremy has worked directly and indirectly with many large, international organizations, including Airtouch, Amgen, Chevron, Citicorp, Diners Club, Eastman Kodak, Enron, Galileo International, International SEMATECH (which includes AMD, HP, IBM, Intel, and Siemens), NASA, Qualcomm, Union Carbide, and the World Bank. His main regions of specialization are Western Europe and East Asia, and his main countries of specialization are France, Germany, Hong Kong (and China), Israel, Italy, Switzerland, the United Kingdom, and the United States.

Maya Hu-Chan is an international management consultant, coach, and trainer, whose specialties are executive coaching, 360° leadership feedback, organizational transformation, diversity, and cross-cultural communications. Maya has coached over three thousand leaders in Global 100 companies to improve their leadership competency and has worked with leaders in countries throughout the Americas, Asia, Europe, and Australia. Co-author of *A Study in Excellence: Management in the Nonprofit Human Services* and *Global Business Skills* for Sematech, she recently completed a new research project "Global Leadership: The Next Generation" for Andersen Consulting and Keilty, Goldsmith & Company (KGC), for which global organizations and high-potential leaders from around the world were interviewed about leadership trends. A book about the research results is scheduled for publication in 2001.

Carlos E. Marin is a senior consultant with Keilty, Goldsmith & Company (KGC). Former vice president of the Human Development Training Institute in San Diego and former academic dean and chancellor of National University, Carlos has national and international experience as an organizational, management, leadership development educator, consultant, and executive coach. Carlos has designed and implemented programs targeted at aligning business strategies with organizational culture modifications. His practice has contributed to the leadership effectiveness of executives in many recognized organizations. An experienced international consultant and leadership development educator, he has worked with such companies as American Express, BellSouth, CASA, Coca-Cola, Ericsson, KFC, Kodak, Merck, Motorola, Northern Telecom, Panamerica Ogilvy & Mather, Sun Microsystems, Telefonos del Noroeste (TELNOR), Texas Instruments, Texaco, and SouthWestern Bell.

Alastair G. Robertson heads up Andersen Consulting's Worldwide Leadership Development Practice. He is also a partner in the organizational and human performance line of business, providing in-depth expertise in strategic change and organizational strategy. During his fifteen-year consulting career in leadership development, strategic change, and organizational behavior, Alastair has worked extensively with clients on the development of leadership behaviors specifically linked to the building of enhanced performance, tailored to an organization's business strategy. He is a specialist in individual, team, and organization leadership assessment and behavior development, building on personal motivational strengths, and is an advisor and coach to many European and U.S.-based executives. His clients include Fortune 500 companies across all industry sectors. In addition to consulting and coaching, Alastair conducts research in leadership and is regularly interviewed by the media on this topic. He is a frequent conference presenter and in 1999 spoke at the Forbes CIO Congress and gave the keynote address at the *Economic Times* Super Achiever Forum.

CHAPTER THIRTY-ONE

THE STANLEY INTERNATIONAL-
LATIN AMERICAN DIVISION CASE STUDY

Robert M. Fulmer

The Stanley International Case presents an opportunity for readers to look at a coaching opportunity from a unique perspective—actually, from three perspectives. The author of this chapter was involved as a consultant on leadership development and corporate transformation at the firm. At an international senior management seminar in Geneva, Ron McIntyre, president of Stanley International, called him aside and explained some of the basic information described below. McIntyre indicated that coaching might be an appropriate approach in this case of executive conflict, but suggested that Fulmer talk to the principals involved to form the foundation for an assessment and recommendation. As you read the following account, you may find it useful to think about the conclusions you would draw from these three accounts of the situation and what approach you might have recommended had you been the coach.

EXHIBIT 31.1. STANLEY INTERNATIONAL-
LATIN AMERICAN DIVISION

Stanley International is a $2 billion division of Stanley Health Products, which was acquired by Cantex, Inc., a Fortune 100 conglomerate, in the mid-1990s. Cantex paid $11 billion (thirty times earnings) for Stanley. After five years of healthy growth, Stanley's operating profits flattened in 1999 to about $400 million. Stanley's R&D

facilities are being consolidated with Cantex's, and unprofitable international operations have been downsized or closed. Employment in the division is down 20 percent from three years ago.

Stanley sales are divided between its three consumer health businesses, including several well-known, over-the-counter products. Analysts expressed concern that Stanley-related debt would exceed the unit's operating earnings.

As part of the major cultural shift within the Stanley organization, Kirby Matthews was moved from head of Stanley International to run Stanley Health in 1998, and Ron McIntyre assumed the presidency of Stanley International from the firm's LA/CAP (Canada, Asia, Pacific, and Latin American) operation. (See Figures 31.1 and 31.2.) Considerable effort has been made to rally the entire organization behind the theme, "Becoming better than the best." Task force groups have looked at each of the key mission areas to determine specific goals for revenue enhancement and cost reductions. Four core values have been stressed as guides for action and decision making. (See Exhibit 31.2, the Stanley International Values Statement on page 347.)

FIGURE 31.1.   STANLEY INTERNATIONAL DIVISIONS

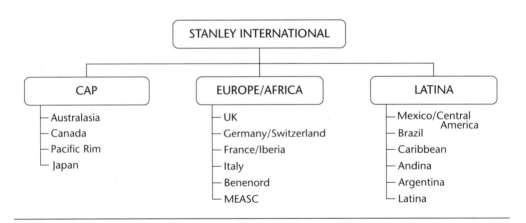

As a result of the strategic framework process, 1999 saw a restructuring and streamlining of operations in nineteen plants. A total of $50 million in savings were achieved through this activity, as well as $28 million being cut from administrative expense. At the same time, their R&D budget doubled from $100 million to $200 million per year, and the advertising budget was significantly increased. As part of the rejuvenation effort, Carlos Guerra was recruited to head up the Latin American Division (Latina), which had responsibilities for all of Central and South America with sales of approximately $200 million. (See Figure 31.3.)

Early in 1999, Carlos Guerra's boss, Gavin O'Reiley, president, LA/CAP, told Ron McIntyre that he was concerned about Carlos' ability to handle the expanded role that

FIGURE 31.2.   STANLEY INTERNATIONAL EXECUTIVE ORGANIZATION CHART

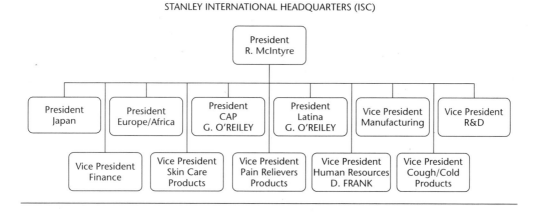

STANLEY INTERNATIONAL HEADQUARTERS (ISC)

FIGURE 31.3.   CAPLA ORGANIZATION CHART

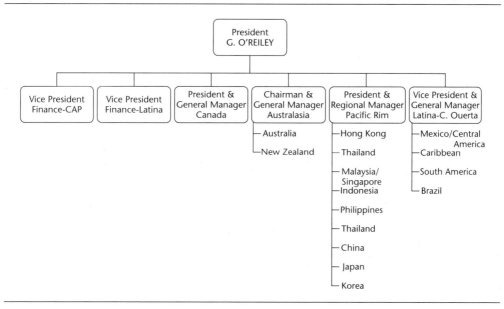

they had envisioned for him. He recommended that Carlos be placed on notice and terminated in six months, unless the situation improved. Gavin planned to meet with Carlos when he returned from a two-week trip to the Pacific Rim, but wanted McIntyre's approval and advice before proceeding.

Three of the key executives are described here, along with their comments about the situation.

Gavin O'Reiley, President, LA/CAP.   "In my opinion, Carlos' job is in danger. I am certain that he is not ready to assume direct responsibility for the Latin American operations. Ron has also expressed his concern both about his ability to perform at a higher level of the organization, as well as some stylistic issues that may be hampering his effectiveness now.

"Perhaps the most serious concern is that Carlos appears to be losing his objectivity about the Brazilian operation. Despite high inflation and the requirement for $200,000 of corporate funds to keep it operating right now, Carlos insists that we need to keep it alive. It is not that I disagree with that assessment just yet; it is the emotional commitment to the concept that disturbs both Ron and myself. I am afraid that Carlos may not be able to adjust to the culture we are trying to build.

"When Carlos first came into the company, he discovered a real mess in Brazil. We had sent a very high-potential young executive from the U.S. down to run the operation as a part of his developmental experience. He is an excellent executive, but his lack of familiarity with Brazilian operations and the language handicap allowed five key Brazilian employees to pull the wool over his eyes. They set up a separate company that was contracting with Stanley Brazil for $1,400,000 of products and services each year. It's common practice in Brazil, and actually saved us time and delivered products at fair prices. As soon as Carlos arrived on the scene, he saw what was taking place and moved decisively to get rid of the people and to straighten out the situation. He takes some justifiable pride in his accomplishments, but I fear this is distorting his judgment about the future prospects for that operation. I also worry that he has turned it into too much of an heroic accomplishment. He talks about it very frequently, and is, in my opinion, overly critical of the Brazilian manager who has been brought back to the U.S. and given other responsibilities. I have told him, 'You are not going to build a reputation in this company on the corpse of Andy Edwards.' He seems much more insecure than when I interviewed him for the job. In fact, he spends a lot of time telling me and other people how good he is.

"About two weeks ago, Carlos made a presentation to the ISC (International Strategic Committee) about Brazil. Ron kept having to interrupt the presentation to ask specific factual questions, because Carlos was too caught up in the long-term importance of keeping Brazil alive. It has, after all, the largest economy in South America. After the meeting, I told Carlos that we were going to have to dramatically reduce costs in Brazil, but not to do anything until we have had a chance to talk further about it. I have concerns that Carlos, whose office is just down the hall, doesn't keep me as well informed as my other reports who are located in Canada or Asia.

"The following week, Carlos told me that he had laid off 250 people in Brazil. I really flew off the handle and reminded him that I had specifically asked that he not do anything until he had let me know. Carlos was extremely apologetic and said that he simply misunderstood me. This, unfortunately, is not the first time this kind of misunderstanding has taken place. As a result of this and a few other things that bothered me, I had a real 'heart-to-heart' with him. I talked about his insecurity, his unwillingness to keep me informed, his overly emotional commitment to Brazil, his over-dramatizing his accomplishments in Brazil, some personal mannerisms I think distract from his executive leadership potential, and the fact that his preoccupation with Brazil was keeping him from sitting on top of some important challenges in Costa Rica and Mexico. Now, he is terribly demoralized. I don't think that my conversation has helped at all. He's clearly not ready to move into a direct reporting relationship to Ron, and I am not sure he's going to make it. My experience is that when a person doesn't fit in an organization, it's better to admit that you've made a hiring mistake and move on rather than waste lots of time trying to 'make a silk purse out of a sow's ear.'"

David Frank, Vice President, Human Resources. "Carlos and I are among five or six of the company's top ten executives who have been with the company for less than a year. Carlos was hired about the same time I was—September of last year. He has a very impressive background. The son of a diplomat from Mexico, he has an MBA from a leading Eastern business school, and was a vice president of International Operations of Acme Pharmaceutical before he was recruited by our executive search to take over the Latin American division. Because Gavin O'Reiley is stretched with current responsibility for about half the world, the game plan, which was discussed with Carlos, was that in a year he would become vice president in charge of Latin America and report directly to McIntyre. This would give him full status as a member of the ISC (International Strategic Committee).

"Immediately after taking on responsibility, Carlos discovered a major problem at our Brazilian operation. A young, highly capable, American general manager had been blind-sided by local corruption. Carlos moved in and fired seven or eight key people, received threatening telephone calls, and subsequently hired a bodyguard for protection. He brought in a CFO (number two person) for Brazil who has excellent experience in the U.S. and Brazil. In addition to his other responsibilities, Carlos remains the general manager of Brazil. I think he has done a good job in remotivating the people in Brazil, but is a bit obsessed about keeping it afloat.

"Ron McIntyre has talked to me about some concerns he has about Carlos' tendency to be overly informal or to make 'disgustingly filthy jokes' at inappropriate times. He also reports that Carlos' tendency to talk about 'my' decisions or 'my' operation makes him think that Carlos may not be much of a team player, which is one of our corporate values. Because of this and continuing emphasis on downsizing, Ron has some reservations about changing the reporting relationship. At the same time, Ron worries a bit that Gavin has changed all of his direct reports within the past year.

"Gavin O'Reiley (Carlos' current boss) shares these concerns and is beginning to question his business judgment as well. I really don't think that Gavin is beginning to have second thoughts about reducing his own area of responsibility, as he has more than enough on his plate with other sections of the world. We have invested a lot of money in the search and relocation efforts for Carlos. We really want him to succeed. We have to help him get over the trauma of this recent confrontation with Gavin and to help a potentially outstanding Latin executive cope with the challenge of re-porting to talented but very 'WASPy' bosses.

"I have recommended that we move Latin American headquarters to Mexico City. This would get Carlos out of New York and closer to his problem operations. Hope-fully, this would allow him to have more warning before meetings with Gavin and reduce the interpersonal conflict."

Carlos Guerra, Vice President, Latin American Division.   "The last few months have been a roller coaster. I knew that this was going to be a challenging assignment, but I didn't have any idea how bad some things were.

"The situation in Brazil was the most corrupt I have ever seen in twenty years of business experience. The most positive thing that I can say about it is that the general manager there may have been incompetent. They never should have sent someone from here with only a three-weeks' Berliz course to run a Brazilian operation. As soon as I was there, I could tell that something was wrong. I began to ask some tough ques-tions and got a lot of superficial answers. It took me less than a week to determine who the culprits were. Even before that, I think people could see the handwriting on the wall. I started getting threatening telephone calls at my hotel that suggested that 'You need to be careful or something bad might happen to you.' Finally, one night, I asked the SOB on the phone if he carried a gun. When he hesitated, I said, 'You damn well better, because I carry one and I am a damn good shot.' After that I didn't receive any more telephone calls.

"I am a little concerned that Stanley International is overly political and not open to non-U.S. values. It is not that I am unaccustomed to dealing with people in high levels of responsibility. My parents were diplomats, and as a result, I lived in several Latin American capitals. In my previous job, I had total international responsibility and experienced no difficulties at all. To my knowledge, no one in top management at Stanley International has an MBA from one of the top five business schools.

"I can't figure out what it would take to please Gavin. Not long ago, he told me I was beginning to lose my objectivity in trying to salvage the Brazilian operation. At his request, I developed a downsizing plan, and even though it hurt me to do this, I went ahead and laid off 250 people, which I thought would really please him. Instead, he came down on me for not having talked this over with him again.

"I think I am building a good esprit de corp throughout the Latin American op-erations. My problems seem to be with Gavin and Ron. Morale is up, and performance (except for the economic instability in Brazil) is better. I feel like I am doing what I was hired to do.

"Except for results, everything seems to be in a downward spiral. I am operating without any staff, except for a secretary. New positions are difficult to come by. I gained authorization for a Vice President Finance-Latina, but I just found out he is going to report directly to Gavin instead of to me. That doesn't make any sense. It also doesn't make any sense for me to be based in New York. I am spending 70 percent of my time in Latin America, which is appropriate. That's my job. I don't see any need for being based in New York. Frankly, I think that is a part of the problem. I am a 'hands-on' type manager. I could save a tremendous amount of time and generate savings for the company by basing our Latin American operations in Rio, where I would have good flights to all of my other reporting units. Dave has suggested moving to Mexico City, but that has little appeal for me. I would be viewed as a 'Local Boy.' Besides, it is very expensive to live there, we have a relatively small Mexican operation, and I'd have to change planes in Miami every time I went to Latin America.

"I realize that there was a need to get better coordination of international operations. From what I hear, Stanley International used to operate as a series of fiefdoms. The strategic framework process has helped give us a sense of direction. I think it is time to move things back to the field for better execution. Europe has just moved its headquarters from New York to Geneva. Pacific is based in Singapore. I could do much better if I were where I could get the job done instead of working on pleasing my boss. I was hired to run Latin American operations, and I would like a chance to do just that."

What Actually Happened

My first challenge was simply to listen. I needed to hear what the various parties had to say, but they also needed to be heard. With Carlos, I listened for almost two hours. He needed to vent his frustrations, and this turned out to be part of the solution.

Kirby Warren, a Columbia colleague, had been doing research for over a decade on various forms of conflict between high-level bosses and their executive subordinates. In looking at almost two hundred businesses that have experienced this type of conflict, the responses seem to be divided into five major categories: *Benign Neglect, Managerial Darwinism, Termination, Separation,* and *Redirect and Redevelop.*

Benign Neglect. Some people in the same position as Herb McIntyre choose to deal with the situation by employing a strategy that could be called "benign neglect." This strategy may be utilized to buy time to prepare for another approach or it may be used rather than planning a different strategy. With this approach, eventually the situation will resolve itself, although perhaps not in the most thoughtful manner. This approach actually evolves into what Warren calls "managerial Darwinism."

Managerial Darwinism.   This approach is usually negative in that it allows for the "survival of the fittest" without ever considering what the survivor may be "fit" for. If the result is provocative or totally competitive, the impact is unlikely to be positive. Should the Darwinism be planned in a constructive manner, with clearly defined rules for engagement, the result may be more positive. The well-publicized competitions for the CEO's position at GE are examples of this approach. Six key executives were given responsibility for specific areas of the business, with the best performer getting the job. After Jack Welch won this competition, he was asked if he would use the same approach to choose his own successor. After pointing out that he liked the outcome of the process, Welch admitted that the approach had left scars in the organization, because various factions were disappointed when their champion did not come out on top. Yet, many firms use alternatives of this approach to select top executives or resolve conflict between senior people. In fact, as this book goes to press, there is another "CEO sweepstakes," as GE gets ready to choose Welch's successor. Herb McIntyre didn't want to have a winner and a loser in this situation, so it was necessary to look for other approaches.

Termination.   In the Stanley case, Ray O'Reiley suggests that the solution may be simply to terminate Carlos. Technically, he has the power to do this, but this would bring significant costs to the organization. While there are the obvious severance and executive search costs, there are more important considerations, such as lost momentum and opportunities, as well as the growing danger that O'Reiley will be seen as a "hatchet man" or someone who is "impossible to work for." When MBA students discuss this case, they often suggest that O'Reiley should be the one to be fired. While there are good arguments that can be made for this decision, the odds are against it happening. In eighteen of twenty-one instances in the Columbia study in which "termination" was the solution utilized, it was the junior executive who left the organization. Loyalty, position power, and corporate leverage are difficult to overcome.

Separation. Carlos argues that "separation" may be enough to resolve the problem. He seems to feel that if he can just be moved to Rio, his problems will be over. (Of course, he doesn't discuss the fact that he has just gone through a painful, expensive divorce and is now engaged to someone from Brazil.) Sometimes a transfer or reorganization can help the symptoms of a conflict disappear, but it may not address the underlying issues.

In this case, if the separation were seen as a win or loss for either of the protagonists, the organization would suffer. The executive coach knew that it was necessary for O'Reiley's concerns to be addressed and for Carlos's diminished self-confidence to be re-established. It was also clear that any solution had to "save face" for the players without significant costs for the organization, given the financial pressure they were operating under.

Redirect and Redevelop. A strategy of "redirect and redevelop" was developed after answering three critical questions:

1. *Is there enough "raw material" to justify this effort?* McIntyre believed that both O'Reiley and Guerra had significant potential to build the team he wanted to put together for Stanley.
2. *Does the most senior person have the time to devote to this effort?* Unfortunately, McIntyre did not think he had adequate time to handle the redevelopment effort. Because of his travel schedule and the demands of trying to keep the restructuring and cost-cutting efforts on track, he decided to bring in an executive coach who knew the organization and was trusted by the major players.
3. *Can we develop a careful plan that will minimize the risks in the situation?*

After listening to the views of the major protagonists, the coach recognized that O'Reiley was not likely to approve any plan that would put Guerra in Brazil, where he felt that Carlos was already overly preoccupied.

He also knew that Carlos needed to build on some of his strengths to re-establish his credentials and self-confidence. Finally, the coach realized that McIntyre and the other executives would positively receive a plan that built on the firm's emerging mission and values statement. Consequently, he began encouraging Guerra to use his MBA skills to develop a series of recommendations that would reduce the overhead and management reporting units (MRUs) in his region as part of the effort to win acceptance for his move out of New York. Carlos was encouraged to use expressions like "build a winning team," "stay close to my Latin American customers," and so forth. He was also told that he could ask that his office be based in Rio, but should be prepared to accept a compromise position that might put him in another location with ready access to his team and customers, but without the costs of an "expatriate" package.

Ultimately, Carlos won acceptance for a plan that eliminated three MRUs in his region. He was able to utilize about one-third of these savings for an office and two staff people in Miami. His personal style, which was much more appropriate for a Latin American operation than for a Park Avenue corporate headquarters, was so effective that two years later Latina produced almost half of the total profits for Stanley International. O'Reiley found more productive areas on which to focus his attention, and Carlos was talking more about the successes of his team rather than his personal success in Brazil.

EXHIBIT 31.2. STANLEY INTERNATIONAL VALUES STATEMENT

Our Values

We Are a Winning Team

We believe that we will succeed only as a team and that the full participation of all is essential to the fulfillment of our mission. It is imperative that we create an environment of mutual respect, candor, and trust; where all can reach their highest potential; where individual initiative and performance are recognized and rewarded; where all identify with the success of the company; and where a winning attitude prevails.

We Are Customer Driven

We believe that the success of our business depends on understanding and satisfying the needs of the consumer. Market needs must drive our choice of products and services and the way we deliver them. At the same time, success in delivering those products and services requires that the recipients of internal services and staff work deserve the same consideration so that all our activities create value.

We Are Dedicated to Continuous Improvement

We believe that sustained success depends on the maintenance of superior quality, which we will only achieve through continuous improvement in everything we do. In a dynamic, competitive world to stand still is to be left behind. We encourage a healthy dissatisfaction with the status quo and the creativity and initiative to do something about it. Openness to change, to experimentation, and to the search for a better way characterizes our attitude to every aspect of our work.

We Have a Sense of Urgency

We believe that being first, speed of action, hard work, and an aggressive determination to get things done are characteristics of every winning team. In our business they are a condition for survival. The first to market has an often insurmountable advantage. The quickest to move keeps everyone else off balance. The will to succeed very often wins the day through sheer determination.

We Act Responsibly

We believe that integrity is an essential asset. Our success is worth having, and ultimately will occur only if our every action is characterized by staying true to our values, and the best of each of the societies in which we live and work. We will always do the right thing.

About the Contributor

Robert M. Fulmer is the W. Brooks George professor of management at the College of William and Mary. Previously, he was a visiting scholar at the Center for Organizational Learning at MIT and taught organization and management at Columbia University's Graduate School of Business. For six years, he was director of executive education at Emory University, where he directed the executive MBA program, as well as public and customized programs for general and functional managers. Bob received his first endowed chair at Trinity University and has served as director of corporate management development for Allied Signal, Inc., with worldwide responsibility for management development. He has also served as president of two management consulting firms specializing in human resource issues.

Bob's writings have been widely read in both academic and professional circles. He is author of four editions of *The New Management* and co-author of *A Practical Introduction to Business, Crafting Competitiveness, Executive Development and Organizational Learning for Global Business,* and *Leadership by Design.* His research and writing have focused on future challenges of management, implementation of strategy, and leadership development as a lever for change efforts.

Bob received an MBA from the University of Florida and a Ph.D. from UCLA. He currently serves on the International Research Advisory Committee of the Strategos Institute and is a senior fellow and special advisor to the president of the EastWest Institute. He served as a subject-matter expert for a 1998 global benchmarking study of leadership development conducted in collaboration with the American Productivity and Quality Center and the American Society for Training and Development.

CHAPTER THIRTY-TWO

COACHING IN THE MIDST OF DIVERSITY

R. Roosevelt Thomas, Jr.

Coaching frequently receives rave reviews as a developmental tool. In fact, successful people in organizations often credit a coach or mentor who guided them to or through the attainment of critical experiences or helped them develop required competencies or pay appropriate dues.

Yet in the past, this tool has been used most frequently by white men to help white men. As the workforce continues to become more diverse, and minorities and women continue to report coming up against glass ceilings in many environments, the question becomes: Can coaching enhance a manager's ability to access talent from a workforce characterized by diversity?

This chapter explores how leaders and managers of an increasingly diverse workforce may offer this developmental tool to those whose attributes and behaviors differ from their own. It first defines coaching and analyzes the dynamics of effective coaching relationships. Then, it addresses the impact of diversity on the coaching process.

Because most organizational settings require collective efforts for success, this chapter focuses on coaching in the context of teams as opposed to individual efforts. Similarly, while workforce participants can differ along an infinite number of dimensions, the discussion here centers around two that receive enormous attention: race and gender. However, the reader likely will find it possible to extrapolate to other dimensions of interest.

What Is a Coach?

A coach is an individual who enables others to achieve collective objectives. Through a variety of activities, coaches seek to foster individual and team achievement. Coaches relish achieving through others and serve in a variety of roles, some of which are described in the following paragraphs.

Mentors (Teaches).   A basic coaching function is that of teaching or mentoring. Comments about great coaches often begin by acknowledging the individual's teaching capacity. This function is probably the cornerstone of the coaching role.

Sponsors (Advocates).   On and off the field, coaches sponsor, advocate, or run interference for their players. This could mean pleading the player's case with an umpire or referee, or it could involve helping to access necessary resources or a promotion or reward for a participant. The coach can perform this function openly or behind the scenes. Players are often unaware of the coach's intervention.

Counsels.   The coach provides a sounding board for players desiring to test or refine their thinking about some aspect of their game. In the coach, players ideally find an individual who cares enough to be open and honest in his or her responses.

Creates a Motivational Environment.   The coach does not motivate, but rather provides an environment that allows each player's personal motivation to come to its full potential. This may require the coach to respond to different players differently, given his or her understanding of the individual.

When players are motivated to satisfy an authority figure, the effective coach assumes the role of a demanding authoritarian. When players are motivated to satisfy an inner drive for excellence and perhaps perfection, the effective coach becomes a facilitative counselor. Phil Jackson, former coach of the Chicago Bulls basketball team, provides an interesting example of creating a motivational environment (Jackson and Delehanty, 1995).

Because Jackson believed that all players sought to connect to something bigger than themselves, he focused on fostering spirituality for team members. Drawing from a variety of spiritual traditions, he created an overarching metaphor that framed basketball seasons as "sacred journeys." His goal was to provide an environment in which the spiritual motivations of his players could manifest themselves and become sources of cohesiveness and collective achievement.

Communicates the Rules. Coaches convey to players how the game is played. They help them to understand the formal and informal (unwritten or not talked about) success requirements. Key to their ability to do so is a sense of timing. They must convey the rules when opportunity knocks. Setbacks or defeats, for example, can provide opportunities to convey lessons about winning that would be difficult to "hear" in the midst of success.

Provides Perspective. In the heat of competition, a participant can lose perspective and focus. From the sideline, coaches often can see things that players cannot. The ability to help players stay in touch with the "big picture" can make the difference between failure and success.

Characteristics of Effective Coaching Relationships

Effective coaching relationships share several characteristics. One key characteristic is *affirmation by the organization that coaching is a legitimate activity.* In many settings, the prevailing culture excludes coaching as a requirement or an expectation. If coaching exists, it is because of the preferences of the coach and it is viewed not as an organizational necessity, but as a quirk of a nice, "people-oriented" individual.

Acceptance of coaching responsibility is another shared characteristic of effective coaching relationships. Yet, even in cultures that encourage coaching, leaders and managers can be reluctant to do so.

Several things contribute to this reluctance. Many managers prefer "doing the work" rather than coaching. Others may believe in "rugged individualism." Within organizations, this translates as "the cream will rise to the top" and "the really good don't need help."

A related hindrance to accepting responsibility for coaching is meritocracy. Some view coaching as an activity that compromises the notion of merit-based success. They contend that recipients of coaching have availed themselves of improper help and cannot claim to be self-made.

Successful coaching relationships also rely on the *potential beneficiary's willingness to be coached*. Great athletic coaches frequently credit their success to having coachable players. In organizations, the factors that inhibit managers from wanting to coach can make potential beneficiaries unwilling to be coached. For example, rugged individualism, meritocracy, and a desire to be self-made can cause individuals to forge ahead alone, depriving themselves of the benefits of any proffered coaching.

There is irony here. Because coaching often occurs behind the scene, individuals who refuse to be coached are often misinformed. They fail to realize that the "self-made successes" they admire have benefited from effective coaching.

Intimacy is part of successful coaching relationships as well. Coaches serve before, during, and after games. Coaches and players spend an enormous amount of time together. The more intimate the relationship is, the greater the potential for effective coaching; the more effective the coaching is, the greater the intimacy that is likely to be shared.

Trust, which grows with intimacy, is also necessary for coaching success. Trust both accompanies intimacy and makes it possible. A by-product of trust and intimacy is caring.

Coaches care for players; players care for coaches and other players. Often successful professional sports teams and high-achieving businesses refer to themselves as "family" or as having a "special kind of chemistry."

Recently, a commentator noted that the chemistry of the Atlanta Falcons was especially good. In response, Coach Dan Reeves noted: "That's been true on all the winning teams I have seen. Football is a team sport. And players have to come to care deeply about each other." This caring reflects the trust and intimacy required for effective coaching.

Effective coaching also requires *shared commitment and ownership*. Coaches and players share a commitment to collective objectives, and while the coaches cannot play, they share ownership in any success or failure that may be realized. This is why coaches frequently accept responsibility for a team's failure.

Presumptions of fairness and equal treatment are essential to quality coaching relationships as well. Effective coaches strive to treat people fairly and equally within the context of collective objectives. However, in quality coaching relationships, *both* coaches and players know that treating people fairly and equally does not necessarily mean treating them the *same*. Unless this understanding exists, coaches risk being accused of favoritism as they respond to their players' different needs.

Who Are the Coaches?

How can we identify coaches within organizations? Some believe that *mentors* are coaches, but not all mentors are coaches. Mentors may agree to teach without sharing ownership or responsibility for outcomes, or without accepting the intimacy that characterizes effective coaching.

The same can be said for *sponsors*. All effective coaches are sponsors, but not all sponsors are coaches. Some sponsors maintain a distance that precludes intimacy or shared ownership of results.

Organizational coaches are likely to be *leaders and managers*. Leaders are responsible and accountable for organizational results. They may be formal heads of organizational units, such as divisions, functions, or departments, or individuals chairing cross-functional teams, task forces, or special projects.

But coaches also can be those with *informal influence*. A valued individual contributor can provide coaching to a network (team) without having formal authority. Alliances such as these may exist around points of view, shared interests, or professional experiences. Within a company, for example, a group of chemists committed to a particular school of thought might be headed informally by one of its colleagues. This individual can influence associates through coaching efforts centered in mutual respect and trust, professional intimacy, shared commitment and ownership, mentoring and sponsoring—all without formal authority or responsibility. As individuals experience success or failure, so do the coach and fellow practitioners.

Impact of Diversity

My research and work with organizations has convinced me that diversity can play havoc with developmental processes such as coaching, mentoring, and sponsoring. A consequence has been less-than-optimal development, opportunity, and utilization of talent with respect to minorities and women. Some issues that the presence of diversity can raise are examined below.

Social Allegiances.   White males coach white males best because of social allegiances and relatively high comfort levels compared to those that they experience with minorities and women. As one white male manager commented, "Mentoring is very important here, but minorities and women don't get the guidance they need, so they walk on land mines that could be avoided." When asked why the guidance was not forthcoming, he replied, "Social allegiance. We don't know how to relate to women and minorities as subordinates or peers. We're more comfortable with white males. Lately, we've made some progress with women, but we're nowhere with minorities."

Another indicator of this "social allegiance gap," is the way in which mentoring and coaching relationships evolve. White males typically report having been chosen, whereas minorities, in particular, describe themselves as having acted proactively to initiate a mentoring relationship. One black woman noted, "I selected the white male I wanted as a coach and approached him. He was reluctant at first and appeared to be uncomfortable, but it has worked out well."

Preferential Treatment.   Concerns about reverse discrimination and preferential treatment can block the establishment of coaching relationships with minorities and women. The desire of minorities and women to avoid being labeled an Affirmative Action hire or promotion can deter them from entering into the informal developmental coaching arrangements that can be pivotal to one's career. Some fear that asking for a coaching relationship will be viewed as a request for favoritism or a sign of weakness, so they wait to be approached.

White males worry that offering coaching to those individuals might spill over into preferential treatment, or be seen as an insulting suggestion that minorities and women need special help to be successful. The fact that coaching relationships in many organizations do not operate in the open, but rather in a shroud of mystery, means that whispers and rumors further complicate matters.

Lack of Confidence.   Many white males possess only a limited history of interacting with minorities and women as colleagues and peers. As a result, they often feel inadequate to the task of creating a motivational environment or providing perspective for minorities and women.

One white woman manager relied primarily on a white male for coaching and developmental assistance, and indeed, he performed well in this role. Her undoing, however, came from being blindsided by women's issues. In retrospect, she feels that she lost touch with the challenges of being a woman in an organization. Her white male mentor lacked experience and knowledge in that arena. Had she had an additional relationship with a more experienced woman manager (who were scarce in her company at that time) or with a network of women, she might have avoided being blindsided.

Lack of Trust.   Trust facilitates effective coaching. When minority and women employees enter a company and see people like themselves clustered or at the bottom of the pyramid, they may find it difficult to trust the organization's process.

In one corporation, a black male learned that effective social relations with white males were required to receive a promotion. Although he perceived some of what was suggested as personally demeaning, he stood ready to do what was necessary. But he did not act on the counsel he received. He realized that the advice had worked for white males seeking promotions, but he did not trust that it would work for him as a black male. His fear was that he would do something he found distasteful, only to have it fail to make a difference for him. Subsequently, he left the corporation in search of another setting, one in which he had more trust.

Fear of Intimacy. Coaching requires intimacy. Some white males worry about establishing such intimacy. One white male remembers, "When women first arrived in numbers, white males here feared closing their doors when they met with a woman."

Minorities, too, can be uncomfortable with intimacy, particularly if they come to the workplace with no history of intimacy with whites. One black woman manager recalls hearing her grandmother, who prospered as an entrepreneur, say repeatedly, "I would just never work for a white person." Now, this black female works in a corporation with white males and white females. Her grandmother's voice lingers, making it difficult for her to be intimate with her white colleagues.

Faulty Presumptions of Fairness and Equal Treatment. Because many companies do not define coaching as legitimate, individuals can presume that it constitutes an unfair practice and fosters inequality. With diversity, perceptions of lack of fairness and equal treatment can quickly evolve into charges of racism and sexism. This reality can lead managers with significantly diverse workforces to avoid coaching out of a belief that doing so could lead to charges of some "ism."

Recommendations

Executives who wish to foster effective coaching in the midst of diversity must begin by legitimizing coaching. They can do this by encouraging potential coaches to accept the responsibility and by encouraging potential recipients to be coachable. They must posit coaching as a necessity that is critical to the organization's viability. In particular, facilitating executives must take care to sanction and reward coaching across racial and gender lines.

Facilitating executives must also encourage potential coaches and recipients to accept responsibility for addressing diverse coaching relationships—for making the coaching experience effective. A critical step here will be to prepare both parties to respond to diversity appropriately.

They must also encourage both potential coaches and recipients to be open to differences that might be uncomfortable, but do not compromise achievement of personal and organizational objectives. They can do this by helping the coaching parties identify and focus on the requirements for success, as opposed to personal preferences or traditions.

Facilitating managers must also help the coaching participants become comfortable with the diversity tension that can characterize relationships in which people have significant differences. They can do so by helping them to accept the reality of the tension, and therefore avoid undue stress when it appears. They can also do this by helping them to maintain a focus on requirements.

Facilitating managers can also help coaches and recipients to become skilled in responding appropriately to diversity issues. In *Redefining Diversity* (Thomas, 1996), I detail *action options* for coping with diversity. The coaching partners will benefit from familiarity with these options and the ability to select the option or blend appropriate for their relationship.

Clearly, coaching in the midst of diversity requires preparation. Unlike coaching relationships between relatively homogeneous pairs, it cannot be left to chance. It is equally clear that although the discussion here has focused on the dimensions of race and gender, it could be generalized to include other variables, such as age, tenure with the organization, sexual orientation, and functional background. As workforce participants become more diverse, executives and managers desiring to access talent will need to become effective in fostering coaching across diversity lines or risk not tapping potential to the degree required for success.

About the Contributor

R. Roosevelt Thomas, Jr. is founder and CEO of R. Thomas Consulting and Training, an Atlanta-based management consulting firm. He is also founder of and senior research fellow at the research-based American

Institute for Managing Diversity. Known for his pioneering work in diversity management, Roosevelt has been sought out by numerous Fortune 500 companies, private sector and government organizations, and academic and nonprofit organizations. He is the author of two groundbreaking books, *Beyond Race and Gender: Unleashing the Power of Your Total Workforce by Managing Diversity* and *Redefining Diversity.*

CHAPTER THIRTY-THREE

COACHING GLOBAL EXECUTIVES: WOMEN SUCCEEDING IN A WORLD BEYOND HERE

Nancy J. Adler

I used to question what executive coaches brought to clients that the executives themselves didn't already know from their own experience. Having had the privilege of coaching many executives, I now understand that the answer is perspective—a perspective beyond that of their own experience, organization, and culture. In particular, given my background, I almost always have the opportunity to reframe issues in a broader, global perspective. More frequently today, I have the opportunity to reframe business realities that have previously been appreciated primarily from a man's perspective into broader possibilities as seen from both men's and women's perspectives.

Part of bringing a broader perspective is to offer a context of meaning beyond each executive's unique position, organization, and industry. By quietly asking questions that are beyond the bottom line, coaching dialogues offer opportunities for executives to consider more consciously the types of contributions they are making to their company and to choose the kinds of contributions they would like to be making more broadly in the world. Examples of these questions include:

- "What does success mean to you?"
- "In which ways is your work helping society?" and
- "Why would your daughter be proud to tell her daughter about what you are accomplishing?"

These questions often appear illegitimate when taken out of the privacy of the executive coaching dialogue. In the public glare of business-as-normal, such questions frequently fail to appear sufficiently pragmatic to warrant executive time. And yet the conversations, reflection, and learning that such questions generate often bring soul, along with deep, personal motivation, back into the pragmatism of professionalism. Context, deep meaning, and purpose are without counterparts in the pragmatism of successful careers, successful lives, and successful societies.

Is Coaching Women Who Are Executives Any Different?

While few people question that the world of business has gone global, most assumptions about building a global career and succeeding as a global executive remain based on the experience of men. Many of the most fundamental assumptions about executive success remain parochial—limited not only to the experience of men, but often to the experience of men working within their own home countries. If companies continue to believe current parochial assumptions about business success, few, if any, women will venture out into the world beyond their national borders, and even fewer will succeed once there. As the twenty-first century begins, one of my roles has become coaching executive women to succeed in a global economy by going beyond the myths and erroneous assumptions of history.

Because so few women worked as international managers in the twentieth century, let alone as global executives, ignorance and misleading myths abound. Not surprisingly, many women, especially in such Anglo cultures as the United States, have been led to believe that they must emulate men to succeed. Fearing to differentiate themselves in any way from their successful male predecessors and contemporaries, many women become reticent to challenge openly the abundant myths about the barriers women supposedly face when attempting to conduct business abroad. One of the most valuable aspects of executive coaching, therefore, has become the private space it creates for women managers and executives to ask societally unacceptable questions, such as:

- "Is it true that as a woman I cannot succeed in the Middle East?"
- "Will I insult their culture if I lead the negotiating team in Saudi Arabia?"
- "How true is it that our company's expansion into South Asia will be jeopardized if I head up the project?"
- "Even if I succeed in getting the CEO to send me to Korea, will I fail once I'm there? I've heard that Korean businessmen just ignore women—that they would never take a businesswoman seriously."
- "Will our joint venture partners be annoyed when they see that my company has sent me as the lead engineer?"
- "Will men in Latin America really think that my company has sent me as some kind of sexual plaything? What do I need to do to get them to respect me?"

As I listen to women telling their stories and asking their "unaskable" questions, my most frequent response is "Why?" Why do you think that might happen to you? What reality do you want to be true for you? How can you go beyond all the negative scenarios of what you and others in your company imagine will occur? Why do you think foreigners will be more prejudiced against you than are some of the executives you have already successfully dealt with here at home? How can you go beyond history's erroneous assumptions to create your own reality? In the privacy of executive coaching dialogues, we laugh, question, and explore a world that has literally been foreign to all too many women and companies. In the process, we lay to rest the misleading belief that women cannot succeed abroad, or, that in order to succeed, they must act like men. Let me give a few examples.

Myth One

Global Experience Is Not That Important. Lisette, an executive in a major consumer products company with two teenagers in high school, recently turned down an assignment in Brussels. Annoyed with her, Lisette's boss told her that he would not consider her for a senior vice presidency because she was not mobile. He emphasized that her promising career would plateau if she did not willingly move abroad to take the expatriate assignment.

Lisette challenges the importance of international experience. She knows that neither her boss, nor his boss—the CEO—have had much experience abroad beyond regularly boarding airplanes. Given that she is currently the highest ranked woman in the company, the requirement that she gain international experience looks suspiciously like another hurdle her boss is putting in the way of her career progress—the latest hurdle defining the glass ceiling.

My response to Lisette's angry phone call is a resounding, "No!" Business has gone global. Requiring international experience reflects neither sexism nor a new variant of the glass ceiling. "Your boss is right. If you choose not to get international experience, it is you who are choosing to remain well below the glass ceiling. No man or woman should be promoted into the executive ranks of a major twenty-first century company without having a deep understanding and appreciation of global business dynamics. Your boss and the CEO grew their careers in another era, an era of domestic or, at most, multi-domestic business. Unless your aim is to progress backward through history and to attempt to have a parochial nineteenth- or twentieth-century career, you don't dare consider limiting your experience to domestic, stay-at-home assignments."

Lisette doesn't like what I am saying, but she believes me. As an executive coach, an outsider, she knows that I am on her side and that I will tell her the truth—even if it is an inconvenient truth that she would rather not hear. Recognizing the truth, however, does not imply resignation to a career stopped by a seemingly impenetrable global glass ceiling. The outwardly paradoxical question I raise with Lisette is: "How can you get significant international experience and keep your commitment to not moving during your children's formative high school years?" Asking such paradoxical questions as: "How can you both move abroad and not move abroad?" and then helping executives resolve them is a significant part of my executive coaching role.

Myth Two

Given Family Commitments, I Can't Take a Global Assignment. In reflecting on her situation, Lisette realized that expatriation, while a very powerful way to gain international experience, was not the only option open to her. As we brainstormed options, Lisette discovered that she could increase her global experience significantly by participating on more global task forces, increasing her international business travel, and—her most creative idea—taking short-term assignments in Europe and Asia while her two teenagers were away each summer at camp. For Lisette, as well as for many other executive women, the problem is the form in which international experience has traditionally been offered (expatriate assignments), not the requirement for global experience itself. The trap for Lisette would have been to reject international experience because it was "packaged" in its traditional, and to her unacceptable, form—as a three-year to five-year expatriate assignment. The trap for me as a coach would have been to accept her boss's definitions of reality, rather than helping Lisette to think beyond the mythology surrounding the corporation's increasingly anachronistic requirements. As Lisette's subsequent discussions with the CEO revealed, expatriation as a developmental strategy was a better fit for the company's needs in the past when business strategy required key executives to have an in-depth knowledge of only one foreign culture. By contrast, today's globally integrated business strategies require key executives to understand multiple cultures and their interaction. The very option that Lisette was suggesting for herself—shorter term exposure to multiple countries—has actually become preferable in many cases to the company's traditional emphasis on a single, longer-term expatriate assignment.

Myth Three

For Global Managers, Being a Woman Is a Disadvantage, Because Certain Cultures Make It Impossible for Women Executives to Succeed. This is a pervasive and erroneous myth that finds its way into the thinking of the vast majority of today's executives, both male and female.

Valana, a senior financial analyst for a major pharmaceutical company, was offered a regional vice presidency in Japan. Given the company's new startup operations in Pakistan, the position in Japan would involve considerable travel to this Islamic country. Valana felt simultaneously excited and cautious. Would she, as a woman, be able to succeed in Japan and Pakistan, both countries reputed to be hostile to women managers and executives? She worried that if she openly raised her fears with her boss, he would change his mind and that, once again, the company would assume that it could not send women abroad. To make sure that she did not ruin the opportunity to work abroad for herself or for other women, she chose not to raise her concerns inside the company, but rather relied on the confidentiality inherent in the executive coaching relationship and called me.

Valana's initial fear was that no woman could succeed in Japan or Pakistan. Her real fear was that if she accepted the position, she would be setting herself up for failure. When I asked her why she believed she would fail in either of these two Asian countries, she immediately sighted the cultural limitations placed on most women in Japan, as well as in most Islamic countries. Unconsciously, yet understandably, Valana had fallen into the Gaijin Trap. She had assumed that, as a woman, she would be treated similarly to the local Japanese and Pakistani women, few of whom are given the cultural latitude to succeed in major multinational businesses. Her mistake was not in her statistics; she was right that there are extremely few women executives in either country. Rather, her mistake was in overemphasizing the salience of being a woman. Based on the actual experience of women executives who have worked abroad, we know that American women are treated as foreigners who happen to be women. They are not treated in the same way as local women. While both the Japanese and Pakistanis limit the roles that local women can take in business, neither culture confuses foreign women with local women. Valana's freedom to succeed lies in the fact that she is visibly foreign. The trap for Valana would be to assume that the Japanese could not tell that she is not Japanese (or that the Pakistanis could not tell that she is not Pakistani); they can.

To get accurate tips on how to succeed in such cultures, I suggested that Valana restrict her advice gathering to conversations with other North

American and European women who had worked for major multinationals in Japan or Pakistan. From them she could learn the nuances of showing respect for each culture without limiting her potential success. I strongly advised that she disregard suggestions made by both men and women who had not had direct experience with women working in the particular countries in which she would be working. Without direct experience, even the best-intentioned colleagues unconsciously pass on myths disguised as advice. The only thing that eradicates the myth that women cannot succeed abroad—and, simultaneously, the fear that such myths engender in both women executives and the companies that consider sending them on international assignments—is learning about the actual experiences of women executives who have worked abroad—the majority of whom have succeeded. (See Adler, 1994, for further research on this topic.)

In the next couple of weeks, Valana did talk with many such women, coming back to me frequently to ask whether I thought their suggestions would really be advisable for her. Among her many questions, Valana asked if it were true that women executives did not have to stay up drinking until late into the night in order to do business with Japanese firms. My answer, "Absolutely true." Whereas male/male behavior in Japan is fairly codified and usually includes a lot of business entertainment and drinking, the newness of women conducting significant business in Japan means that male/female business behavior has yet to become codified. Given the ambiguity at this point in history, women have more latitude than do men to conduct business in ways that feel most comfortable to them. As one highly successful American woman executive, who had been based out of Tokyo for years, laughingly related to me, "Among all of my male colleagues, I am the only one who has consistently maintained relationships with Japanese clients without needing to put my liver in jeopardy! I can get away with conducting business over lunch and a Perrier; the men can't."

Myth Four

Public Is Public, and Private Is Private; To Be Taken Seriously, a Woman Executive Must Hide Her Role as a Wife and Mother. The myth, albeit false, is that foreigners will not take a businesswoman seriously unless she is 100 percent focused on work. American women, who come from one of the most task-oriented cultures in the world, often fall into the trap of emulating American businessmen. They try to focus almost exclusively on business—to the detriment of both their worldwide business success and their private lives.

Perhaps one particularly successful businesswoman's experience says it all. On a business trip to Hong Kong, Katia, a marketing vice president for a global telecommunications firm, was negotiating her first major contract with a consortium of Thai, Malaysian, and Chinese companies. The negotiations were not going very well and looked to be in jeopardy. At a particularly tense moment in the deliberations, Katia glanced at her watch, stood up, and apologized for needing to take a ten-minute break. While receiving quizzical looks from the group of men, she explained that it was bedtime for her seven-year-old daughter back home in Chicago, and that she always called to say good night to her daughter no matter where she was in the world.

Returning ten minutes later, Katia was surprised to discover that the tension around the negotiating table had melted. As she entered the room, the Thai executive asked how her daughter was doing, the lead Chinese negotiator asked Katia if she had a picture of her daughter, and the other negotiators expressed how difficult they imagined it must be for a mother to be so far away from her daughter. After this brief exchange of warm interest and concern, the negotiations continued, now clearly with a focus on efficiently finding a mutually beneficial agreement. At noon the following day, the negotiation that had appeared irreversibly stuck came to a successful conclusion.

Most women from Anglo-Saxon cultures, and especially those from the United States, have been coached by their colleagues to separate their private lives from their professional lives. To succeed abroad, however, these same women need to unlearn the advice that their Anglo-Saxon colleagues have given them. Unlike the task-orientation of Anglo-Saxon countries, most countries emphasize relationship building. In countries such as China, Malaysia, and Thailand, people will only conduct business with people they know, like, and trust. Revealing who you are as a whole person—including unmasking some aspects of your private life—allows colleagues from relationship-building cultures to get to know you, and, therefore, to want to do business with you. It is not that people from relationship-oriented cultures aren't concerned about getting the task accomplished; they are. It's just that relationships must precede task. Katia's relationship with her daughter added the dimension of wholeness that she needed to succeed.

Katia laughs today that a number of her women friends, who are also global executives, now carry pictures of their children very visibly in their business-card cases. Why? Because from the first moment of contact, clients know that they are a whole person—a wife, mother, and businesswoman.

Executive Coaching: Reaching Beyond the Myths of History

The privacy of coaching sessions makes it easier for executives to say, "I'm not certain. . . . I just don't know. . . ." Privacy and supportive advocacy legitimize moments of not knowing. Premature certainty and commitment extinguish innovative possibilities. For both women and men, coaching dialogues can foster a depth of questioning that allows executives to escape the bounded thinking of their own professional, organizational, and national cultures. For women, coaching sessions encourage exploring alternatives that reach beyond the accepted "wisdom" of successful men who have worked worldwide with other men. At their very best, coaching sessions provide the time, space, and learning opportunities that allow executives to offer profound and wise counsel to themselves.

About the Contributor

Nancy J. Adler is a professor of organizational behavior and cross-cultural management at the Faculty of Management, McGill University in Montreal, Quebec, Canada. She received her B.A. in economics and her M.B.A. and Ph.D. in management from the University of California at Los Angeles.

Nancy conducts research and consults on strategic international human resource management, global leadership, international negotiating, culturally synergistic problem solving, and global organization development. She has authored more than one hundred articles, produced the film *A Portable Life,* and published three books: *International Dimensions of Organizational Behavior, Women in Management Worldwide,* and *Competitive Frontiers: Women Managers in a Global Economy.*

Nancy has consulted to private corporations and government organizations on projects in Asia, Europe, North and South America, and the Middle East. She has taught Chinese executives in the People's Republic of China, held the Citicorp Visiting Doctoral Professorship at the University of Hong Kong, and taught executive seminars at INSEAD in France and Bocconi University in Italy. She received McGill University's first Distinguished Teaching Award in Management and has subsequently been awarded it for a second time.

Nancy has served on the Board of Governors of the American Society for Training and Development (ASTD), the Canadian Social Science Advisory Committee to UNESCO, the Strategic Grants Committee of the Social Sciences and Humanities Research Council, and the executive committees of the Pacific Asian Consortium for International Business, Education and Research, the International Personnel Association, and the Society for Human Resource Management's International Institute, as well as having held leadership positions in the Academy of International Business (AIB), the Society for Intercultural Education, Training, and Research (SIETAR), and the Academy of Management. Nancy received ASTD's International Leadership Award, SIETAR's Outstanding Senior Interculturalist Award, the YWCA's Femme de Mérite (Woman of Distinction) Award, and the Sage Award for scholarly contributions to management. She was selected as a 3M Teaching Fellow, honoring her as one of Canada's top university professors, and elected to both the Fellows of the Academy of International Business and the Academy of Management Fellows.

CHAPTER THIRTY-FOUR

COACHING FREE AGENTS

Marshall Goldsmith, Iain Somerville, and
Cathy Greenberg-Walt

The nature of work—and our relationship to major organizations—is changing dramatically. In a time of growing wealth and the age of the knowledge worker, leaders are taking a new look at what motivates star performers.

The management challenge is no longer how to make sure people are doing their jobs; today's manager must be an effective coach who can motivate top performers. Because top performers often see themselves as free agents, an effective manager must build a partnership with top performers that recognizes their needs and keeps them motivated to stay with the company, rather than join the competition.

For insights into the new world of work, Andersen Consulting (with Keilty, Goldsmith & Company) recently completed in-depth interviews with more than two hundred specially chosen, high-potential leaders from one hundred twenty of the world's premier organizations.

Although these star performers varied widely in background, expertise, and motivation, one common theme emerged from our interviews: *these future leaders viewed themselves as free agents.* While interested in pursuing many different goals, they were almost uniformly interested in pursuing what *they* wanted to pursue. They showed little interest in sacrificing their lives for the good of the organization. Most believed that their corporations would "drop them" when they no longer met the needs of the company. Conversely, they were willing to "drop the company" when it no longer met *their* needs. Each person was operating more like an individual small business (ME, Inc., as Tom Peters might say) than a cog in the wheel of a large system.

The Free Agent Economy

As Lester Thurow (1999) notes, "The private ownership of productive assets and the ability to appropriate the output that flows from those assets lies at the heart of capitalism." In the past the key to wealth may have been control of land, materials, plants, and tools; the worker needed the company more than the company needed the worker. Today the key to wealth is control of *knowledge.* As a result, the company needs the knowledge worker far more than the knowledge worker needs the company. To make matters even more challenging for employers, the knowledge workers now clearly *know* that they have the power!

High-performing knowledge workers are becoming increasingly hard to keep and increasingly painful to lose. Many of America's most enlightened corporations, such as Johnson & Johnson, Motorola, Cisco, and General Electric, know that developing and retaining the next generation of leaders is key to their future success. As the free agent syndrome grows, it is impacting not only younger leaders, but also older leaders who have gained financial independence and will soon be leaving their organizations. Meanwhile, there is a dwindling number of proven leaders waiting to take their place.

The Implications for Leadership

It's not only money, but. . . . Economic models historically have assumed that money is the key to changing behavior. However, today's free agent knowledge worker has a far more complex set of motivators that may well change over his or her lifetime. Our interviews indicated that money is only one factor (and often not the most important) in motivating free agents.

There is no denying that money remains an important consideration in high performers' career calculations. Yet, beyond the temptation of simply going for the gold, free agents wrestle with a paradox articulated by Thurow: in a time of rapid change, the economic value of experience falls rather than rises. The shelf life of knowledge, especially technical knowledge, is ever shrinking. Knowledge workers know that it often pays, intellectually, professionally, and financially, to move on to new challenges rather than to keep doing the same thing for the same organization.

Therefore, when dealing with free agents, it is critical to find out what *they* need. The person who sees "work-life balance" as irrelevant at age twenty-four may find it critical at thirty-four. Non-monetary motivators such as challenge, meaning, recognition, and development may mean more than money. Those choosing to look beyond the promise of an early fortune must be offered a powerful alternative, such as those reflected in the following principles:

Free Agents Must Be Treated As Partners, Not As Employees.

An organization's relationship with its top talent is coming to resemble a strategic alliance rather than a traditional employment contract. Free agents can leave at any time. They are not dependent on the corporation. We asked the top one hundred twenty executives at one of the world's leading high-tech companies, "Can the highest potential leader who works for you leave the company and get another job *with a pay raise* in one week?" All executives surveyed said yes! If free agents do not feel that they are being treated as valued partners they will leave (and usually receive a pay raise).

Companies Must Deal with the Self-Interest of the Free Agent.

Historically, large U.S. companies benefited from a one-sided proposition. While the *company* was supposed to maximize return for itself and shareholders, the *individual* was expected to discount his or her own interests and focus on the good of the company. In American business, it has been "politically inappropriate" for an employee to openly demand of management,

"What's in this for ME?" Now that the organization man has been replaced by the free agent, who has no interest in sacrificing self and family for the good of the company, companies that can make the fastest transition to the new world of free agents will have the greatest chance of keeping great people and winning in the marketplace.

Free Agents Can Be Great Team Players. Although organizations err in expecting star performers to neglect their own interests, it is also a mistake to assume that free agents cannot work collaboratively. None of the contributors we interviewed expressed an interest in seeking a short-term gain at a long-term cost to their professional relationships. Their goal was to establish an honest, "win-win" relationship with any organization they joined. Enlightened free agents realize that today's co-worker may be tomorrow's customer, manager, or employee. Their interest is in working to create something meaningful, memorable, and personally rewarding.

Flexibility Is Key to Working with Free Agents. Historically human resource departments have used a "cookie-cutter" approach to dealing with people. A major focus was perceived fairness and "treating everyone the same way." To deal effectively with free agents, this will have to change. Stars have little interest in being treated "just like everyone else." They know they make a unique contribution, and they want to be treated accordingly. Companies offering benefits that can be tailored to individual needs will have a huge competitive advantage.

For example, one of the world's leading financial consulting firms recently tried to promote the company's value of "leading a balanced life" as a reason for its future leaders to stay put. Unfortunately, the firm learned that several top performers were young and single, with no desire to "lead a balanced life." These performers found the entire pitch paternalistic and offensive. Instead they wanted to work as hard as possible and make as much as possible as soon as possible. They believed that they were being asked to make a personal sacrifice *not* to work the extra hours so that others could leave work and spend time with their families.

Leading Free Agents Requires Candor. In many ways the new partnership contract between the large organization and the free agent requires refreshing honesty. Both sides must spend less time playing games. Free agents will be straightforward about what they want. Organizations will have to be equally direct in describing their goals, expectations, and rewards. Successful leaders of free agents realize that loyalty and mutual respect are earned, not given.

Companies that can develop honest, candid, win-win relationships with free agents will lead the way into the next century, and it is the managers who will be forging these relationships. Corporations that in recent years touted the "new employment contract" may not like the "what's in it for me" proposition now that power has shifted to the individual, because in many ways it was easier to live in a world in which every *employee* was expendable. To the free agent every *company* is expendable—and the more valuable the free agent, the more this is true! High potential leaders are special and they know it, and as a consequence of this shift, today's managers and leaders may find their work becoming more challenging, productive, honest, and refreshing.

About the Contributors

Marshall Goldsmith (along with Warren Bennis and John O'Neil) has served as an alliance partner with Andersen Consulting on their groundbreaking research, which focused on the characteristics of the global leader of the future. An expanded version of this research, tentatively titled *Global Leadership: The Next Generation,* is scheduled to be published in 2001. Marshall is a member of the PROVANT advisory board and a member of the board of the Peter Drucker Foundation. "Coaching Free Agents" is an adaptation of one of the many articles that he has written for the Foundation's journal *Leader to Leader.*

Iain Somerville is a partner in Andersen Consulting's Strategy practice, based in Los Angeles, California. He serves the leaders of global organizations, primarily in technology-based service industries, such as communications, media, and education. Over the past twenty-five years, as a top management consultant and executive coach, he has served many of the world's leading private, public, and social sector enterprises. Iain is the founder of the Andersen Consulting Organization Strategy practice and the Institute for Strategic Change—the firm's global business "think tank."

Cathy Greenberg-Walt is the change management managing partner of Andersen Consulting's Global New Business Models Team, a partner in charge of the Executive Leadership Theme Team at the Institute for Strategic Change, a frequent keynote speaker, and an author. With an interdisciplinary doctorate in the behavioral sciences, she focuses on the successful management and integration of business strategy, process, technology, and leadership.

REFERENCES

Preface

Birchall, D. W., and Lyons, L. S. *Creating Tomorrow's Organization: Unlocking the Benefits of Future Work*. London: Pitman Publishing, 1995.

Bridges, W. "Leading the De-jobbed Organization." *Leader of the Future*. San Francisco: Jossey-Bass, 1996.

Drucker, P. *The Effective Executive*. London: Heinemann, 1967.

Hammer, M., and Champy, J. *Re-engineering the Corporation*. London: Nicholas Brealey, 1993.

Handy, C. *The Future of Work*. Oxford: Basil Blackwell, 1984.

Schein, E. H. (See references for Chapter 5 on page 376).

Chapter Two

Goldsmith, M. "Coaching for Behavioral Change." *Leader to Leader*. Fall 1996.

Chapter Three

Kepner-Tegoe, Inc. "Avoiding the Brain Drain: What Companies Are Doing to Lock In Their Talent." Research Monograph One, Executive Summary, 1996.

Rucci, A. J., Kirn, S. P., Quinn, R. T. "The Employee-Customer Profit Chain at Sears." *Harvard Business Review, 76*(1), pp. 83–97, Jan.–Feb. 1998.

Tichy, N. M. "Leaders Developing Leaders." *The Leadership Engine: Building Leaders at Every Level.* Dallas: Pritchett & Associates, 1997.

Chapter Four

Garber, J., and Seligman, M. E. P. *Human Helplessness: Theory and Applications.* New York: Academic Press, 1980.

Kegan, R. *The Evolving Self: Problems and Process in Human Development.* Cambridge, Mass.: University Press, 1982.

Kelly, O. A. *Clinical Psychology and Personality: The Selected Papers of George Kelly.* B. Maher, ed. New York: John Wiley & Sons, 1969.

Miller, A. *The Drama of the Gifted Child.* New York: Basic Books, 1981.

Satir, V. *Conjoint Family Therapy.* Palo Alto, Calif.: Science and Behavior Books, 1983.

Chapter Five

Flaherty, J. *Coaching: Evoking Excellence in Others.* Boston: Butterworth-Heinemann, 1999.

Schein, E. H. *Process Consultation: Its Role in Organization Development.* Reading, Mass.: Addison-Wesley, 1969.

Schein, E. H. *Process Consultation, Vol. II: Lessons for Managers and Consultants.* Reading, Mass.: Addison-Wesley, 1987.

Schein, E. H. *Process Consultation, Vol. I: Its Role in Organization Development* (2nd ed.). Reading, Mass.: Addison-Wesley, 1988.

Schein, E. H. *Process Consultation Revisited: Building the Helping Relationship.* Reading, Mass.: Addison-Wesley-Longman, 1999.

Schein, E. H. "Empowerment Coercive Permission and Organizational Learnings: Do They Connect?" *The Learning Organization,* 1999, 6, No. 4, pp. 162–172.

Chapter Seven

Covey, S. *Principle-centered Leadership.* New York: Summit Books, 1990.

Greenleaf, R. K. *Servant Leadership: A Journey Into the Nature of Legitimate Power and Greatness.* New York: Paulist Press, 1977.

Chapter Eight

Csikszentmihalyi, M. *Finding Flow: The Psychology of Engagement With Everyday Life.* New York: Basic Books, 1997.

Fast Company. "Where Are We On the Web?" p. 306, October 1999.

Kouzes, J. M., and Posner, B. Z. *Credibility: How Leaders Gain and Lose It, Why People Demand It.* San Francisco: Jossey-Bass, 1993.

Kouzes, J. M., and Posner, B. Z. *The Leadership Challenge: How to Keep Getting Extraordinary Things Done in Organizations.* San Francisco: Jossey-Bass, 1995.

Kouzes, J. M., and Posner, B. Z. *Encouraging the Heart: A Leader's Guide to Rewarding and Recognizing Others.* San Francisco: Jossey-Bass, 1999.

New Leadership for a New Century. Washington, DC: Public Allies, 1998.

O'Reilly, C. A. *Charisma as Communication: The Impact of Top Management Credibility and Philosophy on Employee Involvement.* Paper presented to the annual meeting of the Academy of Management, Boston, Mass., August, 1984.

Posner, B. Z., and Schmidt, W. H. "Values Congruence and Differences Between the Interplay of Personal and Organizational Value Systems." *Journal of Business Ethics,* 1993, *12,* pp. 171–177.

Taylor, J. Telephone interview with Jodi Taylor, Ph.D., for Center for Creative Leadership, April, 1998. (J. Taylor now with Summit Leadership Solutions.)

Chapter Nine

Hesselbein, F., Goldsmith, M., and Beckhard, R. *The Leader of the Future.* San Francisco: Drucker Foundation and Jossey-Bass, 1996.

Chapter Ten

Crane, T. *The Heart of Coaching: Using Transformational Coaching to Create a High-Performance Culture.* San Diego: FTA Press, 1998.

Chapter Twelve

De Geus, A., and Senge, P. M. *The Living Company.* Boston: Harvard Business School Press, 1997.

Hoffer, E. *The Passionate State of Mind.* Cutchogue, N.Y.: Buccaneer Books, 1998.

Chapter Thirteen

Argyris, C. *Strategy Change and Defensive Routines.* Boston: Dittman, 1985.

Goldsmith, M. "Ask, Learn, Follow Up, and Grow." *The Leader of the Future.* San Francisco: Jossey-Bass, 1996.

Rogers, C. *On Becoming a Person.* New York: Houghton-Mifflin, 1961.

Chapter Fourteen

Berlin, I. as quoted in P. Bate, *Strategies for Cultural Change*. London: Butterworth-Heinemann, 1994.

Binney, G., and Williams, C. *Leaning Into the Future: Changing the Way People Change Organizations*. London: Nicholas Brealey, 1997.

Birchall, D. W., and Lyons, L. S. *Creating Tomorrow's Organization:Unlocking the Benefits of Future Work*. London: Pitman Publishing, 1995.

Bowen, D. E., and Lawler, E. E. "The Empowerment of Service Workers: What, Why, How and When." *Sloan Management Review*, Spring 1992, pp. 31–39.

Brauer, D. "Human Rights—and Human Duties." *Development and Co-operation*. 1999, *3*, p. 3.

Brennan, E. A. as quoted in R. Wild, (ed.), *How to Manage*. London: Butterworth-Heinemann, 1994, p. 11.

Bull, G. *Tomorrow's Company*. London: Royal Society of Arts, 1995.

Conger, J. A. *The Charismatic Leader*. San Francisco: Jossey-Bass, 1989, pp. 171–172.

Dahl, R. A. "The Concept of Power." *Behavioural Science*, 1957, *2*, pp. 201–205.

Davies, H. "Take a Pay Cut, Bank Chief Tells the Fat Cats." Reported by P. McGowan, in the *Evening Standard*, September 15, 1995.

DeShano, J. "Servant-leadership and Philanthropy." *Servant Leader*.

Ford, R. C., and Fottler, M. D. "Empowerment: A Matter of Degree." *Academy of Management Executive*, Spring 1995, *9*(3), p. 27.

Garratt, R. *Learning to Lead: Developing Your Organization and Yourself*. Fontana, 1990.

Handy, C. B. *Understanding Organizations* (3rd ed.). New York: Penguin, 1985, p. 118.

Hardy, C. *Power and Politics in Organizations*. Hanover, NH: Dartmouth College Press, 1995, pp. xx–xxi.

Heider, J. *The Tao of Leadership: Leadership Strategies for a New Age*. New York: Bantam Books, April 1994, p. 161.

Kaletsky, A. "Why Clinton, But Not Major, May Cling to Power." *Sunday Times*, April 7, 1994.

Kets de Vries, M. F. R *Leaders, Fools, and Imposters*. San Francisco: Jossey-Bass, 1993 p. 224.

Nonaka, I., and Takeeuchi, H. *The knowledge-creating company*. Oxford, England: Oxford University Press, 1995.

Peters, T. J., and Waterman, R. H., Jr. *In Search of Excellence*. New York: Harper & Row, 1982.

Plender, J. "A Balanced Vision For Tomorrow." *Financial Times*, June 7, 1995.

Senge, P. M. *The Fifth Discipline: The Art and Practice of the Learning Organization*. New York: Doubleday, 1990.

Sonnenfeld, J. A. *The CEO as Leader: Concepts of Leadership*. Hanover, NH: Dartmouth University Press, 1995, pp. xi-xxi.

Stewart, T. A. "A User's Guide to Power." *Fortune*, *6*, November, 1989.

Stewart, T. A. as quoted by D. Clutterbuck in *The Power of Empowerment*. London: Kogan Page, 1994, pp. 18–19.

Tam, H. "Recognise Your Responsibilities." *Professional Manager*, March 1995, p. 16.

Townsend, K. *Manhood at Harvard: William James and Others*. New York: W.W. Norton, 1997.

van Maurik, J. (1994). *Discovering the Leader in You*. New York: McGraw Hill, 1994.

Zuboff, S. *In the Age of the Smart Machine*. New York: Basic Books, 1988, p. 395.

Chapter Fifteen

Argyris, C., Putnam, R., and Smith, D. M. *Action Science.* San Francisco: Jossey-Bass, 1985.

Argyris, C., and Schön, D. A. *Theory in Practice: Increasing Professional Effectiveness.* San Francisco: Jossey-Bass, 1974.

Evered, R. D., and Selman, J. C. "Coaching and the Art of Management." *Organizational Dynamics.* 1989, *18*(2), pp. 16–32.

Schwarz, R. M. *The Skilled Facilitator: Practical Wisdom for Developing Effective Groups.* San Francisco: Jossey-Bass, 1994.

Shepard, H. A. "Rules of Thumb for Change Agents." *OD Practitioner,* 1985, *17*(4).

Weisbord, M. R. *Productive Workplaces: Organizing and Managing for Dignity, Meaning, and Community.* San Francisco: Jossey-Bass, 1987.

Witherspoon, R. "Four Essential Ways to Coach Executives. *The Coaching and Mentoring Conference Proceedings.* Lexington, Mass.: Linkage, Inc., 1998, p. 173 ff.

Witherspoon, R., and White, R. P., *Four Essential Ways That Coaching Can Help Executives.* Greensboro, N.C.: Center for Creative Leadership, 1997.

Chapter Eighteen

Betof, E. H., and Harrison, R. P. "The Newly Appointed Leader Dilemma: A Significant Change in Today's Organizational Culture." *The Manchester Review,* Spring 1996, p. 3.

"GE Brings Good Managers to Life." *Fast Company,* Oct. 1998, p. 72.

Goleman, D. "What Makes a Leader?" *Harvard Business Review,* Nov.–Dec. 1998, pp. 94–99.

Manchester Consulting, Survey of 826 respondents, 1997.

Chapter Nineteen

Deming, W. E. *Out of Crisis.* Boston: Massachusetts Institute of Technology, 1986.

McCall, M. W., Jr., Lombardo, M. M., and Morrison, A. M. "The Lessons of Experience: How Successful Executives Develop on the Job." New York: The Free Press, 1992.

Chapter Twenty-Four

Cziksentmihalyi, M. *Beyond Boredom and Anxiety: The Experience of Play in Work and Games.* San Francisco: Jossey-Bass, 1975.

Chapter Twenty-Seven

Folkman, J. *Turning Feedback Into Change!* ® *31 Principles for Managing Personal Development Through Feedback.* Provo, Utah: Novations Group, Inc., 1996.

Chapter Twenty-Eight

Covey, S. R., Merrill, A. R., and Merrill, R. R. *First Things First: To Live, to Love, to Learn, to Leave a Legacy.* New York: Fireside, 1996.

Goldsmith, M. "Ask, Learn, Follow up, and Grow." *The Leader of the Future.* San Francisco: Drucker Foundation and Jossey-Bass, 1996.

Chapter Thirty-Two

Jackson, P., and Delehanty, H. *Sacred Hoops: Spiritual Lessons of a Hardwood Warrior.* New York: Hyperion, 1995.

Thomas, R. R., Jr. *Redefining Diversity.* New York: AMACOM, 1996.

Chapter Thirty-Three

Adler, N. J. "Competitive Frontiers: Women Managing Across Borders." In Adler, N. J., and Izraeli, D. N., *Competitive Frontiers: Women Managers in a Global Economy.* Malden, Mass.: Blackwell, 1994.

Chapter Thirty-Four

Thurow, L. C. *Building Wealth: The New Rules for Individuals, Companies, and Nations.* New York: HarperCollins, 1999.

CONTACT INFORMATION

Nancy J. Adler
McGill University, Faculty of Management
1001 Rue Sherbrooke Ouest
Montreal, Quebec, Canada H3A1G5
    Adler@management.mcgill.ca
    PH: 514-398-4031
    FX: 514-398-3876

John Alexander
Center for Creative Leadership
One Leadership Place
Greensboro, NC 27438
    Alexanderj@leaders.ccl.org
    PH: 336-286-4001
    FX: 336-286-4020

David Allen
David Allen & Co.
1674 McNell Rd.
Ojai, CA 93023
    David@davidco.com
    www.davidco.com
    PH: 805-646-8432
    FX: 805-646-7695

Judith M. Bardwick
Judith M. Bardwick Ph.D., Inc.
1389 Caminito Halago
La Jolla, CA 92037
    Jmbwick@san.rr.com
    www.judithmbardwick.com
    PH: 858-456-1443
    FX: 858-454-3980

Chip R. Bell
Performance Research Associates
25 Highland Park, #100
Dallas, TX 75205
    Chip@beepbeep.com
    www.beepbeep.com
    PH: 214-522-5777
    FX: 214-691-7591

Roger Chevalier
Leadership Applications
924 Hudis St.
Rohnert Park, CA 94928
    Rdc@sonic.net
    PH: 707-584-7160

Thomas G. Crane
Crane Consulting
11052 Picaza Pl.
San Diego, CA 92127
    Tgcrane@craneconsulting.com
    www.craneconsulting.com
    PH: 858-487-9017
    FX: 858-592-0689

Bert Decker
Decker Communications, Inc.
44 Montgomery St.
San Francisco, CA 94104
    Bdecker@decker.com
    www.decker.com
    PH: 415-752-0700
    FX: 415-752-7362

Alan Fine
InsideOut Development L.L.C.
95N 490 W.
American Fork, UT 84003
    Afine@insideoutdev.com
    www.insideoutdev.com
    PH: 801-492-1001
    FX: 801-492-1002

Joe Folkman
Novations Group, Inc.
5314 North 250 West, Ste. 320
Provo, UT 84604
    Jfolkman@novations.com
    www.novations.com
    PH: 801-354-7544
    FX: 801-818-8544

Alyssa M. Freas
Executive Coaching Network, Inc.
7825 Fay Ave., Ste. 200
La Jolla, CA 92037
    Alyssa@ExecutiveCoaching.com
    www.excn.com
    www.ExecutiveCoaching.com
    PH: 858-456-5560
    FX: 858-272-4137

Robert M. Fulmer
College of William & Mary
Pepperdine University
    Robert.fulmer@wm.edu

Marshall Goldsmith
Keilty, Goldsmith & Company
16236 San Dieguito Rd.
Rancho Santa Fe, CA 92067-9710
    Marshall@kgcnet.com
    www.kgcnet.com
    PH: 858-759-0950
    FX: 858-759-1927

Don Grayson
    Dongrayson@aol.com
    PH: 760-944-1861

Cathy Greenberg-Walt
Andersen Consulting
    cathy.l.walt@ac.com
    PH: 215-241-8360

Victoria Guthrie
Center for Creative Leadership
One Leadership Pl.
Greensboro, NC 27438
    Guthrie@leaders.ccl.org
    PH: 336-286-4518
    FX: 336-288-3999

Tom Heinselman
Keilty, Goldsmith & Company
4833 Topeka Ct.
Atlanta, GA 30338
    Tomh@kgcnet.com
    www.kgcnet.com
    PH: 770-604-9784
    FX: 770-395-7520

Paul Hersey
Center for Leadership Studies
230 W. Third Ave.
Escondido, CA 92025
  Campbell@situational.com
  www.situational.com
  PH: 760-741-6595
  FX: 760-747-9384

Maya Hu-Chan
Asian Communcation Professionals, Inc.
  Maya-huchan@yahoo.com
  PH: 619-229-1212

Julie M. Johnson
The Reid Group
258 Mulberry Hill Rd.
Fairfield, CT 06430
  Reidgroup@aol.com
  PH: 203-319-1075
  FX: 203-256-0722

Beverly Kaye
Career Systems Intl.
900 James Ave.
Scranton, PA 18510
  Beverly.kaye@csibka.com
  www.careersystemsintl.com
  PH: 800-577-6916
  FX: 570-346-8606

James M. Kouzes
Tom Peters Company
1784 Patio Dr.
San Jose, CA 95125
  Jkouzes@aol.com
  www.theleadershipchallenge.com
  PH: 408-978-1809
  FX: 408-265-1633

Richard J. Leider
The Inventure Group
601 Carlson Parkway, Ste. 375
Minneapolis, MN 55305

www.inventuregroup.com
PH: 952-249-5222
FX: 952-249-5220

Bruce Lloyd
Strategy Business School at
  South Bank University
103 Borough Road
London SE10AA, UK
  101645.1441@compuserve.com

Laurence S. Lyons
Executive Coaching Network, Inc.
European Office
2 Oak Tree Road, Reading, RG31 6JZ
  England
  Larry@executivecoaching.com
  www.excn.com
  www.ExecutiveCoaching.com
  PH: +44 (0) 118-945-2849
  FX: +44 (0) 870-164-0959
Henley Management College
Future Work Forum Programme Office
Greenlands, Henley-on-Thames,
  Oxfordshire RG9 3AU, England
  laurencel@henleymc.ac.uk
  www.henleymc.ac.uk
  PH: +44 (0) 1491-571454
The Learning Partnership Europe
15A Berghem Mews, London, W14 0HN
  UK
  infoeu@tlp.org
  Laurence@tlp.org
  www.tlp.org
  PH: +44 (0) 20-7371-4141
  FX: +44. (0) 20-7371-6171
The Learning Partnership, USA
317 Madison Avenue, Ste. 805
New York, NY 10017
  infousa@tlp.org
  Laurence@tlp.org
  www.tlp.org
  PH: 212-687-4141
  FX: 212-687-4144

Laurence S. Lyons (continued)
Metacorp Consulting
2 Oak Tree Road, Reading, RG31 6JZ
  England
    info@metacorp.demon.co.uk
    www.metacorp.demon.co.uk
    PH: +44 (0)7050 144412
    FX: +44 (0)870 056-1335

Carlos E. Marin
Keilty, Goldsmith & Company
3506 Avenida Amorosa
Escondido, CA 92029
    carlos@kgcnet.com
    PH: 760-233-2789
    FX: 760-233-2489

Howard Morgan
Keilty, Goldsmith & Company
Leadership Research Institute
4350 La Jolla Village Dr., #120
San Diego, CA 92122
    Howard@lrinet.com
    PH: 858-450-2525

David Noer
Noer Consulting
P.O. Box 35093
Greensboro, NC 27425-5093
    David@noerconsulting.com
    www.noerconsulting.com
    PH: 336-286-0060
    FX: 336-545-9404

Tom Pettey
California Public Employees' Retirement
  System (CalPERS)
400 P St., Rm. 3260
Sacramento, CA 95184
    Tom_pettey@calpers.com
    www.calpers.ca.gov
    PH: 916-326-3068
    FX: 916-558-4001

Elizabeth Pinchot
Pinchot & Company
Box 10328
Bainbridge Island, WA 92110
    Libba@pinchot.com
    www.pinchot.com
    PH: 206-780-2800

Gifford Pinchot
Pinchot & Company
Box 10328
Bainbridge Island, WA 92110
    www.pinchot.com
    PH: 206-780-2800

Alastair G. Robertson
Andersen Consulting
    Alastair.robertson@ac.com
    PH: 617-454-7375

Deepak (Dick) Sethi
The Thomson Corporation
Stamford, CT 06902
    Dicksethi@hotmail.com
    PH: 973-740-1777
    FX: 973-535-1112

Jeremy Solomons
Jeremy Solomons & Associates
303 E. Gurley St., PMB 221
Prescott, AZ 86301
    Jersol@aol.com
    PH: 520-636-5106
    FX: 520-636-5110

Iain Somerville
Andersen Consulting
2101 Rosecrans Ave, Ste. 3300
El Segundo, CA 90245
    Iainsomerville@ac.com
    www.ac.com
    PH: 310-376-2947

Liz Thach
MediaOne Group
   Lizthach@aol.com
   PH: 303-978-9003

R. Roosevelt Thomas, Jr.
R. Thomas Consulting and Training, Inc.
   rrthomasjr@aol.com
   www.rthomasconsulting.com
   PH: 770-234-0222

Dave Ulrich
University of Michigan
3108 W. Dobson Pl.
Ann Arbor, MI 48105
   Dou@ulrich.edu
   www.globalconsultalliance.com
   www.rbi.net
   PH: 734-996-9108
   FX: 734-996-4927

Robert Witherspoon
Performance & Leadership
   Development Ltd.
1825 Eye St., NW, Ste.400
Washington, DC 20006
   Robert@topcoaches.net
   Coachrobt@aol.com
   PH: 202-429-2725
   FX: 202-429-9574

INDEX

This Page Constitutes a Continuation of the Copyright Page